THE **BLUE** ECONOMY

10 YEARS

100 INNOVATIONS

100 MILLION JOBS

Gunter Pauli

REPORT TO THE CLUB OF ROME

Paradigm Publications, Taos, New Mexico, 2010

The Blue Economy
10 Years, 100 Innovations, 100 Million Jobs
Report to the Club of Rome
Gunter Pauli

ISBN 9780912111902

Published by Paradigm Publications, Taos, New Mexico, USA
www.paradigm-pubs.com

Distributed by Redwing Book Company
Taos, New Mexico USA
www.redwingbooks.com

Library of Congress Cataloging-in-Publication Data
Pauli, Gunter A.
  The blue economy : 10 years, 100 innovations, 100 million jobs /
  Gunter Pauli.
      p. cm.
  ISBN 978-0-912111-90-2 (pbk. : alk. paper)
 1. Natural resources. 2. Sustainable development. I. Title.
  HC85.P38 2010
  333.7--dc22
                    2010007905

Graphic Design: Lesley Cox: FEEL Design Associates, www.feeldesignassociates.com

Paradigm
Publications

PRAISE FOR THE BLUE ECONOMY

The Blue Economy describes innovations that are certain to change our habits of production and consumption. It points us in a strategic direction for sustainable development. Dr. Pauli's new economic model gives aspiring entrepreneurs and political leaders the means to contemplate and achieve a sustainable future. They will be able to take advantage of manifold opportunities and make policy decisions that serve both economy and community.

> NOEMI SANIN POSADA
> Colombia Ambassador to Spain (2003-2007),
> UK (1994-1996, 2007-2009), Venezuela (1990-1991) Colombia Minister of
> Communications (1983-1986), Colombia Minister of Foreign Affairs (1991-1995)
> Government of Colombia Peace Negotiator

The Blue Economy is exactly the kind of tool we need to help us repair our broken economy and create a more sustainable model. The new ideas and innovative thinking compiled here give us exciting new options about how to transform our economy so that it can generate new jobs and sustain healthy, happy communities far into the future.

> PHAEDRA ELLIS-LAMKINS
> CEO, Green For All

Over the past 30 years as I have built up the computer industry around ACER, Dr. Pauli has introduced me to many creative ideas, especially through his Zero Emissions Research and Initiatives (ZERI) organization. He has devoted himself for decades to theoretical development as well as practical application of zero emission concepts. The ideas he puts forth in *The Blue Economy* represent a sustainable and competitive business framework based on innovations that offer investors and society financial, social, and environmental benefits. Such opportunities to achieve sustainability, parity, and profitability are not only inviting but tremendously compelling.

> STAN SHIH
> Founder, ACER Computers
> Chairman, IDSoft Capital Venture Fund

Gunter Pauli masterfully elucidates examples from nature that can help us solve our sustainability problems. There are refreshing and competitive options to artificial chemical and technologica! fixes and their unintended toxic consequences.

YVON CHOUINARD
Owner, Patagonia, Inc.

Nature holds all our solutions. Gunter Pauli is a visionary entrepreneur who is able to help us create a Blue Economy based on respecting the Earth's ecosystems and humankind. His book is destined to be the bible of this new economy, meant for all of us who are working to build a better world.

CHRISTIAN COURTIN-CLARINS
Chairman, Clarins (France)

Our current economic crisis is also a crisis of ethics and values which has led to the enrichment of a few and the disempowerment of many. *The Blue Economy* advocates for a new economy, one led by innovation and creativity to cultivate the next generation of social entrepreneurship. We are in need of such an economy and no one is better placed than Gunter Pauli to offer this to the world.

WENDY LUHABE
Chancellor , University of Johannesburg
Chair, Industrial Development Corporation of South Africa

Fifteen years ago Gunter Pauli came to my Tokyo office where I was serving as Rector of the United Nations University. He explained his concept of "Zero Emissions" and I immediately hired him as my Special Advisor. In a very short time, the Zero Emissions concept was thoroughly disseminated in Japan and other countries. Private Japanese companies quickly began to invest in technologies and facilities to implement, in practical terms, that original concept.

   Gunter's new work, *The Blue Economy*, presents excellent innovative ideas with practical applications that will help entrepreneurs and consumers to significantly impact the economies of the world, while earning money, generating jobs, and protecting the environment. In envisioning the future, Gunter continues to be an optimist. I am one too. As you read *The Blue Economy*, you will be introduced to these ideas and their concrete applications. Don't miss it and recommend it to your friends.

PROFESSOR HEITOR GURGULINO DE SOUZA
Rector, UN University, Tokyo, Japan (1987-1997)
Secretary General, IAUP (International Association of University Presidents) Brasilia, DF Brazil

Ultimately, our civilization will survive if we are able to emulate nature. *The Blue Economy* illumines the way.

LESTER R. BROWN
President, Earth Policy Institute
Author, *Plan B 4.0: Mobilizing to Save Civilization*

Though I know too little of ecology, the rich ideas and inspirations set forth in *The Blue Economy* are worthy of our greatest attention.

ELIE WIESEL
1986 Nobel Peace Laureate

The Blue Economy shows us that by securing materials and aligning production schemes as nature does, many problems of environmental degradation and pollution would disappear. However, economic policy and core business models largely ignore integrated solutions. Future economic models would do well to take into account the strategic advantage of a portfolio of innovations based on nature and physics. That will be a tall order, but Gunter Pauli´s book, with its rich presentation of how nature and economy can and must collaborate, convincingly shows the way.

ANDERS WIJKMAN
Member, Swedish Royal Academy of Sciences
European Parliament (1999-2009)

The Blue Economy is an exceptional vision of what is truly possible in the context of a sustainable economy. Gunter Pauli has worked tirelessly for many years to put substance to the promise of a Blue Economy. His book is the fascinating result of true dedication to unlocking the potential for sustainability that is universally practiced in Nature's ecosystems. As investments managers we always seek great, unique ideas that can make money while solving the world's greatest challenges. I would urge anyone who is interested in going beyond shallow notions of sustainable business to read this book and be inspired by the real opportunity we now have to create a truly enduring and sustainable economic system based on Nature's profound wisdom.

COLIN M. LE DUC
Partner, Generation Investment Management LLP (London)

Gunter Pauli is an inspired and visionary entrepreneur. He is the kind of business leader and educator the world needs. His concepts and ideas for creating sustainable business and social enterprises are based on a deep understanding of ecosystems. This book belongs in the library of every university, business school, and entrepreneur who wants to make a difference in the world today.

HAZEL HENDERSON
Author, *Ethical Markets: Growing the Green Economy*
President, Ethical Markets Media (USA and Brazil)

The Blue Economy describes in a clear and inspiring manner a systems approach that models Nature and provides a way forward. For anyone who wants to profit from the economic opportunities concomitant with 21st century changes, Gunter Pauli explains how to restructure economies and reshape societies.

HARVEY STONE
President, Open Circle Innovations

Gunter Pauli has formulated an entrepreneurial business model that can respond to basic needs, build social capital, and achieve sustainability. His current economic development work with READ in Bhutan is focused on introducing a portfolio of the innovations described in this book as tools to improve the National Happiness Index and foster environmental and social entrepreneurship. Given the mission of the Social Venture Network, his message in *The Blue Economy* is certain to resonate with a growing community of business and social leaders.

OMER L. RAINS
Chairman, Rural Education & Development (READ)
Global Director, Marshall Plan Venture Capital Fund
Member, Social Venture Network (SVN)

Gunter Pauli has carefully gathered many concepts that can achieve harmony with nature, wealth for entrepreneurs, and opportunities for food and livelihood security for all. *The Blue Economy* is important reading for all entrepreneurs who embrace environmental awareness and celebrate human evolution.

PAUL MAHAL
Co-founder, CoroCare

Hawaiʻi is moving to revitalize the *ʻāina* – (the land and the ocean) using the principles of prosperity from the *ahupuaʻa* model, originating from the indigenous culture, aligning with the ancient systems of the Earth and the values and spirit of Aloha and Pono. The innovations described in ***The Blue Economy*** honor this spirit. *Aloha ke Akua, e mālama kakou.*

MARK MCGUFFIE
Managing Director, Enterprise Honolulu.

Japan was among the first to support Gunter Pauli's early work with zero emissions. I am certain that the innovative approaches he describes in ***The Blue Economy*** will give the entire world a powerful engine for a new kind of economy.

PROFESSOR KIYOSHI KUROKAWA, M.D.
Special Science Advisor to the Prime Minister of Japan (2006-2008)
President, Science Council of Japan (2003-2006)

The Blue Economy fosters our transition from a product-based economy to a system-based economy. Such a cultural leap requires all of us to see – and move beyond – the connections that have gone into an oblivious core business strategy subject to market tyranny.

DR. CATIA BASTIOLI
President, Novamont SpA (Italia)
European Innovator of the Year (2007)

As a species we have evolved in interdependence, formulating the tools for brilliant co-existence. The novel ideas and breathtaking concepts presented in ***The Blue Economy*** resonate with our deepest knowing. We are led to recognize that Nature devises systems perfectly suited to continuance. The model of cascading energy and nutrients from one kingdom of nature to the next offers us a necessary paradigm that allows us to envision our place in nature's congruence.

AMY MCCONNELL FRANKLIN, PH.D, M.ED., M.P.H.
Emotional Intelligence Education Consultant and Lecturer
Author, *Choose to Change*

In *The Blue Economy* Gunter Pauli exposes readers to a brilliant compendium of innovations that hold the potential to intertwine profitability with sustainability. He shows us how business, science, civil society, and community can partner and profit in meeting the needs of all. This work will energize entrepreneurs to meet the challenge set by former United Nations Secretary-General Kofi Annan: *"Let us choose to unite the power of the markets with the authority of universal ideals. Let us choose to reconcile the creative forces of private entrepreneurship with the needs of the disadvantaged and the requirements of future generations."*

FREDERICK C. DUBEE
Professor, World Peace Academy, University of Basel
Senior Advisor, United Nations Global Compact, China Network
Executive Director, International Global Management Education Institute

The Blue Economy holds a special place on my desk – front and center. In my 30 years of working for a sustainable future, it is rare to come across a book with such a high level of both intellectual rigor AND joyful wonder. I consider both essential. Gunter Pauli's insights and extraordinary breadth of solution-oriented scenarios can make your head spin and your heart beat fast. As a student of systems thinking and design, the 100 innovations described fill me with a sense of hope and thrill me with the possibilities for a future I'll be happy to leave to upcoming generations.

KRIS HOLSTROM, REGIONAL SUSTAINABILITY COORDINATOR
The New Community Coalition
Colorado organic farmer

The Blue Economy reveals, through the eyes of an economist, a panoply of technological innovations based in nature. It shows us that environmental sustainability and company profitability are far from mutually exclusive.

ANDREW PARKER, PHD
Research Leader, London Natural History Museum & Green Templeton College,
Oxford University; Blue Economy Innovator

From the GREEN (initiative)
Jump into THE BLUE (economy)
Your RED (balance sheet) becomes BLACK (wealth)!
With the true dynamic of GAIA (naturally . . .)

TOMOYO NONAKA
Chairwoman, Gaia Initiatve
CEO, Sanyo Electric Group (Japan) (2005-2008)

CONTENTS

FOREWORD

The ideas you are about to encounter are among the most tantalizing prospects for realizing a low carbon, resource-efficient, and competitive economy in the 21st century. It is remarkable that some of the greatest opportunities for jobs will come from replicating the waste-free efficiency of ecosystems. The natural world, in all its splendor and diversity, has already solved many of the sustainability challenges humanity faces in ingenious, unexpected, and even counterintuitive ways. If humans could only unravel the fascinating chemistry, processes, structures, and designs that organisms – from bacteria and mollusks to reptiles and mammals – have evolved and tested over millennia, perhaps then we would have new and transformational solutions to the many challenges faced by a planet of six billion people, rising to over nine billion by 2050.

Gunter Pauli's book, *The Blue Economy*, opens the door to this fresh, forward-looking field. The pioneering advances it profiles will quickly persuade business and government leaders to explore and develop the cutting-edge sciences at the foundation of these new developments. It highlights the innovative work of many, including Emile Ishida (Japan), Wilhelm Barthlott (Germany), Andrew Parker (UK), Joanna Aizenberg (Russia/USA), Jorge Alberto Vieira Costa (Brazil), and other front-line scientists who refuse to accept either the conventional wisdom or the status quo. In featuring their work, *The Blue Economy* demonstrates that we can find ways of utilizing physics, chemistry, and biology with renewable materials

and sustainable practices just as ecosystems do. This is no longer the realm of science-fiction; it is actually happening here and now. With appropriate policies to support research and development, with promotional strategies delivered through market mechanisms, these materials and methods offer abundant opportunities for accelerating adaptation to pressing global issues.

In turn, widespread adoption of the framework proposed in *The Blue Economy* can provide a solid rationale for implementing the agenda of the Convention on Biological Diversity and the missions of organizations like UNEP and IUCN. Currently, species are being lost at an unprecedented rate. Many scientists believe that the world is now undergoing the sixth wave of extinctions, primarily caused by economic models and human behavior that undervalue the contributions of species, habitats, and ecosystems to our lives and the planet's life support systems.

These species within ecosystems underpin our mega-trillion dollar economy by providing essential services at the local, regional, and global level. Many ecosystem species and processes hold clues for potentially significant achievements in the production of medicine, food crops, biofuels, and low-energy materials. These could prove to be essential for societal measures to mitigate or adapt to climate change. Such achievements will certainly be needed to catalyze new sustainable businesses and industries to provide decent, sustainable jobs. For the 100 innovations it describes, *The Blue Economy* estimates an employment potential of 100 million jobs. The plausibility of this estimate is enhanced by the fact that there are today more people employed in renewable energies than in the oil and gas industries combined, and that investment in wind, solar, and geothermal power generation exceeds investment in new fossil fuel power plants.

The United Nations forecasts that by 2025, 1.8 billion people will be living in countries or regions suffering from water scarcity. Two thirds of the world's population could be living with conditions of water stress. Meanwhile, climate change is expected to aggravate water problems via more extreme weather events. Consider a water-collecting system modeled after that of

the Namib desert beetle. This resourceful creature lives in a location that receives a mere half-inch of rain a year, yet it can harvest water from the fogs that blow in gales across the desert several mornings each month.

Researchers have recently designed a surface that is inspired by the water-attracting bumps and water-shedding valleys of scales on this beetle's wings. These scales allow the insect to collect and funnel water droplets that are thinner than a human hair. Trials have been conducted to capture water vapor from cooling towers by using a technique modeled after the beetle's skill. Initial tests have shown that this film invention can recover 10% of the water lost. This lowers energy bills for nearby buildings by reducing the heat island effect. An estimated 50,000 new water-cooling towers are erected annually and each large system loses over 500 million liters of water per day. Thus a savings of even 10% is significant. Other researchers are adapting the beetle's water collection system to develop tents that collect their own water, as well as surfaces that will mix reagents for "lab-on-a-chip" applications. Twenty people are employed on this fledgling development but the true world-wide potential might be as many as 100 thousand new jobs.

The Blue Economy cites a project in Benin where a novel farming and food-processing system emulates the way an ecosystem "cascades" nutrients. Animal wastes from the slaughterhouse are processed in a maggot farm to feed fish and quail; biogas provides electricity and plants purify water. The project is a microcosm of the Blue Economy. For the same Dollar, Euro, Rupee, or Yuan it generates, it produces income, livelihoods, and food security while recycling and re-using wastes. To date 250 people are employed. There is a potential of 500 thousand jobs if this cascading model were used in every African abattoir, and five million jobs worldwide.

It has been nearly 70 years since Swiss engineer George de Mestral, having examined the natural hooks of the burdock seeds that stubbornly attached to his clothes while on a countryside stroll, came up with an invention we know as "Velcro™." More recently, buildings such as a shopping centre in Zimbabwe, a hospital in Colombia, a school in Sweden, and the Zoological

Society of London are cooled by structures inspired by termite mounds. Meanwhile, engineering schools around the world are racing to develop far more efficient solar power based on the molecules and processes of photosynthesis. What **The Blue Economy** emphasizes is the vast potential of such innovations. It spotlights the tipping point inherent in the immense number of such breakthroughs currently in the laboratory, under development, or being commercialized.

The world has been racked by food, fuel, environmental, financial, and economic crises. Ecosystem and biodiversity loss has led to an emerging climate crisis and a looming natural-resource calamity. A Blue Economy, able to deal systematically with these many challenges, and ready to seize the manifest multiple opportunities, is now essential. Our Earth has always been our greatest resource, and this book cites 100 new reasons why investing in both local and global ecosystem sustainability is even more valid and central today. If we follow the logic of nature we can create a foundation for societal sea-change and economic transformation that manifests from the ground up.

Leonardo da Vinci neatly summed up the power of ecosystems and nature's material efficiency in his **Codex Atlanticus**: *"Everything comes from everything; everything is made of everything; everything turns into everything, for all that exists in the elements is made of these elements."*

ACHIM STEINER
Under-Secretary of the United Nations
Executive Director, UN Environmental Programs (UNEP)

ASHOK KHOSLA
President, International Union for Conservation of Nature

DEDICATION

Let us not demand more of the Earth.
Let us do more with what the Earth provides.

— GUNTER PAULI

The endeavor to grasp new insights based on the elegance of nature's ecosystems is anything but a solitary exercise. While this book was written by one person, the impulses, energy, and support emerged from a diverse network, ranging from old friends, close family, and surprising new arrivals. Since 1982, Yusuke Saraya, my long-time friend from Japan, often conspired with me to explore the possibilities offered by ecosystems. The strongest encouragement for this project came at the start from my friend Yasuhiro Sakakibara. After a memorable visit to Reims, France, in 2006, the moment I first discussed the idea with him, he offered his full encouragement. His unconditional support, combined with his admonition that it had to make business sense, typifies the personal generosity that accompanied his promise of funding.

The intellectual supports from Ashok Khosla, Anders Wijkman, and Heitor Gurgulino de Souza, who have been fellow co-inspirators and members of the Club of Rome, have offered structures for debate. From the beginning they provided generous support for this endeavor to identify real breakthroughs beyond "green" batteries and corn-based plastics. Jorge Reynolds, whom I have had the privilege to follow and work with over a quarter of a century, provided first-hand and deeper insight as to how single discoveries into the functioning of the whale heart could impact society beyond the health of heart patients. His inventions provide a fresh look at how innovative advances in health care could provide breakthroughs for

planetary health and simultaneously build a competitive industry, in effect achieving a powerful and deliberate synchronicity. Jorge is also part of a small nucleus of individuals who witnessed Paolo Lugari's emerging dream at Las Gaviotas that used the powers of symbiosis in natural ecosystems to heal centuries of thoughtless human abuse of the land.

The technical and innumerable pages of listings of what nature and ecosystems accomplish, gathered with painstaking effort, came to life only when scientists like Joanna Aizenberg, Andrew Parker, Peter Steinberg, Christer Swedin, Jorge Alberto Vieira Costa, Peter Steinberg, and Fritz Vollrath plumbed the depths of their insights and described opportunities with passion and clarity. These efforts, complemented with the entrepreneurial pragmatism of Curt Hallberg, Emile Ishida, Mats Nilsson, and Norman Voyer, provided a wealth of content that helped establish the vision and the foundation for the ideas that stand at the core of this book. When I subsequently contemplated the work of systems integrators like Paolo Lugari (Gaviotas), Father Godfrey Nzamujo, John Todd, and Anders Nyquist, I realized the tremendous power of bundling these technologies into systems to achieve something that is economically viable, eminently natural, quite complex, yet very simple. I knew that their energy had set me on track toward something truly worthwhile. Without the generosity of time offered by over a hundred scientists and entrepreneurs, I would never have had their perspective for my goals to describe how adapting the logic of ecosystems to economic models can generate sustainable livelihood and provide the basic needs of all.

Then, there is the energy to pursue this endeavor against all odds. When my partners of the moment abandoned larger goals and chose to control intellectual property for personal benefit, it was the ethical leadership of my mentor, Elie Wiesel, that helped direct my focus to the greater good. It permitted me to drop the excessively romantic view of each species that had diverted my attention from the real power of ecosystems and the vast portfolio of entrepreneurial opportunities. Within that changing world my wife, Katherina, provided the greatest support. Her unconditional backing helped me realize the importance of discarding the superficial calculations of idealized businesses in favor of a vision of systemic job generation that could redefine competitiveness and offer a new economic framework to a global population.

Several organizations around the world invited me to share emerging insights, engage dialogues, focus proposals, and prioritize the cases. Addressing Bioneers at the Bay (Massachusetts, USA – organized by the Marion Institute); the governing council of UNEP in Nairobi, Kenya; the COP on Biodiversity in Bonn, Germany; the Industry Leaders' Summit in New Delhi, India; bankers and farmers at ABSA in Stellenbosch, South Africa; Al Gore's Expert Panel on Solutions for Climate Change in New York, USA; the GLOBE Meeting at the G8 in Tokyo, Japan, the LIFT Conference in Marseilles, France; the Annual Congress of Engineers (ANPEI) in Brazil; the APEC CEO Summit in Singapore; the General Assembly of UNIDO in Vienna, Austria; and the 2009 Annual Meeting of the Club of Rome in Amsterdam, Netherlands, are some of the valuable exchanges that enriched my insights.

Perhaps the greatest gift over the past decade was the spider bite (from the brown recluse) that put me on crutches for nine weeks and in a wheelchair for four. While this did not stop me from scouting the world for solutions, it did offer me time in Marion, Massachusetts to reflect upon pathways towards the future. Michael Baldwin, founder of the Marion Institute, and Peter Dean, his fellow board member, offered me a rare chance to think and rethink, while a new world emerged on my horizon.

It was at this nexus in time that Peter Dean and Erin Sanborn's crystallizing energy provided the platform this project has deserved ever since Achim Steiner, the Executive Director of the United Nations Environment Programme, opted to support this initiative. I am very grateful that Achim has continued to support this effort to look at the emerging Blue Economy. Then the editors appeared who could convert the spirit of this epochal insight into language that reaches everyone. Martha Fielding and Bob Felt

translated my insights into this emerging world into a fluid chain of words and concepts that reaches a larger readership, beyond the experts and the converted.

In 1979 Aurelio Peccei, founder of the Club of Rome and a personal mentor, invited me to attend the annual meeting of the Club in Salzburg, Austria. Three decades later, the members of the Club have considered this book worthy of being named a Report to the Club of Rome, in the rich tradition of milestone publications like **Limits to Growth** and **Factor Four**. It is a humbling honor. Thus it is with deep gratitude that I undertake to merit these expectations. My deepest wish is to fully contribute to the vision and the shaping of the sustainable society articulated by the founding fathers of the Club of Rome.

There are many people who have been key to making certain that this book came to be; but perhaps the most momentous inspiration has been my son, Philipp-Emmanuel, who just arrived to this world, opening wide my eyes and making me look positively into the future, reawakening that fundamental feeling that parents have a responsibility to create an environment that is conducive to a better future. My older sons, Carl-Olaf and Laurenz-Frederik, were the first readers of this book. My adopted daughter Chido deserves full credit for demonstrating that all in this book is not fantasy. It is reality in the making as described throughout the chapters of **The Blue Economy**. This is what offers hope.

PREFACE

If we teach our children only what we know,
they can never do better than we do.

— GUNTER PAULI

In the 1980s when I read the books of Lester Brown and his team at the Worldwatch Institute, I had the urge to make available to everyone this wealth of data concerning global environmental issues. The onslaught of negative statistics and trend analyses, based on data assembled in Washington DC, showed only a few positive lights on the horizon. Consequently I created a dedicated publishing company to bring the *State of the World* and *Vital Signs* to a recalcitrant listener: the business community in Europe. As an entrepreneur who had established a half-dozen companies by then, I was also a concerned citizen. In the early 1990s with the arrival of my two sons, Carl-Olaf and Laurenz-Frederik, a reflection crossed my mind as happens with so many young fathers and mothers: we want to leave the world to our children in a better condition than we received it from our parents. As my first sons graduate from high school nearly two decades later, I must confess it seems a Herculean task.

However, as life matures and wrinkles unveil deep concerns, we cannot simply remain concerned citizens, worried about the future, sorry about every error. Rather we must regroup and find ways to create the foundation on which we can allow the next generation to surpass our achievements. Perhaps the greatest freedom we can offer our children is to allow them to think differently and, more importantly, to act differently. It is therefore helpful to reflect on what we can bequeath future generations as a structure for positive thinking and a platform for concrete action. This is perhaps the

greatest challenge. The bad news is not only about the health of our planet. For the first time in decades we are realizing that the economic system is also crumbling.

As an early member of the Club of Rome, the informal gathering of concerned policy makers, scholars, business leaders, and international civil servants, I know all too well the importance of sounding a wake-up call. The ***Limits to Growth*** report put forth by the Club of Rome clearly delineated the vicious cycle of population explosion, environmental degradation, unbridled industrial growth, and collapse of ethical standards. As a publisher of the Worldwatch ***State of the World*** in selected European languages, and as an avid participant in the Club of Rome for three decades, I could never separate the negative conclusions from the need for positive action.

I began working with Ecover, a Europe-based producer of biodegradable cleaning products. When even the largest manufacturers adopted our biodegradable ingredient – the fatty acids of palm oil – as an industry standard replacement for petrochemical surfactants, it dramatically increased demand for this alternative. This spurred many harvesters, especially in Indonesia, to replace vast swathes of rainforest with palm tree farms. In destroying the rainforest, much of the habitat for the orangutan was also lost. Thus I learned to my chagrin that biodegradability and renewability do not equate with sustainability.

In my first article on the subject, published in Seoul, Korea in 1991, I exhorted the industry to emulate the efficiency of ecosystems. The wisdom of an ecosystem is not just that it provides services like fresh water and clean air, replenishment of topsoil, balanced control of bacteria, and a never-ending evolutionary pathway, always searching for better solutions and higher efficiencies. Ecosystems are also an inspiration for changing our highly wasteful production and consumption model. The article suggested that sustainability is only foreseeable when our system eliminates the concept of waste, and starts cascading nutrients and energy as nature does.

After the disenchanting experience with Ecover, I was challenged by Prof. Dr. Heitor Gurgulino de Souza, the Rector of the United Nations University hosted by the Japanese government, to model an economic system that generated no waste and no emissions, yet created jobs, contributed social capital, and did not entail a higher cost. I accepted this challenge three years before the Kyoto Protocol was approved. Thus I had the opportunity to imagine, from an academic ivory tower, how we could emulate the productive and evolutionary interactions of natural ecosystems where waste for one is food for another. Following three years of research, and in cooperation with the United Nations Development Programme, the ZERI Foundation was established in Switzerland with its sole objective to implement pioneering cases that could demonstrate a scientifically feasible and economically viable model of production and consumption.

Celebrating the first decade of pioneering around the world, the Board of ZERI commissioned an inventory of innovations inspired by natural systems. Although the starting point was nothing more than assembling peer-reviewed, publicly accessible scientific literature, it quickly evolved from a romantic and fascinating search for the brilliance in each species that dramatically enriches biodiversity, to a quest for an economic model that could inspire entrepreneurs to put humanity in general and its production and consumption in particular on a viable and sustainable path. At the outset of this search I had the opportunity to work with Fritjof Capra to edit the book, *Steering Businesses towards Sustainability*. This project triggered a deluge of ideas. I realized that my search for a next generation of business opportunities was based on the conviction that if I could portray the models I envisioned, it might inspire others to become entrepreneurs. The review team ploughed through and annotated thousands of pertinent articles in English-language scientific publications. These were complemented with similar Spanish, German, and Japanese publications. My task was to sift through one after the other and imagine which one of over 3,000 cases would present an opportunity to move industry and commerce toward sustainability independent of subsidies or tax breaks. I pondered which innovations could be bundled into a system that could

work the way ecosystems do, clustering innovations developed by diverse players, making a more efficient use of all the existing, unfailing forces described by the laws of physics for which there are no exceptions.

As an entrepreneur who embraces innovation, I submitted a shortlist of 340 technologies to a team of corporate strategists, expert financiers, investigative journalists, and public policymakers. This exercise happened prior to the current recession, while the world was still building castles in the sky with money that did not exist. Over a period of two years I met with inventors and entrepreneurs in all four corners of the world. I held dozens of meetings with financial analysts, business reporters, and corporate strategy academics. This helped sharpen the logic behind the ultimate selection of the 100 most remarkable innovations cataloged in Appendix One. Then, the recession hit. At the end of 2008 when the United Nations announced that the collapse of the financial markets had cost developing countries over 50 million jobs, a sense of realism emerged. I could find no satisfaction in matching a captivating photograph to a scientific explanation. I needed to communicate something more than the inspirational brilliance of every species we had examined.

A new team undertook a complete reassessment of all the information before us and examined the dynamics of the current economic model's demise in the light of the innovations we had cataloged. We spotted the phoenix of new growth that seemed to shift the logic of short-term results and bonuses to one that gives a world constrained by limited resources the ability to respond to people's basic needs with what we have. I saw a clear model emerging that could offer entrepreneurs around the world a unique window of opportunity to change the dominant business paradigm. It was not about cloning and genetic manipulation, protected by patents that appear closer to bio-piracy than actual innovation. It was about the pervasive logic and sensibility of ecosystems. This short list of 100 innovations drew inspiration from the ability of ecosystems to always evolve to higher levels of efficiency, to cascade nutrients and energy, to leave nothing to waste, to utilize the abilities of all contributors, and to respond to the basic needs of all.

Such insights into ecosystems logic have crystallized into the underpinnings of this book, allowing me to establish the framework for a Blue Economy and to realize that the current economic upheaval is a blessing in disguise. It may be that we are finally calling a halt to the unrealistic consumerism that has propelled the economy into insurmountable debt. Exhorting consumers to spend more is a stereotype of the blind logic that cajoles citizens to buy their way out of crisis by indebting all of us as well as subsequent generations, beyond our capacity to ever repay. This unconscionable approach siphons the entire world's liquidity into an elite "bankonomy," denying credit for everyone else. Such actions are at the base of a bankrupt economic model, a Red Economy model that borrows – from nature, from humanity, from the commons of all – with no thought of repayment beyond postponement to the future. Insatiable economies of scale callously search for ever lower marginal costs for each additional unit manufactured, making dismissive abstraction of all unintended consequences. The financial crisis of 2008 stemmed from bankers and corporate decision-makers embarking on a merger and acquisition frenzy, leveraging assets and amassing such enormous debt that the growth became self-defeating. Such is the tale of an "In-the-Red" (debt) Economy that failed.

In comparison, a Green Economy model has required companies to invest more and consumers to pay more, to achieve the same, or even less, while preserving the environment. While this was already a challenge during the heyday of economic growth, it is a solution that has little chance in a time of economic downturn. The Green Economy, in spite of much goodwill and effort, has not achieved the viability so greatly desired. If we shift the spectrum, we see that a Blue Economy addresses the issues of sustainability that go beyond mere preservation. A Blue Economy engages regeneration. We might say that the Blue Economy is about ensuring that ecosystems can maintain their evolutionary path so that all can benefit from nature's endless flow of creativity, adaptation, and abundance.

It is the young at heart who will seize upon the entrepreneurial opportunities that emulate ecosystems and cascade energy and resources to add value

and generate multiple exchange benefits, translating them into income and employment. When we implement the concepts of a Blue Economy, the decisions of millions of actors can supercede the *dirigisme* of a few market makers, monopolistic companies, or state controls, and a powerful new social and economic structure manifests. The engagement and commitment of citizens is what will change the rules of the game and what will effect a real shift. At a moment in history where peak oil and peak food are clearly hovering, we can draw practical ideas and inspiration from ecosystems as we witness their ability to apply creativity and evolution in overcoming challenges to survival. This book aims to contribute to the design of a new economic model that is not only capable of responding to the needs of all but converts the artificial construct called "scarcity" into a sense of sufficiency and even of abundance.

While the waste of material resources exemplified by modern landfills and incinerators is to be deplored, the waste of human resources is absolutely unacceptable. When the numbers of unemployed youth oscillate between 25% in industrialized countries and over 50% in the developing world, it is easy to imagine what it means to our global society if its leaders consider the next generation useless – or even worse, if the young and disadvantaged consider themselves useless. It is indicative of a system in severe decline, a society in extreme crisis, underscored by mounting statistics of violence, criminality, terrorism, drug abuse, illegal immigration, relinquished education, and the deplorable treatment of populations or communities already at-risk or underserved.

Abdul Samer Majali, who served as President of Jordan University as well as Prime Minister, once said, "*Expose – do not impose.*" If our aim is to create a better world for all, not just a fuller bank account for a few, if we are prepared to counter risk with gain, then thoughtful considerations, based on solid science and documented illustrative cases, can help us envision and achieve it. A strong platform for entrepreneurship could emulate the success of ecosystems in eliminating waste and achieving full employment and productive capacity. Multiple small initiatives around the world could provide the basis for new entrepreneurial opportunities that would permit the shift to a macro-economic system. Instead of deferment as policy-makers reach agreement, the direction we take is to expose individuals everywhere to the open-source opportunities provided by nature.

It is amazing how little natural logic there is in modern society. To cool a building, air-conditioning experts pump cold air "up"? To clean water we dump chemicals in it to kill all life? Greenhouses heat the air, not the roots? We pay upwards of $100 per kilowatt hour for electricity provided by a battery that toxifies our environment? When we drink a cup of coffee we give value to only 0.2% of the biomass while the rest is left to rot, generating methane gas, or stressing earthworms, who suffer as much from the neurotoxin called "caffeine" as we do. A hundred thousand tons of titanium, mined and processed at high temperature, are flung into landfills when we "discard" our "disposable" razors. Humanity makes excessive use of energy, emits greenhouse gases beyond reason, and causes havoc in the environment. We can hardly be surprised that we face climate change. Indeed, the only excuse for what we do and the way we do it is that we are ignorant about unintended consequences. Once we know, we not only have the clarity needed to change, we are also empowered to consciously make it happen.

Chido Govero, an orphan who lost her mother at the age of seven and never knew her father, turned immediately from a young girl to the head of her family with the responsibility to provide food for her grandmother and little brother. Although such tragedy is real, it is far too common. There are millions of people, many of them women and children, who must tolerate abuse to guarantee a semblance of food, water, and shelter. As someone who quickly learned how to survive for years on nothing more than a bowl of peanuts a day, Chido also quickly learned to appreciate the generative capacity of ecosystems. In Africa, these natural systems have been pillaged by the irresponsible farming of settlers who brought their traditions from temperate climates with four seasons, whose techniques not only denuded the land of its natural vegetation but drastically eroded the rich topsoil.

Yet Chido does not judge the errors of the past. She has grasped the opportunity to redefine the potential of coffee-crop agro-waste to achieve food and livelihood security for herself and her fellow orphans in Zimbabwe. Given food and livelihood security, abuse – both of young girls and of natural systems – can be eliminated. Chido's vision is to accomplish this in her lifetime.

What more do you expect to achieve in your lifetime? Do you mind waiting to answer until you have read this book?

Gunter Pauli
10th of January 2010
La Miñoca, Columbia

CHAPTER ONE

TIMELESS RESOURCES
FOR THE CHALLENGES
OF OUR TIMES

Some dream to escape reality.
Some dream to change reality forever.

— SOICHIRO HONDA

This book is about adopting a new awareness that it is not so very difficult, provided we are prepared to leave old habits behind and are ready to embrace new ones. It is a wake-up call to those of us who feel that the chances are simply too unique to let pass by. The opportunities before us will make a difference – now. It must be now. Deep ecology, permaculture, and sustainability are concepts that planted the early seeds of green thinking. Such ideas taught us to appreciate the use of sustainable materials in our structures and products. Though we have begun to understand the importance of sustainable processes, few know how to make these economically viable. If we begin to understand and utilize nature's brilliance, economy, and simplicity, we can emulate the functionality embedded in the logic of ecosystems and achieve a success unrivalled by current massively globalized industries.

PHYSICS AND PRACTICALITY

Ours is a physical universe. All life, and all matter that surrounds us, perform in accord with the very predictable laws of physics. The vital relationship of the laws and theories of physics to the essential conditions of how we produce, consume, and survive are not given much attention in today's physics classroom. Yet it is in observing the basics of physics that we realize how minute shifts in pressure, temperature, and moisture content create outstanding products that in their elegance, simplicity, and effectiveness far outshine the results of genetic modification. Instead of manipulating the biology of life, let us find inspiration in the ways that nature utilizes physics.

From the first nanosecond of creation, our universe, our world, and ultimately our species' evolution have been influenced and shaped by the dominant forces of temperature and pressure. Within the framework of fundamental physical forces – gravity, electromagnetism, and weak and strong nuclear forces – our Earth's species underwent interactions and reactions, translating their evolutionary experience into remarkable diversity. Ecosystems developed that are shared by millions of unique species operating within the realms of physics and biochemistry and evolving biologically.

It is amazing how everything in nature learned to use physics to their advantage. Perhaps this is due to the fact that, unlike natural language grammars, or biology, there are no exceptions to the rules of physics. The sun rises every morning, apples drop from the tree, and low and high pressure fields cause wind. When it comes to chemistry, it all depends on temperature, pressure, and a catalyst. And, as the progeny-bearing male seahorse demonstrates, when it comes to biology, there is always an exception to the rule.

Scientists posit that for the past several billion years all life on Earth has evolved and adapted in relatively stable ambient water and air temperatures and pressures. Every living species has learned to work with what is locally available. Shaped by the inevitable laws of physics, every species that has navigated millions of years of evolution has learned how to solve challenges to survival, simply by using what they have and doing what they do best.

When a human infant is born, the pathway to individual life includes the experience of tremendous pressure, passing through a narrow ten-centimeter opening to the air-breathing world. The child's shoulders and chest are compressed so that all liquid is expelled from the lungs.

By emptying the lungs, the first breath of air can be taken. This pressure is an indispensable preparation for life, evoking a sense of stress and providing a contrast that permits savoring the beauty of arrival on Earth. It is similar with all life. When a butterfly leaves its cocoon, a patient observer will see how hard it must struggle, even for hours, to complete its transformation into a beautiful winged creature. Early scientific observers, cutting the cocoon to facilitate the butterfly's emergence from its tight protective shell, found that it could not fly, and in fact died moments after its painless birth. Thus pressure can be seen as ushering in life, catalyzing the complex dynamics of form and function, from pulling muscles, to the beating of the heart pumping blood, to the animation of all the joints and the inhalation and exhalation of breath.

It seems that crisis is another form of pressure that is capable of energizing us to reach for new solutions. Likewise, it reminds us to savor the beauty of living.

WASTING AWAY

After a billion years of species evolution, mankind alone seeks to control nature's dynamic balance of life guided by physics. We harnessed energy to use at will – at first fire, then fossil fuels and nuclear power. We exploited and shaped matter to our invention, often achieving the remarkable, sometimes less so. Yet the achievements of our industrial age also brought a strain on the carrying capacity of our planet. The profligate generation and consumption of energy has brought us things no one desires, and has destroyed or compromised much of what natural systems contributed over millennia. We find ourselves at a crossroads where we must examine the choices for our future. Are we to live in harmony with our Earth and its species, or will we continue our consumptive and destructive flagrancies? Will we learn to peacefully and productively cohabit or will we extinguish ourselves, as we have already begun to extinguish so many other species, drowning in our unproductive excesses and volumes of waste?

Nearly all the hundred thousand different molecules that comprise petroleum are taken up in the process of synthesizing fuel, plastics, building materials, or any of the myriad petrochemical products in daily use. Yet, the concomitant waste stream that accompanies this masterful achievement is everywhere to be seen. No longer hidden, we now see the environmental costs entailed in the extraction and refining of petroleum, the dramatic impact on climate change caused by the release of carbon into the atmosphere, and the tremendous burden of waste accumulated from petroleum-derived products. The creation of covalently bound molecules that made plastics possible has surely been a remarkable innovation. Yet the chemical processes that synthesize plastics, requiring careful management of pressure and temperature as well as the administration of catalysts, result in products composed of super molecules that degrade only with difficulty. There are massive islands of accumulated plastics slowly degrading in a vast area of the Pacific Ocean. Small particles now admix with beach sand. Massive landfills overflow with discarded hunks of these same stubbornly fixated petroleum polymers. Think of it: a single-use water container made of plastic can remain intact in a landfill for hundreds if not thousands of years! Surely we can do much better.

Much of our agriculturally based production creates a similarly excessive stream of waste. A brewery uses only the starch from the barley, and discards the remains. Rice is farmed only for its kernel, and the rest, especially the straw, is simply waste. Corn is farmed solely for the seeds that become feed, plastics, or fuels. Since all three applications compete for the same little kernel, demand sends the price of corn spiraling upward. Many people in developing Latin American countries can no longer afford the cost of *arepas* or *tortillas*, basic foodstuffs to stave off hunger and starvation. Then there is coffee, farmed only for its berries, with the rest left to rot; or the production of sugar from cane, using only the 17% that is sugar content, while the rest is burned. Trees logged for making paper only use the cellulose; over 70% of the tree is incinerated as waste. The methane released from untreated decomposing dairy manure tops the list for greenhouse gas emissions. Whenever we do not know what to do with a "waste," we "discard" it. That is antithetical to the way natural ecosystems operate.

Most of our industries generate massive amounts of waste. For every ton of municipal solid waste, there are 71 tons produced from mining, manufacturing, and product distribution. We have nuclear waste, soil laced with heavy metals, chromium-contaminated groundwater, landfills bursting with cast-off plastic containers. The residues of our consumption are buried in highly centralized areas and are burned when the volume accumulates. It is misleading to claim that burning waste generates energy. Much of the waste that is incinerated is merely reduced in volume because burning reduces the moisture content. Most of the components remain, except for water.

It is estimated that the total spent in the US each year just to transport waste to landfills reaches a staggering $50 billion dollars. If we add to this the cost of collecting, hauling, sorting, and disposing waste from construction, agriculture, mining, and industry, the price tops an incredible *one trillion* dollars. This means that the money wasted on waste every year is more than the 2009 stimulus package for the entire US economy, and more than the massive deficits undertaken by European governments to pump comparable amounts of cash into ailing banks. While these trillions count as productive activity in the national accounts, it is clear that waste management is a non-productive activity. The jobs generated should never be classified as green jobs. The use of land for waste storage is not productive. The toxic seepage and containment costs are unacceptable, and are billed to society as a whole – an externalized cost that corporations are not required to deduct from profit margins.

This prevailing economic model has fueled two centuries of an unending cycle of growth, consumption, and disposal, feeding an insatiable appetite for material wealth for which societies have accumulated more debt than can ever be repaid. We reached all too eagerly for the easy credit offered by banks to buy what we often did not need. Meanwhile massive and critical demands, especially those of peoples living in developing nations, have gone unmet. World demand has grown beyond the Earth's ability to provide potable water and a daily meal for far too many families. Despite the gains we have made, our present means are not capable of responding to the needs of all. Our material lifestyles and desires require ever-larger levels of energy production that use fossil fuels, coal, nuclear power, and even photovoltaics (which require copious energy inputs) and windmills (which need electricity to power up). We can – we must – do better.

Over the past decade there have been calls by prominent environmentalists and economists for industrialized nations to dramatically reduce their material intensity. Prior even to these voices, the call for more material efficiency was admirably articulated in Ernst Ulrich von Weizsäcker's book, **Factor Four**, which became a Report to the Club of Rome. William Rees' concept of an "ecological footprint," offering a calculable means for evaluating human demand in the context of renewable ecological capacity, entered the professional lexicon and expressed our excessive use of materials in an easily understood metaphor. If our habits remain unchanged, we will need more than one additional Earth to sustain our present production and consumption level and to hold the accumulation of waste that we have nowhere else to dump. The economy is not crumbling simply because of the disintegration of financial markets where mythical money flowed. Our economy is stressed because our material world operates on the basis of physical resources we do not have, and waste we have nowhere to hide. Perhaps the first change we should make is to stop producing and consuming things we do not really need that make the waste that no one wants, especially waste that is toxic to ourselves and our fellow beings on this planet.

HOW TO WELCOME WASTE

With any luck, what we will realize is that making waste is not the problem we must solve. If a living species does not generate waste, it is most likely dead, or at least very ill. The problem we have, and that we must address, is that we waste the waste we create. Consider that the conversion of waste into nutrients both requires and generates energy. While we are always looking for sources of energy for commercial and home applications, ecosystems never need to be wired. No member of an ecosystem needs fossil fuel or a connection to the grid to achieve output; nor is waste an outcome in natural systems. In nature, the waste of one process is always a nutrient, a material, or a source of energy for another. Everything stays in the nutrient stream. Thus the solution not only to the environmental challenges of pollution but to the economic challenges of scarcity may be found in the application of models we can observe in a natural ecosystem. Perhaps we can turn dilemma into solution by broadening our perspective and abandoning the concept of waste.

With green chemistry, polymers derived from petroleum were replaced with polymers derived from natural raw materials as varied as starch, amino acids, sugar, lignin, cellulose, and many more. We can now acknowledge that not only the product but the whole process can be inspired by natural systems. Rather than accomplish substitution of a toxic component or ingredient with one that is less polluting, if we emulate how natural ecosystems utilize everything, we will in effect achieve sustainable systems that provide jobs and outperform waste-spewing industries. This means that the resultant product, whether a natural color, a building material, or a water repellent surface, can not only be manufactured in recognition of its interplay with the environment but can achieve economic success and garner appreciable market share.

Unique solutions perfected by desert insects, spiders, and sea algae can replace toxic products that are today's standards with products that are manufactured with truly renewable materials and means. Such solutions are important because they can noticeably improve our daily lives while reducing levels of toxic pollutants. Toxin-spewing, inefficient, old-model industries will lose competitiveness and thus their ability to employ. Ideally, the whole cycle of production, consumption, and post-consumption becomes sustainable. This is what will permit the fundamental shift to a Blue Economy. The first step is to search for ways to convert waste into contribution, and to identify inputs that are widely and cheaply available because they are of little or no value to anyone else in the system. That is how nature works.

Under the chairmanship of Hiroyuki Fujimura, Japan's Ebara Corporation embarked on a quest for a "zero emissions" strategy that would leave nothing to waste. Everything – even waste – was to generate value. Ebara funded and supported Prof. Yoshihito Shirai at the Kyushu Institute of Technology to pursue solutions for plastics manufacturing using the logic of cascading nutrients and energy. Shirai and his staff developed a process that uses a fungus to convert starch collected from restaurant food waste into polylactic acid at nearly ambient temperature. In effect they devised a way to make plastics from kitchen waste! Although the raw materials are agricultural and renewable, they never draw down the supply of a staple food the way that corn used for biofuel or for biodegradable plastic has done. Nor does the waste end up in a landfill, where it emits methane gas.

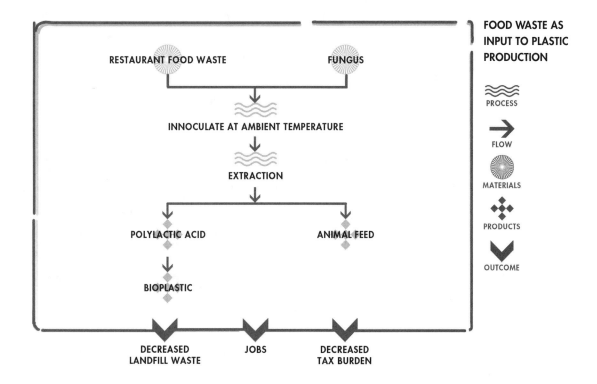

FOOD WASTE AS INPUT TO PLASTIC PRODUCTION

Industry leaders have the opportunity to accomplish similar successes in the area of biodegradable soaps and detergents. Sugar-derived surfactants (alkyl-polyglucoses), which are mainly used in the pharmaceutical industry, offer an ideal alternative to soaps made from palm oil. Another option would be to use d-Limonene, an extract of citrus fruit peels ideal as a substitute for diverse harsh cleaning agents. If industry could forego the use of chemicals and waxes to preserve fruits stored for months or shipped over long distances, such "waste" from the production of citrus juice could be used for animal feed or as a source of pectin (a jelling agent), and could be given greater value as a truly green biodegradable soap.

Paper manufacture has a comparable option. Cellulose and lignin are traditionally processed with alkali-sulfates. This traditional wood separation process chemically burns everything but cellulose so that the fibers used in commerce are the sole output. The residue, known as "black liquor," is incinerated. Professor Janis Gravitis from the Wood Chemistry Research Institute in Riga, Latvia, has studied alternative processes for paper production, including the creation of a biorefinery to extract for commercial use all the components of a tree, from cellulose, to hemi-cellulose, lignin, and lipids. Once scientists and industrial engineers begin to design processes that cascade nutrients, so that the waste from one is a readily available raw material for another, we are closer to achieving whole systems design.

Given the availability of new alternatives without the drawbacks of harmful side effects or toxic byproducts, it is timely to motivate the scientists and entrepreneurs to embrace such sustainable manufacturing processes. Industry and commerce require our encouragement to recognize the business opportunity embedded such an approach, while recognizing as well the value of supporting environments that are health-promoting and conducive to life.

ACHIEVING ABUNDANCE

While skeptics may argue that modeling from natural ecosystems can only succeed against all odds, in reality these systems are designed such that it is actually difficult to fail. Natural systems provide fascinating operational models of efficient production and consumption. Although it is often an individual species we most admire and lyrically describe, it is ecosystems, with great diversity around the world, that demonstrate efficient ways to respond to everyone's basic needs with what is locally available.

This is a fundamental principle for the Blue Economy that contrasts to the current episode of economic history where we have designed a system based on what we do not have. Stop and reflect: every ecosystem has achieved a state of self-sufficiency. Although we may initially perceive scarcity, a closer look shows that abundance and diversity are the reality. The greater the abundance generated, the more that can be achieved with less, and the greater the biodiversity that emerges. Ecosystems do not evolve towards monopolies with few dominant players. Ecosystems more closely exhibit the market conditions proposed by Adam Smith, the founder of modern economics: thousands of players fine-tuning their actions as if an invisible hand were directing them to the best allocation and use of resources.

Engineers and agronomists who might reject a whole systems model as unrealistic are unacquainted with the remarkable projects that have already achieved effective outcomes. Output is high, with low material input; energy consumption is low, and in most cases the system produces more than is needed. Health enhancement, food security, and potable water, are additional – and not inconsequential – benefits. Cascading nutrients and energy from one species to another in a continuous cycle and within a framework provided by physics is demonstrably applied in an industrial context.

Highly productive Blue Economy industries, capable of generating employment for all, are on the horizon. They are based on how nature uses physics and biochemistry to build harmoniously functioning whole systems, cascading abundantly, transforming effortlessly, and cycling efficiently without waste or energy loss. These forces not only determined the parameters of life on Earth but also helped shape life itself. As we move from a linear perception to seeing a cyclic, regenerative model, we too can shape our behaviors and practices to assure that everyone's basic needs are met and that our blue planet Earth, with all its inhabitants, progresses towards an optimum future.

CHAPTER TWO

EMULATING ECOSYSTEMS FOR A BLUE ECONOMY

Motanai (Waste not, want not).

— JAPANESE PROVERB

A vibrant economy is essential to sustainability. The reverse is also true. Without true sustainability no economy can continue to function. With that in mind, perhaps it will not surprise you to learn, as you will while reading this book, that a solution to our current economic malaise lies in understanding and applying ecosystems logic. Nature demonstrates true economy – and true sustainability – all the time. If we were to develop our economies following nature, we could use energy and resources efficiently and without waste, and create hundreds of millions of jobs. Ecosystem models offer the keys to abundance, and the means to share with all. An economic system inspired by ecosystems would work with what is locally available, such as naturally recurring energy resources that express the laws of physics first and foremost. Physics describes the underlying forces that are dynamically utilized by every species on Earth. This insight is the pathway to sustainability. Transforming the current economic down-cycle by emulating the logic modeled in ecosystems will allow us to meet basic needs and create a true economy, a Blue Economy, an economy of abundance.

Emulating the functional and material efficiency of ecosystems and natural habitats is a pragmatic way to achieve sustainability and high resource efficiency while remaining competitive and generating added value. Cascading nutrients and energy is another ecosystem elegance that we would do well to emulate. It is nature's method for transforming apparent scarcity to sufficiency and ultimately abundance. We can picture a cascade as a waterfall, as a flow of nutrients that requires no power source, merely the force of gravity. It offers a visual metaphor to help us comprehend how nutrients are transported from the species of one biological kingdom to another, for the benefit of all. Absorbed minerals feed microorganisms, microorganisms feed plants, plants feed other species, with the waste of one being nourishment for another. Cascading energy and nutrients leads to sustainability by reducing or eliminating external inputs such as energy and by eliminating waste and its cost, not just as pollution but also as inefficient use of materials.

Around the world there are successful and well-established examples of entrepreneurship that illustrate how a Blue Economy can not only benefit the land but also its inhabitants, with the result that food security, livelihood security, and contributory occupations are available to all. We can look to the remarkable transformation of the Vichada savannah in Colombia accomplished by Paolo Lugari at Las Gaviotas. We can study a project for West African food and livelihood security established in Benin by Father Godfrey Nzamujo. We can follow the vision of Håkan Ahlsten and the citizens of Gotland to sustain and renew their land and culture; or the efforts of Picuris Pueblo in converting small diameter wood from a fire hazard to raw materials for an integrated biosystem that sustainably generates jobs, food, fuel, and construction materials. These have in common emulation of nature's nutrient cascade and utilization of energy sources that function according to the laws of physics. As well, each achieves food and energy security while generating multiple benefits, including positive cash flow, reduction of material intensity, and energy savings.

PLENITUDE FROM PAUCITY

When Paolo Lugari proposed regenerating the Vichada savannah in Colombia into the rainforest it once was, no one thought it possible based on the prevailing science of the time. A track of savannah on the Western side of the Orinoco River was worthless. The pH was low, the water was not drinkable, and there was no easy land, water, or air access. Who would purchase even an acre? The land was obtained through land grants, which cost approximately $2.50 per acre. The bank funding was made possible by Mario Calderon Rivera. Lugari persevered, planting with neither experience nor funding, using a creative approach to regenerate the dry, despoiled savannah and transforming it into a haven of lush tropical biodiversity. Now, a quarter-century later, Lugari welcomes visitors to 20,000 acres of restored rainforest. He and his team discovered that the symbiosis between mycorrhizal fungi and the Caribbean pine tree not only secured the survival of 92% of the seedlings planted, but also changed the physical attributes of the region. How?

When innoculated with the fungus *Pisolithus tinctorius*, the small Caribbean pine tree, *Pinus caribaea*, creates a discrete shaded space protecting the soil and roots from the sun's ultraviolet rays. Although the heat stress remains high, causing a thick carpet of pine needle droppings, the pine tree grows to maturity because it is well nourished by the fungus. The carpet of pine needles improves the moisture content of the soil, simultaneously trapping composting debris that would otherwise wash away.

Importantly, this debris cover also moderates the temperature of the soil. When rain falls on a hot soil, it cannot penetrate even the porous surface and thus more readily washes away, lost to erosion. When rain falls on a cooler soil, it is more likely to be absorbed into the ground. Thus the increase in soil permeability caused by inversion of the temperature differential between the rain and topsoil creates an environment for new seeds to gain hold. As the emerging forest grows, diversity flourishes and rain becomes more abundant. The dry savannah with poor drinking water and overly acidic soil now becomes not just a forest, but a rainforest abundant in potable water, with a richer soil ideal for flourishing plant life.

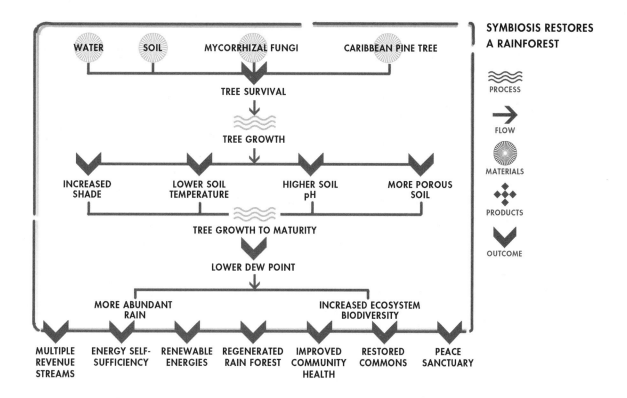

SYMBIOSIS RESTORES A RAINFOREST

≈≈≈ PROCESS

→ FLOW

⊛ MATERIALS

❖ PRODUCTS

⌄ OUTCOME

A Japanese film crew, arriving in Gaviotas to record what few could believe, observed clouds approach and float above the savannah. The moment these clouds drifted over the forest's cooler sphere, the crew was amazed to experience the refreshing rain that began to fall. Indeed, the green forest is fresher than the heat-absorbing plains. Thus, when the surface is cool, the clouds drop their moisture thanks to the lower dew point. Leaving behind 450 years of slash-and-burn agriculture and the cultivation of invasive grasses used as cattle fodder, Las Gaviotas enfolded fungi and trees in elegant symbiosis, creating the conditions that revived an entire forest.

Despite these stunning meteorological and soil shifts, perhaps the most highly touted result of all has been an equally stunning increase in land value. Land that produces is land that has value. Over a 21-year period, the value of each acre of savannah converted to rainforest, measured solely on the values of potable water, harvestable food, and available livelihood, increased as much as 3,000-fold. Before restoration, people in the region around Las Gaviotas had no chance of employment. They suffered from gastrointestinal diseases, could not obtain safe drinking water, and lacked reasonably available medical care. Just one generation later, water is a commons distributed nearly for free. The sale of surplus water to the rich in Bogotá, who are prepared to pay the same price they pay for a bottle of imported San Pellegrino or Evian water, provides Las Gaviotas a cash flow that never previously existed.

Inspired by its healthy cash flow, its portfolio of technologies licensed worldwide, its generous wages, and its contributions to the local community of 2,000 inhabitants, William B. Harrison Jr., the Chairman of JP Morgan, championed the expansion of Las Gaviotas from 20,000 to 250,000 acres. Based on JP Morgan's Emerging Markets analysis, he offered Alvaro Uribe, the President of Colombia, a $300 million investment package. Such an expanded initiative could generate an estimated 100,000 jobs over the next decade, while offsetting the carbon emissions of countries like Belgium and the Netherlands.

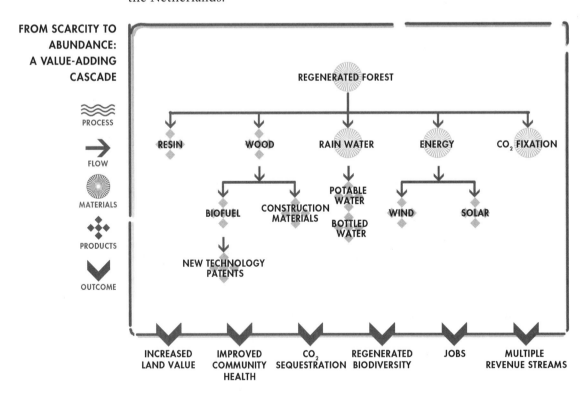

FROM SCARCITY TO ABUNDANCE: A VALUE-ADDING CASCADE

PROCESS
FLOW
MATERIALS
PRODUCTS
OUTCOME

REGENERATED FOREST

RESIN — WOOD — RAIN WATER — ENERGY — CO₂ FIXATION

BIOFUEL — CONSTRUCTION MATERIALS — POTABLE WATER / BOTTLED WATER — WIND — SOLAR

NEW TECHNOLOGY PATENTS

INCREASED LAND VALUE — IMPROVED COMMUNITY HEALTH — CO₂ SEQUESTRATION — REGENERATED BIODIVERSITY — JOBS — MULTIPLE REVENUE STREAMS

Where government services and traditional business never benefited the local population, one man's vision and his seminal work met the people's needs. This accomplishment of social and environmental caretaking, embracing the ideals of entrepreneurship, achieved success by emulating the natural processes of ecosystems. The success of Las Gaviotas illustrates that it is the interplay of pressure, temperature, surface tension, conductivity, magnetism, and so much more that makes the wind blow and the trees grow. Once we understand the dynamic connections and interactions of nature's interwoven tapestries, whole new approaches will unfold.

FOOD SECURITY IN AFRICA

The Songhai Center in West Africa, located in Porto Novo, the capital city of Benin, is run by Father Godfrey Nzamujo, a Dominican priest. In 1985, just a year after Paolo Lugari launched his Las Gaviotas reforestation scheme, Father Nzamujo undertook a program to reverse hunger and provide food for Africans. It began on a few acres of swampland granted by Benin's former president. Today, a quarter-century later, it has moved full circle from environmental degradation to an impressive endorsement of the possibilities for African food and livelihood security.

Under Father Nzamujo's guidance, Songhai developed a logical system for cascading nutrients and energy to achieve remarkable outcomes. Waste water (both gray and black) from toilets, washing, and all animal and human waste is collected in a three-chamber digester. Chopped water hyacinth, a local invasive aquatic plant, is added. In the digester the combined biomass produces methane, providing energy for local use. After mineralization, the remaining material becomes feed for zooplankton, phytoplankton, and benthos, which in turn feed fish in the aquaculture project. The digester design provides a high level of curing and gas production, imitating the acid-alkaline switch our body uses to restrain detrimental bacteria. The pH evolves from acidic in the digester to highly alkaline in the neighboring algae ponds. Anaerobic bacteria, complemented by sunlight, aid the powerful transformation of CO_2 into oxygen by microalgae, and complete the natural systems design that eliminates pathogens. Professor George Chan, who dedicated his life to the design of such integrated farming and waste management systems, would be proud of the outcomes.

Songhai faced another major hygienic challenge: flies. Although chemical spraying was considered, this could not be recommended in a food-producing environment that aspired to the organic label. The strategy pursued by Father Nzamujo was extraordinary. He turned to maggots, the larvae of flies, to solve the problem.

All slaughterhouse waste at Songhai is collected in a special area where hundreds of small, barely hand-width deep cement squares are completely surrounded by canals patrolled by carp. The open area is covered with a huge net so that birds cannot enter. The mesh is just large enough for hungry flies to pass through. Flies thrive on the castoffs of slaughter – what cannot be turned into edible product. This feast for flies turns the area into a massive maggot farm, with a production capacity of nearly one ton of maggots per month. Yet, there is not one fly to be spotted anywhere else at the center. All the flies converge on what is for them a delectable soup of nutrients, gorging themselves and laying larvae in abundance. Water is then sprinkled over the half-digested waste, so that the maggots float to the surface, to be easily harvested.

What can you do with maggots? The primary local economic use is as an inexpensive feed for fish and quail. Both quail eggs and fish contribute to good nutrition and food security. However, it is the maggot enzymes that offer an even greater potential for economic value. They have medicinal properties that are proven to heal wounds by stimulating the growth of fibroblast cells. How do you extract the enzymes while reserving the live maggots as feed for fish and quail? A brilliantly simple solution: maggots regurgitate when they are immersed in salt water!

Here is another case of elegant ecosystems design. Father Nzamujo's initial goal was to reduce disease by finding a natural means of eliminating flies.

That solution in turn provided the enzymes that effectively accomplish natural healing. While the biology and biochemistry of maggots clearly demonstrates medicinal properties, a new hypothesis proposes that these enzymes generate a barely measurable electrical pulse, undetected because there is no appropriate instrumentation. This pulse stimulates cell regeneration and promotes healing. Maggots have learned how to apply the laws of physics (electricity and magnetism) as a stimulus for healing.

Maggot treatment is approved by governments worldwide, especially for diabetic patients. The "purified" version – without the maggots – seems to have a chance for fast-track regulatory approval. This would be most welcome, since the main cause of amputations in Africa is untreated wounds.

AN ISLAND AFLOAT A DREAM

Nearly a millennium ago the greatest merchants of Florence and Russia built churches and warehouses on Gotland, a small but remarkable island in the center of the Baltic Sea. Arriving in Visby, the capital city, leaves a lasting impression on visitors. The large stone wall that surrounds the city encompasses not only the historic buildings and cathedrals, but generations of tradition.

As the twenty-first century arrived, the island's inhabitants struggled to find ways to prosper in a globalized world economy. It seemed that tourism was the only option. Indeed, with just under a million visitors annually, tourism is the largest contributor to Gotland's economy. During the summer holidays the local population grows ten times in size, only to implode for the rest of the year.

Yet it was the wish of its citizens to create a future for their land, and particularly for succeeding generations who would otherwise leave the island as soon as possible. Their vision was to design a sustainable community, in harmony with the resources of the land, juxtaposed against the background of its great historic accomplishments, and its recognition by UNESCO as a World Heritage city. At the invitation of Prof. Dr. Carl-Göran Hedén, a member of the Swedish Royal Academy of Sciences, the community undertook an envisioning exercise that gathered together students, bankers, policy makers, researchers, and businessmen to seek solutions.

Any observer looking for development opportunities other than tourism will immediately focus on the countryside. Dotted with picturesque churches and domiciles, the agricultural landscape has been lovingly shaped throughout the centuries. When sugar beets were introduced 100 years ago, they were successful enough to create a new industry. Lacking appropriate economies of scale, the sugar mill closed as globalization consolidated. There was little incentive to pursue agriculture, except carrots. Famous for their "sandy" look, carrots from Gotland acquire a superior taste in the island's alkaline soil. Although producing carrots was not a problem, selling them from the middle of the Baltic Sea was a challenge. Furthermore, it was common for grocery store purveyors to reject a substantial portion of the harvest that did not meet their rigorous shape conformation standards.

The citizens evolved an innovative approach that took advantage of this natural cascading of nutrients while generating value and jobs. Håkan Ahlsten, the local banker, liked the idea of manufacturing a simple product: oven-fresh carrot cakes. With such ready access to fresh and abundant raw material, a carrot cake enterprise was impossible to ignore. Agreement was reached, and a delicious carrot cake recipe was quickly developed. Baked, then frozen, the Gotland cakes became much in demand throughout Sweden and as far overseas as Asia. In five years, employment at the local bakery jumped from a mere five to thirty.

The next major initiative was precipitated by the desire to achieve better market value by utilizing the entire harvest. Mr. Yngve Andersson, another of Gotland's upstanding citizens, invested in the design and construction of a carrot-sorting center where nearly the entire harvest could be stored, sorted, and processed using sophisticated machinery. The massive harvest was machine-sorted into specific categories. Every variety was individually packaged, from baby carrots, to long, thin carrots, to stronger and shorter carrots, to odd-shaped roots. Surprisingly, cleaned and packaged baby carrots, which were formerly considered too small to have any market value, could be sold for four times more than standard carrots. The largest carrots are not packaged but become carrot juice, a very profitable niche market. Interestingly, the largest carrots produce the most juice – as much as 40% more by volume. The shredded carrot pulp, rather than becoming waste, is an ideal pig feed.

Carrot sorting to generate higher value from the existing harvest posed major challenges. The machinery could only cope with processing the entire harvest if the total volume were distributed over the entire year rather than concentrated in the six-week harvest season. However, processing the harvest over twelve months required an investment in cooling the warehouse to a constant temperature of 32° F. When the economic persuasion of better price supported the feasibility of this undertaking, the next challenge was meeting the operation's now dramatic energy requirements.

With the figures before him, Mr. Yngve Andersson decided to take the risk of exclusively powering the facility with wind energy. The entire operation – warehousing, sorting, processing, packaging, selling into market segments, including deep-frozen carrot cakes, is entirely powered by wind energy. The capital investment in wind energy was easily recovered from international sales. The total estimated direct and indirect employment sums to 250 jobs. Rethinking carrots generated jobs, cut costs, and successfully pointed the Gotlanders to a progressive path for job generation and livelihood security.

Finding value in what is locally available creates sustainable and competitive industries that can influence economies, even when they are located on an isolated island in the Baltic Sea. To the islander's credit, this is not their only initiative. Other breakthroughs demonstrate Gotland's pioneering spirit. Carrots are the most impressive case, but the combination of beer and bread is just as commendable. The Gotland Brewery supplies excellent beer to the local population. The spent grain left from the brewing process is shipped to the local bakery, Eskelunds Hembageri AB, where it is made into bread – another fine example of turning waste from one process into raw material for another. By using what is locally available, cascading nutrients, and encouraging entrepreneurs to implement competitive ideas, the citizens of Gotland are years ahead of their peers.

PROGRESSIVE PUEBLO SOLUTIONS

Raging forest fires often make the news. Each year wild fires devastate vast ecosystems in the western US. The New Mexico Bureau of Land Management obtained a grant from the federal government to pay for the removal of small-diameter wood (up to seven inches) from the lands of Picuris Pueblo. Whether burned or dumped in a landfill, this cleared debris would contribute to the atmospheric carbon load. Lynda Taylor and Robert Haspel proposed an alternative, and worked with the Picuris Pueblo elders to design a solution that cascades nutrients and energy in harmony with Pueblo customs.

Removal of the small diameter wood and reduction of forest fire risk was quickly accomplished. The bulk of the cut wood was dried, then placed in recycled 40-foot shipping containers and subjected to an incomplete combustion process by containing the fumes, thus converting the wood to charcoal. However, to honor Pueblo tradition it was necessary to eliminate the equipment tracks left in the forest by the brush-clearing vehicles. Mulch made from the small diameter wood was inoculated with a native mushroom spore, then spread on the equipment tracks. Remarkably, just two years later, no tracks were to be found. The mushrooms are gathered as food by tribal members, while the mushroom substrate and waste, rich in amino acids, serve as feedstock for the Sam family bison herd. With a sufficiency of livestock feed and ongoing support from Taylor and Haspel, the Sam family locally supplies buffalo meat to commercial markets.

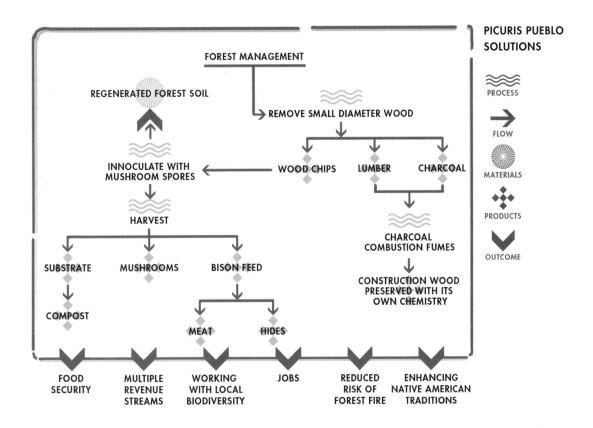

PICURIS PUEBLO SOLUTIONS

≈≈ PROCESS

→ FLOW

◉ MATERIALS

❖ PRODUCTS

❯ OUTCOME

What started as an effort to reduce the risk of fire became an integrated biosystem generating jobs, food, fuel, and construction materials while replacing chemicals and gasoline. The Picuris Pueblo experience is an example of economic development based on natural systems, using what is locally available and building on the traditions of Native Americans.

When we replace old standards with something completely different that cascades nutrients and energy, an entirely new economic paradigm emerges. Remarkable solutions emerge from reinterpreting the nature and function of energy and nutrients, allowing us to achieve greater resource efficiency, to build competitive industries, and to adopt innovations that generate jobs and create added value. This is how ecosystems evolve to ever more efficient systems, requiring ever less energy expenditure for ever more species. It is an all-inclusive cascade that leads to abundance at every level.

BAGASSE, A SWEET SOLUTION

The massive volumes of agro-waste our food industry produces can also be deftly handled by mirroring ecosystems. Take the case of sugar mainly sourced from cane. The sugar content of cane is around 10-15%. Thus, each ton of sugar produced accounts for only a small portion of its source biomass. The rest, waste known as *bagasse*, is typically incinerated. Natural systems seldom use fire as a source of energy, whereas we humans use fire all the time. Burning bagasse provides a cheap and available fuel source, but the only component that really supplies energy is the lignin. The rest, composed of hemicellulose and cellulose, creates massive carbon emissions when burned, because these substances incinerate without contributing useful heat.

Were we to use bagasse to produce paper, paper products, and cardboard, as has commenced on a small scale, it would clearly be a better outcome. Even though this tropical fiber does not fit the current supply chain management model, which is based on massive worldwide plantings of pine and eucalyptus, a quick calculation produces some astonishing figures. At the annual rate of 15 to 30 tons per acre, bagasse provides 100 to 200 tons of fiber in the seven years it takes the fastest growing pine trees to reach maturity. In terms of fiber, sugar cane handily tops the volume produced by trees from temperate climates.

Thus we begin to see how we can use what is renewably generated while building viable clusters of industries. It is our adherence to a wasteful industrial logic that uses only the sugar in sugar cane and burns the bagasse, at the high cost of damaging levels of carbon emissions. It is the same allegiance to short-sighted accounting that causes us to extract only the cellulose from pine trees to manufacture paper and waste the remaining 70-80% of the tree. There are many other examples. The harvesting of coffee beans leaves a staggering 99.8% of the total biomass as waste. The latest studies on solid municipal waste in the US indicate that for each dollar spent on handling household waste in landfills, $70 dollars are spent dealing with the waste from agriculture, mining, and industry!

Imagine that we produced food like the rest of nature, cascading through living kingdoms from plants to mushrooms to animals to bacteria to algae, and back again in different directions and combinations according to specific habitat. The only energy sources needed are light and gravity, which are readily and freely available! Here are the glimmerings of a new economy, rooted in robust models that cascade nutrients, and generate food, habitat, employment, energy, and currency in renewable ways.

URBAN WHOLE SYSTEMS

This cascade model is also functioning in urban and industrial settings. The Eco-Town Research and Development Center in Kitakyushu, Japan, has risen from the ruinous remains of a contaminated landfill at the edge of Dokai Bay, once called the "Sea of Death." As a burgeoning iron-manufacturing base, Kitakyushu was abandoned to its citizens when international competition drove down the price of steel. The provincial government took a major role in underwriting a structural shift from heavy industries to environmental industries. Under the directorship of Yoshihito Shirai, the Kitakyushu Eco-Town Plan transformed the entire eastern portion of the Hibiki landfill area, developing and promoting environmental industries and advanced technologies. Each year, thousands of international trainees and volunteers go to Eco-Town to study and learn cutting edge "3R" technologies (Reduce, Reuse, Recycle), returning to their homelands to establish projects and share their newly acquired know-how.

Clearly it is not only effective but essential for governmental and industrial leadership to seize the moment. At the same time, a new economic model will only succeed if it fosters grassroots business initiatives. This is where the capacity to inspire the uninspired, to reach the unreached, the opportunity to work communally with others who often are neither considered nor given a chance, offers the core perceptual shift for how we can make a difference in this world. Empowering young people, especially those in global pockets of unemployment and poverty, can achieve enormous economic impact.

The constructs of scarcity are unappealing to those who must endure it. If you are without a job, hungry, abused, or frail, sustenance is more than polite conversation. It is a matter of immediate survival. If we operate the way natural systems do, it is entirely possible to create more jobs while increasing productivity and improving resource efficiency. You will never hear of unemployed trees, fish, or mushrooms!

How can we achieve abundance as a society? How can we continuously obtain renewable sources for food, shelter, livelihood, and wellbeing? In mirroring the successful methods found in natural ecosystems, we can begin to choose models with a generous scope, a propensity to cascade, a goal of planetary and species stewardship, and a future of perpetuity. Therein is true economy. As we begin to grasp the fullness of this paradigm, the image of a Blue Economy rises like a phoenix from the ashes of economic instability, drawing strength and inspiration from nature.

CHAPTER THREE

NATURE'S RESOURCE EFFICIENCY

Nature uses the longest threads to weave her patterns.
Each small piece of her fabric reveals
the organization of the entire tapestry.

— RICHARD FEYNMAN

STRUCTURE AND FLOW

Simple and pragmatic approaches to indoor comfort are lessons we can learn from the physics of moving water and air, as well as from the elegantly simple methods perfected by species as varied as the termite, the zebra, the Namibian desert beetle, and the mussel. If we follow this new framework, we can achieve more with less energy and ensure better health conditions than ever imagined. We can even eliminate components and products that are considered indispensable in modern construction. How is that possible?

Buildings that are entirely closed and fully insulated to reduce energy consumption have little chance to self-regulate. Air pumps are required to push controlled air volumes through the building to maintain the occupants' comfort. Unfortunately, closed buildings accumulate humidity; especially in the basement (moist air is heavier and moves downward). Bedrooms are heated with dry air that burdens our respiratory systems, while dust particles accumulate from the ample use of electronic equipment. Many of these particles are electrostatic. Mites proliferate in the carpets because triple-glazed windows with an ultraviolet filter provide them the best-ever breeding ground.

Dust mites are microscopic relatives of the spider. These tiny creatures live by eating the detritus of a building's occupants. The dust mite is a common culprit in dermatological and respiratory allergies such as eczema and asthma. Removing mites requires harsh chemistry, which may circulate for months in a closed building, along with the volatile organic chemicals that compose most furniture and carpet glues. This is not how one might imagine an energy-efficient "ecological" building! Though we may have a 30% energy savings – in fact all power could have been generated by solar cells – the costly use of chemicals and the stress to our immune systems are unintended side effects. On the other hand, if energy-efficient building design included solutions with a proven track record, benchmarked for millions of years by species living in a similar habitat, then we would notice a radical difference in what healthy buildings looked like and how their systems functioned. Indeed, healthy buildings can be doubly efficient by reducing both energy and health care costs, requiring less risk capital to build and securing a better return on investment. How?

TERMITES, THE MASTERS OF FLOW

The first farmers on Earth were termites and ants. Perhaps as early as 100 million years ago, termites responded to the need to survive changing weather conditions. Their successful adaptation involved a greenhouse-like farming system. They perfected a method whereby the nest's internal temperature and humidity was under their full control, permitting efficient harvesting of fungi, the termites' primary food. They successfully achieved food security and evolved from hunter-gatherers to domiciled species well before *homo sapiens* evolved.

This admirable mastery of temperature, humidity, and atmospheric pressure follows the laws of physics as well as the application of complex mathematics to engineer farming and construction. Termites have perfected the design of chimneys where air warms and predictably rises, creating a pressure differential within the nest below. Since the nest is connected to its ambient surroundings by tiny underground tunnels, the outside air flows into the nest to equalize the air pressure. This precisely illustrates Newton's Third Law of Motion, "For every action there is an equal and opposite reaction."

However, since the air that flows through underground tunnels is within a narrow temperature range that is kept stable by the temperature of the deeper soil, the humidity and temperature of the exterior determines how much moisture remains in the air that enters the greenhouse nest. Termites know how to calculate and construct their nests anywhere in the world, in any climate, securing ideal growth conditions for the rich white mycelium that is their principal source of nourishment.

Swedish architect Bengt Warne observed termites in Zimbabwe in the late 1950s. His original drawings of termite mound airflows, published in *På Akacians Villkor (On the Conditions of the Acacia)*, look simple but are challenging to adapt to modern architectural purposes. It took another brilliant Swedish architect, Anders Nyquist (who met Warne but never collaborated with him), to develop mathematical formulas that codified Warne's insights in a model that makes present automated climate control systems obsolete. Based on studies of termite architecture, Nyquist discovered that energy-saving buildings can be designed that are warming or cooling when needed, providing comfort without locking inhabitants into an airtight and heavily insulated room. Where air cannot flow, harmful bacteria and microbes readily proliferate. In such a space, when one person sneezes, everyone catches cold. This cannot be the purpose of saving energy!

The Laggarberg School in Timrå, just outside Sundsvall, Sweden, was Nyquist's design adaptation of the genius that both termites in nature and ancient civilizations throughout history have used to keep warm or stay cool without guzzling energy or using elaborate chemical insulation to keep heat out or freshness in. A system of vents and channels achieves air conduction that moderates temperatures and maintains freshness.

The termite's skills are exceptionally instructive, even though the insect is subject to obliteration around the world for its supposedly voracious appetite for wood. Were we to consider that termites are traditionally responsible for the long-term fertilization of soil, we might have less animosity and greater appreciation for them. In fact, typically 15% of the Earth's vegetation becomes the nutrient source for the fungi that termites consume. The decomposing debris produces heat that warms them in the winter while enriching the deep soil for decades to come.

From the termite we can learn how to continuously refresh the air in a building without heating or cooling. If the air is refreshed, there will be less risk of a building developing what is known as "sick building syndrome," where stagnant, microbe-laden, stifled air is trapped inside and leads to illness as a result of fungal and microbial contamination. In the termite's world, this same system controls humidity, which determines the productivity of the fungus on which termites rely for nutrients. The termite's airflow system precisely and permanently secures 86° F and 61% humidity. The only variable that the termites do not control is water. If heavy rains flood the land, the nest can be inundated. This stressful environment is the signal for the *Termitomycis* mushroom – a gourmet delicacy even for humans – to ensure survival by reproducing. The termite queen as well knows how to carry spores to safety in her mouth to start farming at a new nest.

It is fitting that the first multi-story building emulating the ingenious work of termites was erected in Harare, the capital city of Zimbabwe. The Eastgate Shopping and Office Centre, a 10-floor edifice built in the late 1980s by the UK engineering group Arup, is heated and cooled solely by natural airflows. The economics of this innovative system are convincing. Eliminating the space between floors used for air ducts drops the break-even point from 55 to 46%, essentially adding an extra floor in the same elevation while reducing investment costs (in this case, a savings of $3.5 million dollars) and operational expenses by 10 to 15%. Banks fund construction projects that can demonstrate lower risk and better returns, while requiring less capital and offering better rental rates to occupants. Sustainable features such as low cost, maintenance-free, passive air conduction instead of expensive mechanical air conditioning also attract financing options.

A STRIPE OF A DIFFERENT COLOR

The zebra offers an additional insight into technologies that would reduce or in some cases even eliminate the need for insulation in many parts of the world, through control of surface temperature. The zebra is capable of reducing its surface temperature by 17.5° F with air currents generated by the interplay of its black and white stripes. Here is another ingenious distillation of the laws of physics that is taught at school but perhaps not well understood in practical application. Although architectural design looks for moderation of temperature through the heat-reflective properties of white, the case of the zebra would argue that buildings should rather be painted black *and* white. We know that the color white reflects the sun, and thereby reduces heat. The color black absorbs the sun, thus increasing surface temperature. The air above the white stripes is thus cooler than the air above the black stripes. The heated air above the black stripes rises, creating a pressure differential with the higher air pressure above the white stripes. This generates micro-sized air currents that cool the surface without mechanical ventilation. Does this make a notable difference? Can this be commercially developed?

A Daiwa House office building in Sendai, Japan, also designed by Anders Nyquist, capitalizes on this interplay of black and white. While controlling the surface temperature on the exterior of the building, the interplay between the oppositely colored surfaces decreases the building's indoor temperature in summer by 8.5° F. By extrapolation, we can see that the mere physical effects of black and white surfaces reduce interior temperatures, saving an estimated 20% in energy usage. Though not as impressive as the zebra's 17.5° F, we humans have been at it for only a few decades, while the zebra has mastered the technique over hundreds of thousands of years. The low and high pressures are leveled thanks to micro-gusts of wind. Instead of insulating the interior, the interplay of physics removes heat from the exterior, reducing the need for polyurethane (with fire retardants) or glass fiber on the interior. Actually, the zebra has an insulating layer of fat only under its black stripes, since the tissue below the white stripes does not need it. It makes sense; it saves materials; it is very simple. It never stops working as long as there is interplay of black and white, which is guaranteed as long as the sun shines and the laws of physics apply.

Aiming to save energy, architects today recommend insulation on the inside of a building and beneath the roof to block the transfer of heat or cold. Builders typically use polyurethane chemicals, or glass fibers produced with mined materials and processed at high energy cost, to insulate the indoors from the outdoors. The zebra shows how taking advantage of the predictable laws of physics to first reduce heat or cold at the exterior can translate to less need for chemical products or expensive heating and cooling installations. This interplay based on pressure and temperature requires no additional expense and works all the time. Indeed, the laws of physics have no exceptions.

A DESERT OF PLENTY

The dark coloration and extraordinary life span of *Welwitschia mirabilis*, a desert plant species, give us further cause to consider that white alone may offer only short term comfort when it comes to beating the heat. The Namib Desert has been arid for at least 55 million years and is believed to be the oldest desert in the world. A grasshopper accidentally jumping from a stone into desert sand would scorch and die in only a few minutes. In this water-starved environment, with only one rainfall every seven years, the *Welwitschia* not only survives but, with an estimated life span of 2,000 years or more, seems to hold the record as the oldest living plant on Earth. The *Welwitschia* mastered the capture of dew on its two leaves to near perfection, as well as the ability to source moisture from two meters deep.

Lighter colors reflect sunlight and reduce heat absorption at the surface. While humans value cooler temperatures, these have a disadvantage in a desert setting. In the desert the main target is not coolness, but rather decreasing the dew point so that a minute quantity of moisture can be predictably captured. A cooler surface increases the dew point and thus

reduces the quantity of moisture available for harvest each morning. Darker colors induce a lower dew point with a warmer surface and a cooler air. This would imply greater heat absorption during the day, except that plants and beetles can conduct heat away. Members of this desert ecosystem survive through heat reduction achieved through ventilation and conduction, another demonstration of the ecological use of physical principles.

The Namib Desert is also home to a large array of lichens. These are actually not a plant species, but rather a symbiosis or composite of two organisms, namely a fungus and an alga. The fungus functions as the body and harvests water for the lichen as a whole from morning and evening fog. By photosynthesis the alga produces the nutrients required for survival. Though their mycelium may be barely two cells thick, these lichen are perhaps the best miners in the world, able to penetrate seemingly solid stone.

"However is that possible?" we may ask. Our logic to penetrating rock has been shaped by Alfred Nobel, who invented the chemical reaction known as "dynamite," our only current means of extracting mineral ores from deep within the Earth. Humanity takes recourse in chemistry, while natural systems first exploit physics. Lichens do not use dynamite; actually nothing in nature would use such an excessive and destructive force. The microscopic size of the lichen's mycelium allows it to easily navigate the spaces between rock crystals. When a magnesium molecule is found, it is moved to the surface for plant, bird, or animal life to partake. As a result of the lichen's fine and precise mining technique, Namib fauna and flora gain access to the trace minerals needed to function in this delicate environment. The contribution of each species ensures survival for all those living within this framework of temperature, moisture, and light.

COLLECTING WATER BY ATTRACTION AND REPULSION

The *Onymacris plana*, a beetle also indigenous to the Namib Desert, is not simply dark, but intensely black. It achieves better dew-point management results than plants in the same habitat by using heat conductivity with the addition of another physical effect: extreme hydrophobia. At first, a desert beetle's capacity to repel water may seem as irrelevant as windshield wipers on a submarine. However, the careful analysis undertaken by UK scientist Andrew Parker reveals that microscopically small drops of dew form each morning as soon as the sun tips over the horizon. These droplets are rapidly rejected from the hydrophobic (water-fearing) wing surface of the beetle or the leaf surface of the plant before they evaporate. The minute droplets of rejected water are collected on extremely hydrophilic (water-loving) patches around the beetle's wings. This interplay of hydrophobic and hydrophilic surfaces assures the Namibian desert beetle an ample daily water supply, enough in fact to shower and to drink. Curiously, this system of water and temperature control is counter-intuitive: black creates survivability in the hottest climate and water-repellent surfaces secure drinking water.

SOPHISTICATED STICKING

Geckos do not mind a storm. They are unmoved by most anything, effortlessly adhering to surfaces wet or dry, rough or smooth. The gecko uses attractive and repulsive intermolecular electrostatic forces called "van der Waals," after the Dutch physicist who first scientifically identified them. Amazing! Things stick together because of the underlying physics! One day innovative products inspired by the intermolecular manipulations of the gecko could compete with Velcro™, itself inspired by the hooks on cocklebur seeds that have applied a "sticking without glue" solution for ages past. We might even suggest that the geckos and cockleburs have greater sophistication when it comes to "sticking" than, say, mussels. Geckos and cockleburs use physics first, guiding their biology to grow cells that achieve the desired performance. Mussels rely on chemistry. This does not mean that mussels do poorly by relying on a chemical solution. In fact, they are a remarkable inspiration for how we can replace the toxins that chemical engineers have heretofore developed for any number of commercial adhesives.

Mussels are constantly battered by waves. As a consequence they have perfected a glue to attach themselves to rocks. They have learned how to build such great elasticity into their water-resistant glue that even the strongest surf will not detach them. Kaichang Li from Oregon State University (USA) studied the resin that mussels produce and applied his research conclusions to develop a commercial glue that Columbia Forest Products uses to replace formaldehyde-based epoxies, the standard glue for particle fiberboard. Indoor air quality is markedly better when formaldehyde is not a component of the building materials.

When market leaders use green chemistry to replace toxic chemistry by putting nature-inspired innovations into their products, they achieve profitability concomitant with sustainability. Thus, while we admire the gecko and the cocklebur for elegant use of only physical forces without the need for chemistry, we give the mussel all our respect for teaching us how to eliminate toxins from our homes, schools, and offices.

VORTEXES AS VIABLE BACTERICIDES

Natural systems don't solve problems with a shower of harsh chemicals. There are a few well-publicized biological exceptions, such as aggressive snakes, toxic frogs, venomous spiders, and deadly mushrooms. However, their toxicity is nearly always directed against another species, hardly ever members of the same family – though the black widow spider is a notorious exception to the rule, as is always found in biology. Prior to reverting to any form of deadly chemistry, and certainly chemistry that could be mutagenic or carcinogenic to members of the same family, natural species apply the forces of physics. Where living species, especially fauna and flora, are an easy inspiration for humans from poetry to technologies, the inanimate part of nature also has lessons to share.

Have you ever wondered how rivers cleanse themselves? They use physics and the nutrient needs of two diverse families of bacteria. The pervasive movement of a river allows the continuous creation of vortices in the water. A vortex increases pressure at the core of its swirl to the point that nano-scale pressure and friction rupture bacterial membranes. Bacteria are thus rendered into nutrients for other species further downstream to enjoy. These finely-distributed nutrients, combined with spaces enriched with dissolved oxygen and areas where air is eliminated from the water, allow bacteria and microalgae to mineralize any excess biomass quickly and efficiently. At the same time, this shift from spaces rich with dissolved air to spaces vacant of air makes it impossible for detrimental aerobic bacteria to flourish.

The power of the vortex, induced merely by flowing water abiding the laws of gravity, is among the most impressive demonstrations we have studied. Have you ever seen a river flow in a straight line? What might be the logic in a river's meanderings? Curiously, modern industrial engineers design everything in straight lines with 90° turns. Yet, the famed 20th century Viennese artist-designer-architect Friedensreich Hundertwasser once declared, *"The rigid straight line is fundamentally alien to humanity, life, and the whole of creation."*

Viktor Schauberger, a brilliant Austrian inventor and the founder of implosion technology, spent much of his career as a forester. He observed that the dual vertical and horizontal swirl of river vortices caused solids to deposit in the center of the river bed, while eroding the rock and soil along the banks. One of his early design breakthroughs was a log transport system that curved as a river does, allowing logs to pass without jamming or blocking. Remarkable! Straight transportation systems block, meandering ones flow. Straightened rivers accumulate sediment and meandering rivers provide fresh, clean water!

Swedish innovators Curt Hallberg and Morten Oveson developed a non-linear mathematical model that made the power of any vortex predictable. With developing vortex technology, we can now replace polluting chemical solutions with physical solutions. The potential energy savings from vortex technology, and an increased understanding of the natural geometry of a vortex, makes possible a plethora of opportunities for businesses and societies. If we combine these insights with hydrophobic and hydrophilic checkered rooftops borrowed from the Namibian beetle, we reduce energy and material consumption, and can generate water on the top of a building. From there it can follow the law of gravity and flow into the premises. With vortex technology, the same gray water that washes clothes on the tenth floor can be reused just one or two floors below, thus reducing the water wasted by a factor of five to ten.

The Swedish startup company, Watreco, offers a device that uses their patented Vortex Process Technology® to eliminate air from water. This is an attractive proposal for anyone needing to produce or maintain large amounts of ice. When you produce ice, you freeze both water and air. Air is an insulator. The energy needed to freeze and maintain the ice in hockey rinks and ice arenas, for example, is thus dependent on the amount of air the water contains. Because the vortex technology eliminates the air, the energy savings (up to 43% according to Ohio State University trials) is a positive contribution. It reduces costs and decreases the input to climate change by eliminating the greenhouse gases from icemaking that are produced by 100,000 kW hours per year of electrical generation.

What clinches it from a business standpoint, however, is that the ice produced from the vortex water is crystal clear, permitting advertising displays placed beneath the ice to be highly visible. Ice normally cracks under the weight of the hockey players, since the air bubbles cause imperfect ice crystal formation. With air removed, the ice remains clear even under the weight of the crisscrossing players. Surely advertisers with diminished budgets would comprehend the added advantage of their logo easily viewable on sports broadcasts. Then again, perhaps advertisers could even be motivated to foot the bill. This could be a strategic new business tactic: advertisers paying for energy-saving devices!

The income generated by additional advertising revenues is a multiple of the energy savings and can be measured by multiple means. While substantial sums might be contracted with large hockey league sponsors around the world, at thousands of smaller ice rinks the use of vortex technology to clarify the ice could generate additional revenue and reduce the pressure on local government budgets. Interestingly, the town-owned ice rink in Telluride, Colorado is second only to their water treatment plant as the biggest energy consumer in town. The town recently purchased a vortex system for their ice rink. They anticipate greatly reduced energy costs starting in 2010, once the system is fully installed. Elsewhere, the city of Malmö, Sweden quickly realized this savings/earnings potential and installed a full system of ice-making using vortex technology. David Henderson, head coach of France's men's national ice hockey team, reports on his team's evaluation of the vortex-produced crystal-clear ice: *"Elite players have been unanimous in their praise of the improvement of ice quality in regards to hardness and durability. The ice has also become more transparent, which leads to a second major improvement: the visibility of on-ice publicity for the sponsors."*

Value created by such extrapolations of physics is enormous, and far outpaces investment costs. It actually makes the energy savings seem like an added benefit! A simple technology created a new competitive edge in advertising that at first glance had nothing to do with air, energy, or ice. There are an estimated 16,000 indoor ice rinks around the world. The total savings in electrical expenditures could reach approximately $200 million per year if all were to adopt this technology. Better yet, the costs would be well below the first year's savings.

NATURAL WAYS TO AVOID FIRE AND FLAME

Asbestos was once appreciated as a naturally-occurring mineral fiber that provided roofing and insulation that did not burn. Unfortunately, it was conclusively identified as a carcinogen. Yet decades after incontrovertible scientific and medical studies have proven this beyond any doubt, asbestos remains available on the market. Even more ironically, countries like Canada that pride themselves on a progressive approach to sustainability still permit open-pit asbestos mining in the 21st century.

Both Europe and the US have sharply restricted the use of asbestos. A few billion-dollar out-of-court settlements suppressed industry's appetite to pursue its use. However, there is another side to the coin. Legislation around the world mandates the use of fire and flame retardants in many things, for example, children's clothing, car seats, interior textiles, airplanes, and office furniture. The quest for a family of chemicals that lowers the possibility of fire from cigarette butts or candles has stimulated the development of bromine and halogen-based chemicals. These fire and flame retardants work. The only inconvenience is that they also seem to cause cancer. Worse, mammals in the Arctic accumulate these fire retardants in their fatty tissues in general and their reproductive organs in particular. Everyone agrees that these chemicals find their way to the Arctic. However, since no one can explain the pathway by which they arrive, there is no verifiable link to bromine and halogen-based products. Thus, no legal responsibility can be assigned. Industry will continue to manufacture and sell these products.

Will consumers continue to ignore the havoc caused by the dumping and incineration of halogens and bromines? Scientists wonder if polar bears will become extinct more quickly from chemically-induced infertility or from habitat disruption through climate change. A few substitutes like phosphorus-based retardants have been introduced to the market; however, industry claims that there is no substitute for the effectiveness of bromine.

Mats Nilsson, a scientist and researcher with the Swedish firm, Trulstech Innovation, has developed a portfolio of gels and powders made from abundantly available food-grade ingredients that he calls "Molecular Heat Eaters." This makes sense. Our bodies have a unique capability to manage heat and oxygen. If heat is channeled away from a fuel source, and if oxygen is converted to carbon dioxide, there is no risk of fire. Most chemistry students learn this as the Krebs Cycle. This is a worthwhile substitution: replace carcinogenic chemicals that have a negative impact on our health with food grade materials that are available in abundance at comparable prices. Imagine the competitive advantage of Nilsson's fire and flame retardants. It is no longer necessary to choose between immediate death by fire or slow death by cancer! We can replace products that destroy life with products that promote life. The biochemicals needed for Nilsson's inventions could be derived from grape pomace, a by-product of wine making, or citrus peel that is waste from juice production.

These products succinctly illustrate the advantages of the Blue Economy model. The crowning beauty of Nilsson's technology is that it has the potential to solve massive ecological challenges. When wildfires devastate California or Colorado, the U.S. Forest Service rushes to spray chemicals by plane. Now, we can blanket the area with food-grade chemicals, instead of phosphorous, and secure fast relief from fire without detriment to the ecosystem.

In the future, the same technology could be used to eliminate the risk of explosions in mines. Excessive concentrations of naturally-occurring methane fill mining tunnels and create underground disasters if sparks occur as the mining equipment gouges out rock. At present, mining equipment is manufactured from expensive nickel and cobalt metal alloys to reduce the risk of sparks. Using the air channels already in place to mist the mining space with food-grade fire retardants could suppress sparks and prevent explosions. This would additionally reduce the demand for cobalt and nickel mining, and the subsequent expensive processing into high-performance metals.

These advances in applied physics, physical chemistry, chemistry, and biology give us reason to believe that innovations inspired by nature are shaping a new economy. In a recent interview, Achim Steiner, Executive Director of the United Nations Environment Programme, declared, *"Many technologies are in commercial use. We're not talking about theory any more; these are real results occurring in the real world and in the real market."*

UNLOCKING SOLUTIONS TO THE CHALLENGES OF SUSTAINABILITY

The vital relationship of the laws and theories of physics to the basic conditions of how we produce, consume, and survive are not given much attention in today's physics classrooms. Yet, it is in observing the basics of physics that we realize how minute shifts in pressure, temperature, and moisture content create outstanding products and processes that far outshine the results of genetic modification with their artfulness, precision, and effectiveness. Instead of manipulating the biology of life, we can find inspiration in the ways that nature uses physics.

Quick, one-off solutions don't appear to be resolving the complex problems we are confronting, both in our individual domiciles and our greater domicile, our Earth. Successful future industries will reexamine the basics of science and seek inspiration for innovative solutions that apply physics first and chemistry second. If we consider the underlying forces and the systemic conditions that predict the results prescribed by physics, then we will understand why chemistry in nature differs markedly from the chemistry that dominates our lives today. The few molecules retained in natural products and production processes reflect the best possible use of physics. The gecko and the mussel demonstrate two sticking systems, each of which performs within clear physical parameters. While green chemistry and even sustainable biology are important goals, if we look more deeply we will grasp the forces that determined both. Whenever possible, Blue Economy models follow the physics. Such a different approach is unmatched by market leaders.

This may well be the logic that we need to pursue in an era of economic crisis. Instead of using chemistry – traditional or green – nature shows us ways to eliminate chemistry. Green chemistry and sustainable biology face the challenges of finding funding and navigating the lengthy approval processes required by the government authorities of developed nations. Such drawbacks hamper the rapid business reconfigurations required by economic crises. The market's competitive framework needs encouragement

44

to help fast-track procedural regulatory requirements as new insights unfold from our observation and implementation of what nature achieves.

Imagine the impact such innovations can have on building design. There are nearly 50 on our list of 100 that could be utilized in homes, offices, and factories. Buildings that use these technologies are first and foremost healthier for their occupants. The additional benefit, as demonstrated by Jean Noel's Centre Pompidou in France, is that everyone who has the chance to explore such a building sees the elegant application of the laws of physics. As we adopt the principles of a Blue Economy our use of non-renewable resources can dwindle to just a fraction of what it once was, requiring less investment and less cost.

A Blue Economy goes beyond efficiency and better return on investment. Much of what we believe we need is entirely unnecessary, and can be replaced by products and methods that are better and simpler than those most widely used today. Rather than diminishing our economy, these alternatives can make it stronger, freeing up material resources and currency. Thus with a bundled portfolio of innovations based on pragmatic solutions to critical issues that have already been faced and solved by many species on Earth, we can redefine the competitive model. Such insights can help solve many of the sustainability challenges we face while giving power and precedence to entrepreneurs. When we create pathways for strengthening our capacity to respond to the basic needs of all – water, food, health care, housing, and energy – with what is readily available, we are building an openly sourced Blue Economy from the ground up.

The few insights shared here, from dew point management through the interplay of color, heat conductivity, and hydrophilia, put us on track for new thought patterns. The design of a building or home need no longer be about saving energy. Instead it can be about replacing old ideas like polyurethane with new ideas beyond insulation. This is a refreshing approach. The growth economy was always driven by consuming and investing more. Here,

a reduction in consumption provides a stimulus to the economy, whereby a material or a process that uses a harsh chemical solution is replaced by a solution that utilizes merely the properties of physics.

Something … is replaced by … nothing. This sets the tone for our emerging model of the Blue Economy.

CHAPTER FOUR

LEADING THE WAY FOR MARKET LEADERS

Today we have a temporary aberration called
"industrial capitalism" which is inadvertently liquidating
its two most important sources of capital –
the natural world and properly functioning societies.
No sensible capitalist would do that.

— AMORY LOVINS

OAK FROM SEED

Starting from a cautious investment of less than a half-billion dollars ten years ago, 2008 saw venture capital funds channel an estimated 8.4 billion dollars toward developing "green technologies," despite the inhibiting effects of worldwide recession and compromised liquidity. Today, the 100 innovations showcased here have generated an estimated 20,000 jobs. While this is encouraging, it is a mere trickle for a world that needs a vast river of one billion new jobs. Where the bailout of defunct industries and financial institutions may be money down the drain, investments in innovations that are part of a systemic portfolio can provide the catalytic effect the world economy urgently needs. Even someone without business experience and only a grasp of the fundamental principles of a Blue Economy can have an entrepreneurial chance to succeed. If a new solution requires less expenditure or energy, or if multiple income opportunities are available, then start-up capital or microinvestments may be all the encouragement needed to make it happen.

Crisis generates a unique degree of freedom to innovate, and a window of opportunity to fast track businesses that meet basic needs, where the status quo has no interest to act and no chance to succeed. The ventures we contemplate may be once-in-a-lifetime opportunities to reorient our economy. In inner city, rural, and ex-urban environments, in the North and South, East and West, we have a chance to introduce innovations and business models that respond better to our economic needs than two hundred years of industrial progress.

In the last two months of 2008 alone the worldwide financial crisis caused an estimated net loss of 50 million jobs in emerging nations. A continuing crisis could push another 200 million people into extreme poverty. The International Labor Organization reports that the number of "working poor" could reach 1.4 billion, or half the working population of the world's developing countries. How do we condone such travesty? How can we abide such loss of human potential? It is with a sense of urgency that we focus on the solutions that can make a difference in the lives of many. Achieving livelihood security means individuals can obtain food, shelter, and comfort, provide for their families, and experience a measure of dignity and satisfaction from the contribution of their labor. Innovations that emulate nature's cascading effect can offer an invitation to a greater and more abundant future, thriving with diversity. The jobs potentially created may well be counted in the hundreds of millions.

NEW POSSIBILITIES, NEW PERSPECTIVES

We might compare the current economic upheaval that has gripped the world to what nature accomplishes with volcanic eruptions and tornadoes. Although such natural disasters wreak destruction and cause tragic loss of life, such extreme, out-of-bounds states also restore the prevalence of ambient conditions. They are the exceptions that confirm the rule. Such exceptions put whole systems under enormous stress, yet they also provide an opening for new possibilities and new solutions where none were evident before.

In economic terms, when disruption occurs at such a fundamental level, a completely new pathway to the market becomes available. Innovations that can emulate nature's cascading effect and that make use of the laws of physics have the chance to succeed because they have little to gain from existing business models. They simply do not compete by the same rules. Batteries are replaced by no batteries; medical devices, surgery, and pharmaceuticals are replaced with "none of the above!" Instead of dealing constantly with waste, the "residues of production" are used to realize greater income than that generated by the core business of another totally unrelated business. In essence, this is why now, more than at any time in recent history, we have the opportunity to generate millions of jobs while moving away from scarcity, pollution, and waste. Thousands of people in hundreds of countries will intuitively grasp the principles and realize the opportunities in what is before them. Their work will cascade and conjoin with the work of others and create opportunities for even greater numbers of people. This fundamentally rooted approach emulates nature's models. Such innovations are benchmarked, and the solutions are real.

These opportunities are tied to the reality that the use of non-renewable resources is a weakness. The use of toxic components is an even greater weakness. Failing to use or even destroying resources not considered part of the core business definition are lost opportunities and significant weaknesses. Shedding thousands of jobs does not promote customer loyalty; resisting change and receiving government bail-outs are simply other forms of energy wasted. They engender no confidence and have no chance of long-term success.

For the past two decades, prominent and eloquent scholars, academics, and leaders have lectured on and presented many of the breakthroughs described in this book. Introduced by various researchers and with various names, examples of nature technology have been put forth around the world. Many brilliant and enthusiastic researchers and innovators have contributed to the growth and interest in the field. As the first awareness of nature technology achieved international prominence, research dollars were allocated to study innovations that could direct business towards sustainability. The media reported these innovations in stories accompanied by marvelous photographs and films. Televised presentations all found large and appreciative audiences eager to know of the next fascinating flora or fauna performance unimagined by humans.

Yet top business management remained disaffected. With the exception of a few cases, notably in Germany and Japan, market leaders fell short of adopting or promoting any of these technologies. Industry barely paid lip service to the possibilities and hardly responded to proposals. Business executives attended presentations that outlined these marvelous opportunities and voiced their enthusiasm. Yet they returned to their offices to continue business as usual. At Vice-President Al Gore's Expert Panel on Solutions for Climate Change held in New York in January, 2008, it was common to hear that although venture capital had its antennas directed towards nature technology, most of the proposed innovations were simply "too different to get traction on the ground." Perhaps this is true, for these innovations essentially alter the current business model, and business experts unwilling or unable to adapt will have little understanding and little in common with the emerging approaches.

If we are serious about designing a new economic model richly inspired by natural solutions that have evolved over time, then it is not enough to attend lectures, read reports, watch colorful documentaries, and contemplate connections. There is a major hurdle that must be surmounted to move from talk to action. The key is to achieve a competitive and strategic positioning of these innovations by vigorous operators in an open economy, mapping a pathway within the competitive environment from discovery, to understanding the science, to replacing the present unhealthy and unsustainable production and consumption model with something better.

How do we transform our present socio-economic downturn, and our present economic system that is woefully in need of improvements, into a system that promotes life, strengthens resilience, relies on what is available, builds on sustainable practices, works with the flow of physics, offers innumerable opportunities to learn, adapts to changing conditions, responds to basic needs, builds community, instills a sense of responsibility beyond oneself, generates jobs, creates multiple revenues, and provides challenges? We risk that our children will confront the same mistakes we have endured – wars waged, human rights violated, worldwide hunger and poverty rampant, as society at large remains distracted and disengaged. There is a need to encourage the freedom to improve, the liberty to rethink and re-imagine, to find solutions that are just, equitable, and stabilizing. Whether theirs are fresh young faces in posh Manhattan preschools, or faces streaked by grime and hardship in the *favelas* of Ecuador, the new generation is easily inspired by opportunities that are alive and present around them. Why are our business leaders missing out? Are there enough entrepreneurs to transform our economic systems so that as a society we can move beyond behaviors of consuming more and exhausting the resources available to us?

Certainly, the wealth of innovations before us provides an impetus to this urgently needed economic shift. Imagine an economy without a scarcity syndrome. Imagine an economy that evolves to sufficiency, where moments of stress catalyze us to abundance, where the abiding impetus is to realize ever more creative ways to stimulate innovation. Imagine an economy that encourages new generations to greater success than their parents achieved – greater even than their parents could imagine.

GETTING OUT OF THE BOX

Although applying the cascading model may be most attractive to innovative business organizations with broader and stronger social missions, the opportunity to generate jobs in the new economy will not be based on the time and motion studies that brought us 19th and 20th century labor productivity. New job generation opportunities will emerge from "eco"-facture, not "manu"-facture. The new industries that emerge will utilize processes that conform to the same physical rules that nature follows.

Harsh chemicals, refined metals, and other polluting and non-renewable materials will be replaced by solutions achieved through simple physics – gravity, pressure, and temperature. Eco-facture will replace energy-intensive and toxic processes with ambient temperature operations that make use of natural variations of pressure and other principles of physics to produce goods. Waste will become a resource. Locally available materials will be incorporated into the materials stream. Market standards will be transformed, and creative ideas will take precedence over stagnant business norms where the status quo rules out changes to revenue streams.

Many companies today still operate under established management school doctrine that does not encourage thinking "out of the box." This is a model that cleaves to five management principles outlined below. In actuality these principles can be a hindrance to progress, and even antithetical to a model that can deliver the means we need to meet the critical needs of our times. Our challenge is not only to get out of the box, but to find a way to work with the landscape of these management principles, while replacing old limitations with new opportunities.

Many years ago, Mr. Soichiro Honda, founder of Honda Motor Company, was asked if he had run a business analysis based on the strengths and weaknesses of his own company and those of his competitors when considering whether to evolve from a motorbike manufacturer to an automobile producer. He responded, *"If our team had run a business analysis, we would never have ventured into the car business."* He quickly added, *"I simply made a list of the weaknesses of the world's biggest carmakers – and that list was quite long."*

MANAGEMENT PRINCIPLE 1:
CORE BUSINESS DEFINED BY CORE COMPETENCE

Graduates of modern business schools follow the axiom that any initiative must subject itself to a thorough business analysis, producing detailed reports and mapping out clear-cut strategies for how to succeed and how to fend off major competitive forces. Corporate CEOs and managers are trained and expected to operate within well-defined fields that have clear parameters for success. If a company is not competitive, it is not viable. Achieving market share means consumers repeatedly buy a product when offered at the perceived ideal combination of cost and quality. However, once mainstreamed this model resists change, and often excuses collateral damage to the environment and even to society at large. The blinders of a core business approach can even disconnect managers from social ethics, creating a moral double standard. Remarkably, business often concludes that doing "less bad" equates to doing good.

The concepts of core business and core competence have dominated management directives for the past half-century. If a new approach emerges that falls outside the scope of a core competence, it is extremely difficult for management to accept. Furthermore, a new technology cannot be brought to the market solely on the basis of core competencies. Even though a market leader may be persuaded that a new technology is an opportunity to gain competitive edge and market share, there is no guarantee this technology will be approved for development. Often these new fields are more easily engaged by entrepreneurs outside of so-called market leaders. The shift in technological platforms and the need for new competencies liberates a start-up company from needing previous experience in the industry.

Take the case of the pacemaker. For 50 years this surgically implanted medical device has been the solution to irregularities in cardiac rhythm. The pacemaker is powered by a battery located near the collarbone. Our current stress-filled lifestyles insure that millions of pacemakers – at a minimum cost of $50,000 each – will be needed in the years to come. While everyone is focusing on developing more efficient batteries, the next generation of cardiac rhythm solutions requires neither surgery nor battery. The cost of this new intervention technology could be as low as $500 dollars; the cost of the nanotubes is not more than a few dollars.

The introduction of a nanotube conductor that channels electrical current from healthy tissue to afflicted areas of the heart was inspired by studying the channels of cells that provide conductivity around and through the heart of a whale. This is a knowledge base that is foreign to pacemaker manufacturers. No mainstream medical technology company has the foundation on which to build this new business. This innovation requires a conductor, carbon tubes, communication capabilities, natural energy sources, and chip designs. Such a retooling implies a deep chasm of unknown factors, making market leaders disinclined to invest. This sort of "disruptive technology" would further require new staff, components, and business planning, comparable to the creation of an altogether new business division. Most challenging of all, adopting such an innovative approach could very well undermine the lucrative income stream enjoyed by medical equipment companies.

Who would venture into the unknown, particularly during a recession? Industry giants like Boston Scientific or Medtronic are not apt to lead the way. If a top business executive has made the decision to acquire, at great expense, a gadget with guaranteed revenue potential from a proven and successful technology, why would they promote research funding or approve an investment that would undermine it? Who would accelerate the shift to this non-surgical approach when the revenues generated would be only a fraction of the cash flow each operation generates for the whole medical system, including surgeons, anesthesiologists, pharmaceutical companies and battery makers? The answer is obvious: no one who benefits from the market today.

Another example is the innovative use of the physical properties of vortexes. Currently, industries that desalinate, de-scale, and purify water depend on chemistry and reverse osmosis. Chemicals like chlorine kill bacteria, other acids de-scale, and a pressure of up to 800 PSI separates salt from seawater to create potable water. New technology is benchmarked that utilizes mounting pressure in a vortex to convert calcite to aragonite. Ever higher vortex pressure ruptures bacterial cell membranes, while the increased water density naturally achieves 39° F, thus expelling salt, leaving the center of the water flow pure and clean. This is a fundamentally different approach than that taken by market leaders, although some market leaders, such as Nitto Denko, Siemens, and GE, may be ready to pursue these new developments. It requires not only forward thinking but the appetite to master the challenges of new technology and the willingness to learn new competences.

Management Principle 2: Supply Chain Management

Supply chain management involves the oversight of materials, financial transactions, and market delivery as products move from harvest or collection, to manufacture, to consumption. Even though a market leader may be persuaded that a new technology is an opportunity to gain competitive edge and market share, there is no guarantee this innovation will be approved for development. It must fit a manufacturing and distribution system – a supply chain – that predates the innovation and can carry the breakthrough. The strategic management team must make sure that research ideas make sense to marketing and manufacturing.

Many activities within a company need to converge around the introduction of new technologies and emerging product portfolios. Lack of a joint commitment from all departments, especially finance, supply chain management, and marketing, could unleash overt and covert conflicts based on personal interests ranging from career plans and year-end performance bonuses, to corporate policies such as depreciation rules, tax planning, and quarterly earnings targets. In the end, these conflicts often undermine any innovation strategy. There are in fact remarkable innovations described herein that perfectly fit an existing supply chain model. Nevertheless, developing market share is a challenge that requires enormous fortitude and perseverance.

Here we would take the example of vaccines that traditionally require a complete cold-chain from production to transportation, delivery, and storage at the dispensing medical facility. The supply chain management is based on strict temperature control. If one link in the chain fails, the spoiled vaccines must be discarded and replaced. In developing countries, where access to refrigeration often depends on an irregular electrical power supply, the solution has been to invest in solar- or propane-powered refrigeration to eliminate the risk of spoiling vaccines. Yet viable innovative solutions are available.

Thermo-stabilizing technology inspired by the resurrection fern (*Polypodium polypodioides*) and a microscopic invertebrate, the tardigrade, or water bear, has been developed by Bruce Roser and his venture company, Cambridge Biostability. They offer a freeze-drying system using tardigrades for preserving vaccines, applying this innovation with off-the-shelf equipment. This could handily facilitate a speedy integration of the innovation into the supply chain.

Another innovation that closely fits the supply chain model has been developed by Canadian researchers Sylvie Gauthier and Normand Voyer, marketed through the venture firm CO_2 Solutions, which is listed on the Toronto Stock Exchange. Theirs is a proprietary technology that utilizes the natural ability of a biocatalyst to manage CO_2 emissions at industrial scale. This technology fits easily into the scrubbing systems of coal-fired power stations and cement factories. It requires only minimal refitting. Since this is an add-on to existing technology, there is no disturbance of the existing production and supply. Their innovation thus has a better chance to penetrate the market through agreements with leading engineering firms.

Mats Nilsson's fire and flame retardants, made of natural food-grade ingredients, have successfully integrated the supply chain for use in particle board (for furniture or housing), polyurethane (widely used in cars and homes), and carpet fibers (for offices, homes and airplanes). There are hundreds of additional applications that need to be developed. Even though he can offer these non-toxic chemicals in gel or powder form, bonding with the materials to be treated requires minor adjustments for each application. The research to make this possible takes time and money. Treating materials as varied as latex, nylon, and cellulose requires a detailed understanding of how to bond the food-grade retardants with the production processes for different materials. Lack of major investment funding has so far compromised Nilsson's ability to complete the necessary research and make the bonding specifications each material and process requires. Need we wait decades before halogen and bromine toxins have been replaced by Krebs Cycle inspired molecules? Perhaps a clear preference expressed by consumers would encourage the world's largest homebuilders to test, approve, and utilize this product. It may be hoped that mainstream companies like Albemarle, Chematur, or BASF would be ready to move forward with such breakthroughs.

MANAGEMENT PRINCIPLE 3: OUTSOURCING

Innovations that succeed in meeting core competence and supply-chain management requirements must also fit with the management principle of outsourcing. Outsourcing is the process of subcontracting to third-party companies so that management can dedicate time, people, and resources to its core competence. This requires more than the mere adoption of a new technology by corporate management. The company must act as change agent for all its suppliers and subcontractors. If Daiwa House (Japan), the world's largest homebuilder, decided to replace the fire retardant chemicals they currently use, it would require developing and testing distinct product variations for each field of application, approval from industry regulators, determination of new adoption specifications, and coordination with the procedures of over 600 suppliers and subcontractors. That would be a significant task.

When this innovative flame retardant does not contribute additional revenue, only better indoor air quality, then the shift of one technology to another during an economic downturn diverts significant management attention from its perceived core responsibilities – securing sales and improving cash flow. The will to change would of necessity come from some greater sense of allegiance to health and the environment than that given to ingrained management principles.

Another technology based on the Fibonacci sequence demonstrates proven energy efficiencies that could save computer server companies millions by cooling their servers with natural geometry. Overheated computers and game consoles like the X-box from Microsoft are a well-known problem. The noise generated by ventilators is a nuisance. Naturalist Jay Harman, while working with the Australian Department of Fisheries and Wildlife, observed the flow geometries of ocean and air currents. His observations led him to formulate what he terms the "Streamlining Principle," which translates nature's flow efficiencies into streamlined design geometries. What he learned from the nautilus shell and kudu horn significantly improves the performance, output, and energy usage of a wide range of fluid-handling mechanical movements while reducing noise. He founded Pax Scientific in 1997 and raised capital through the sale of sub-licenses, since the proof that this technology saves energy is beyond debate. Yet not one of his applications has been successfully mainstreamed. The delays he and his team face are in accessing supply chain management, responding to fast turn-around cycles in the computer industry, and coordinating with the computer industry's worldwide outsourcing. The patents accumulate and the revenue from advances on sub-licenses continues to provide the cash for further research. But to close the first mega-sale a fourth obstacle must be overcome: the seal of approval of the vice-president for finance.

Management Principle 4: Cash Flow as King

Even though new products may reduce costs by saving money or energy, while simultaneously benefiting the environment, they may not automatically produce sales. In standard business practice improved margins are great, because they generate additional cash with which new investment can be funded. But shelf space is expensive for consumer goods, and fast-moving consumer products, heavily advertised in the media, mean that the cash flows faster. In the current economic downturn, giant international companies with a wide portfolio of products are dramatically reducing the number of their offerings and brands, limiting their catalog to products that have the fastest turnaround and not necessarily the highest profit margin. The overall cash flow is much greater on a product with daily sales and a five percent margin as opposed to a 50% margin on a product that sells only once a month. Just-in-time inventory turnover eliminates holding products in a warehouse, freeing the capital locked in stored consumer or industrial goods. Fast-turnover goods are attractive to investors and shareholders, especially industries that manufacture and deliver basic necessities like food- and health-related products not as subject to up-and-down economic cycles.

Another aftermath of the financial crunch is that credit is hard to get. When a technology like Watreco's vortex-based device to remove air from water might save 10-12% of energy usage, corporate financial management will conclude that this reduction in energy cost does not justify committing scarce cash. The money spent on marketing and manufacture may take years to recoup. That is sufficient to derail a purchase decision. Innovations providing energy savings of even 20-30% are unlikely to be adopted during an economic downturn. The idea of securing investments out of the savings they offer is part of an unacceptable model. Innovations must offer more than energy savings; simply costing less is not good enough. Market leaders have the confidence to make the necessary capital investment only when additional revenue can be assured.

MANAGEMENT PRINCIPLE 5: CROWDING OUT

Even when the corporate strategist, the supply chain manager, and the finance director have endorsed an innovation, the marketing team remains to be swayed. Inventors and innovators must develop a unique selling proposition that gets a product on the shelf and into the catalog, while successfully communicating its "story" to prospective consumers. In an atmosphere of concern about scarcity, the on-the-shelf reality is that everyone operates in a market characterized by oversupply. Our present variety and choice of consumer products is aptly described by the French proverb, *"l'embarras du choix,"* "an embarrassment of riches."

With so many alternatives, success is not a given even when a new product is better and cheaper. The first difficulty is getting attention and the next is attracting purchasing dollars. This is mainly due to the fact that established market leaders pursue a strategy known as "crowding out." This means that a product based on the same technology is made available with minor variations, absorbing all the possible shelf space, or responding to slightly different industrial requirements. The idea is to give buyers the sense that they have exactly what they need. This does not leave much room for a new arrival.

Products and services are standardized; production and distribution are streamlined and simplified. Diversity is reduced to marketing gimmicks and packaging design – whatever is underneath is much the same everywhere. There is essentially only one diesel engine on the world market, although it is used by a dozen carmakers. The electric motors for home appliances are nearly identical everywhere in the world. Such manufacturing processes universally consolidate market share into the hands of a few whose goals are economies of scale: producing more of the same at an ever lower marginal cost. Once an item is mainstreamed, the associated and secure money flows inhibit and discourage change.

The adhesive products market superbly illustrates this dilemma. There are hundreds of glue and sticking solutions on the market, dominated by giant companies such as 3M. Henkel, a German company, markets adhesion products derived from plant starch. In effect, the market is inundated with "solutions." The world demand for adhesives and sealants approaches $50 billion in annual sales. The adhesives and sealants sector in Europe alone invests $200 million in research and development each year. This is a huge market with lots of research power concentrated in the hands of a few who already have such a breadth of products that it is difficult for a new product, however creative and however appealing, to build a niche and crowd others off the shelves, gain space in the sales catalogs, or acquire the attention of buyers. An article in *Time Magazine* or *The Economist* may provide some visibility, but as long as there is no actual accompanying order form, it will make little difference. Despite the many solutions that could some day replace the unsustainable products now for sale, present market leaders are disinclined to endorse such change.

This brings up another aspect to developing and maintaining market share that can threaten or obliterate a product on its path to the mainstream market. "Suffocation" can preempt the necessity for crowding out. Once a new product is selling in a niche market, and is perceived as a threat to the market standard, the giants of industry may act to acquire the emerging business and its patented technologies. The inventor will be offered a favorable buyout, and the new technology may simply be buried, never reaching consumers, simply because it disrupts an existing cash flow and profit margin.

THE DOWNSIDE OF THE UPSIDE

SO MANY SOLUTIONS, SO LITTLE TIME

Over and above the range of synthetic solutions already competing in the market, there are numerous known innovations inspired by natural systems. The gecko is the popular new arrival, while Velcro™ has successfully created a multi-million dollar niche of its own. The paper wasp native to central Europe has pincers that enable it to break down wood mechanically (physics first). It then eats these pieces and mixes them with aqueous digestive juices. This chemically shortens the length of the fibers. On drying, water evaporates, the cellulose fibers form a mat, and the adhesive hardens. The nest is ready.

In contrast to paper wasps that use a water-based adhesive, the adhesive used by honey bees for comb building contains wax. Wax is a liquid at a bee's body temperature. Only on cooling does it solidify and adhere. Bees' wax hence meets the ideal requirements for modern adhesives, e.g., heat melts. It is solvent-free but can be applied as a liquid. Barnacle larvae can bond to virtually any hard marine material. The bonding is achieved through a secretion from cement glands. This secretion is a reactive adhesive possessing a high resistance to water. New adhesive is constantly secreted to ensure that the bond remains intact.

Such competition in the glue and adhesion sector alone illustrates that that opportunities using natural solutions abound. Thus, even an alert management team can have a difficult time choosing which innovation to support. Where do you start if your research department has hardly any biologists or biochemists, and the marketing and production strategies remain bound by the straightjacket of core business based on core competence?

Greenwashing

While many of us would consider ourselves positive and pro-active, consumer enthusiasm and the desire of concerned citizens to contribute to solutions for sustainability can end up an obstacle to embarking on real change. In our quest for green solutions we are keen to quickly embrace what seems an obvious path towards sustainability, though in reality it may not be such a good idea after all. In 2006, Europe rushed to promote biofuels, only to realize that this sudden massive demand for raw materials, spurred by consumers wishing to buy green fuels, would affect the availability of corn grown for food. Instead of maize corn for human consumption, farmers planted field corn – suitable for livestock or biofuel manufacture. Prices for this staple food increased, making food security in the developing world even more difficult to achieve. The rush to secure corn supplies helped the world's largest traders and processors of agricultural output achieve record profits, yet it caused enormous hardship elsewhere. The United Nations issued a warning, and corn and palm oil were discouraged as biofuel sources.

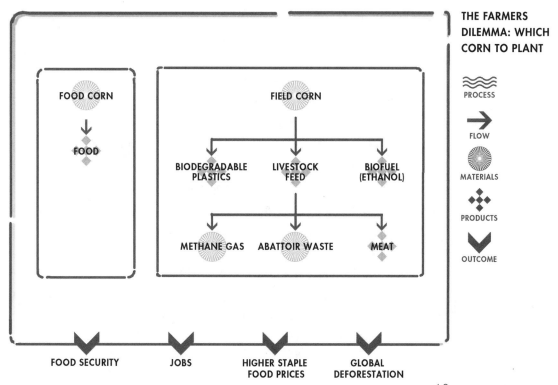

THE FARMERS DILEMMA: WHICH CORN TO PLANT

PROCESS

FLOW

MATERIALS

PRODUCTS

OUTCOME

Similarly, we rightly question the sense of biodegradable soaps made of fatty acids derived from palm trees planted on denuded land where rainforests once stood. We ponder the rationale of consuming delectable *shiitake* mushrooms cultivated from felled oak forests in China. If we can be mindful of the larger picture, we can avoid too readily embracing an obvious solution only to later discover compromising harm.

The conversion to biodegradable soaps in Europe and America destroyed the habitat of the orangutan. When ecologically minded companies developed a line of biodegradable soaps derived from the fatty acids of palm oil trees, their success in taking market share incited the major market players to follow suit. To meet burgeoning international demand, millions of acres of rainforest were cut down and replaced by cultivated palm oil trees. Such unintended harm is a hard way to learn that biodegradable does not equate to sustainable. Green solutions that put the livelihood of the poor and the life of primates at risk are morally and ethically unacceptable, and are just another form of greenwashing.

"Green" solutions that have toxic inputs or processes and unintended side effects should not be in line for sustainability awards. It is irrational to offer congratulations for doing less harm, especially when the damage is inflicted upon the whole ecosystem on which life depends. The ethically correct choice is to achieve greater benefit, not create less damage. Substituting asbestos with halogen- and bromine-based fire retardants, for example, does not offer a real solution. A less toxic solution is still a toxic solution. We must seek out solutions that neither pollute our food chain nor our personal environment. We can adjust our thinking and increase our ambitions. The argument that a little toxin load does no harm relies on the pretense that something proven detrimental, mutagenic, or carcinogenic can be tolerated in minute quantities. There is no such diagnosis as "a little bit of cancer" – you either have cancer, or you don't! The same applies to the notion of making as much money as possible by whatever means, then reserving some of that gain to do something special for society. Such a compensation game is unethical, although unfortunately widely played.

The inability to see connections beyond the obvious is a major challenge we must surmount when designing the Blue Economy. Several innovations have succumbed to flawed or shortsighted processes. A new molecule for controlling bacteria promoted by Biosignal (Australia) used toxic solvents in the production of the synthetic analogue. The first hydrophobic/hydrophilic sheets manufactured by QinetiQ (UK) to capture dew in the desert used a chemistry that created a potential health hazard for workers and consumers. Compact fluorescent lighting pioneered by Osram (Germany), provides major energy savings and is widely accepted by consumers, yet the mercury used in manufacture is a toxin. It is released into the environment when the light bulbs are discarded and not recycled. We cannot with a clear conscience defend saving energy while releasing mercury into the ecosystem. We can do much better.

FROM 20 THOUSAND TO 100 MILLION

When the markets soften and margins are under pressure, it may be that the last thing established management wants is anyone in the research or product design departments promoting a creative new idea inspired by nature. Within this context, it is a challenge to introduce innovations, even those with many applications. While we may lament the difficulties in convincing market leaders of this brilliance, we may more reasonably be delighted that such innovations will generate enormous numbers of entrepreneurial ventures and sustainably based jobs. The inaction of today's market leaders may turn them into the dinosaurs of tomorrow, leaving tremendous opportunities for those who are ready to change the rules of the game. Of course, it is possible that mainstream management may be convinced to think out of the box. We all know from our own experience that when you are desperate you are more willing to try a new approach.

Re-imagining the future requires entrepreneurs in science, social affairs, business, environment, and culture. It requires drawing back from an economy where the engine of growth is indebtedness loaded upon our children and grandchildren, squandering those future generations' material resources. Perhaps now, as we continue to voice our desire for change, having witnessed the tsunami-like destruction wrought by greed, lies, and blindness, we may find that government, business, and industry are ready to alter their perceptions and allocate the resources to support and develop a Blue Economy. Perhaps now they can move forward with the will to respond to the needs of all with what we have and what we can share with those who have not.

CHAPTER FIVE

NATURE'S MBA
(Mastery of Brilliant Adaptations)

How strange that Nature does not knock,
and yet does not intrude!

— EMILY DICKINSON

An MBA (Master of Business Administration) degree confers a status to the holder that makes them desirable as business managers and leaders. They have learned to analyze transactions and interactions that help pinpoint cost reduction for labor and raw materials, maximize cash flow, increase market share, and fine-tune supply chain management. Unfortunately these experts, who are today's dominant business leaders, seem on the verge of disconnection from the habitats and inhabitants of our planet. Worse, their narrow focus on one core business blinds them from recognizing viable opportunities outside their sphere of interest or knowledge. Our production and consumption schemes are outdated, incapable of responding to the basic needs of all. They must either evolve or be replaced by ones that thrive by functioning harmoniously with all life, promoting diversity, and fairly ensuring food, shelter, health, and livelihood for everyone. It is with this conclusion that we turn our admiration and attention to nature's MBA – Mastery of Brilliant Adaptations.

Ecosystems offer tremendous inspiration for devising economic models capable of responding to the needs of all. Natural systems always change, always evolve. That is their power and their beauty. When we attend to nature's MBA, we can begin to understand how to integrate innovations into multifaceted models cascading nutrients and energy, supplying energy from integrated and renewable sources, designing structures that capture and utilize what is minute and transform it into what is grand, into networks that become so efficient that nothing is wasted and we have a net energy gain.

Industry is resistant to continuous change. Predictability is the name of the game. The model of core business and core competence pursues productivity in a manner that actually inhibits the natural path of evolution and change. This is in fact the logic by which industry arrives at solutions based on genetic manipulation. Once you know how to alter genes, you believe you know how to predict their outcomes. Where industry leaders prefer a predictable production system that uses harsh chemistry to stabilize molecules forever, and genetic modifications that stifle natural evolutionary tendencies, natural systems offer a different solution. Water is the solvent; molecular bonds are temporary to permit high biodegradability, so that molecules can be combined over and over again. Genetic modifications naturally occur in the realm of bacteria as this is part of their evolutionary pathway.

These differing frameworks explain why natural systems are always changing while industrial systems are inherently resistant to change. To avoid change and to provide more of the same, industrial systems create global standards that apply everywhere, under the pretext that this reduces costs. In contrast, ecosystems source everything locally. They satisfy their needs with what is readily available. Since ecosystems thrive on local biodiversity, standardization is of little use. After all, biodiversity is based on – as the word implies – diversity. This helps elucidate why new business models based on bundled portfolios of innovations will be implemented through thousands of entrepreneurs, each of whom will find their niche and their chance. Industry's desire is to control and standardize, to merge and expand on the imaginary curve of economies of scale, externalizing all costs outside their narrow focus. The fact that only a few varieties of tomatoes and potatoes are commercialized, while there are hundreds of varieties, and that our main crops are primarily wheat, corn, and soy monocultures, makes it evident why soils are depleted and disease infestations meet little resistance.

If we observe nature we see that ecosystems evolve towards ever-higher levels of efficiency and diversity thanks to contributions from all players. A 500-year-old cedar tree and a majestically erect bear may be the most remarkable inhabitants we notice when hiking the Rocky Mountains, but a closer look shows that millions of other species, mostly invisible to the eye, are not only contributing but are critical to the whole system. Evolution implies a constant trend towards greater efficiency and greater diversity. So may it be with economies, shaped by entrepreneurs at all levels in business, science, culture, and education.

As Fritjof Capra has pointed out, ecosystems are networks of networks. The same management principles can be observed layered within each network. Indeed, ecosystems are all about connecting, about allowing everyone to contribute to the best of their abilities, while operating within clearly defined boundaries where nutrients and energy are endlessly cascaded and the laws of physics are followed without exception. Following a cascading model and capitalizing on the principles of physics makes it possible to respond to basic needs, in every location, with whatever is locally available. Instead of contrived scarcity and shortages, what we see in a Blue Economy model is abundance – of food, energy, jobs, and revenue. How many communities would oppose? Given the potential outcome, how many entrepreneurs would refuse the risk of bringing such innovations to the market?

Everyone can also imagine what it means to have the benefit of a platform technology that replaces chemicals with purely physical effects, as the vortex has been documented to do. Everyone can understand what it means for food security when coffee waste, or other agro-waste, turns into protein-rich mushrooms, contributes income from both the waste and the mushrooms, and provides high-quality animal feed from the spent mushroom substrate. We are building up social capital and eliminating abuse. We are turning a globally traded commodity like coffee into a resource for food security. Surely everyone can understand such value.

EMPOWERING ENTREPRENEURS

The model for a Blue Economy is based on what is real. While job losses and youth unemployment are dramatic in the industrialized world, the reality we must confront is that the present economic disarray leaves no place for the one billion new arrivals entering the labor market, especially those from developing nations. The incapacity to imagine meaningful jobs and to provide worthy challenges to a whole generation equates to telling the young that there is no future for them, that their generation is lost. Every night over a billion people go to sleep hungry. Nearly two billion have no access to safe drinking water. Worse, the current economic system is based on the bankrupt notion of scarcity where growth is funded with debt perpetually carried over to future generations. Shortages and deficiencies are considered the logical base and a necessary evil from which a more efficient allocation of resources will evolve. This same scarcity mentality also foments debate and social resistance to innovation, because it portrays such change agents as threats to job security, by proposing to replace labor with no labor.

Thus it will require creativity and inclusiveness of the entrepreneurs in science, social affairs, business, ecology, and media to move us toward a Blue Economy. Natural systems can build local entrepreneurship much as evolution embraced innovations through diversity. There may be no greater power for change than the young at heart, ready and willing to assume the risk. It requires as much clarity of purpose as it requires perseverance. Fortunately, it does not require experience in a given sector, nor a lot of money. It does require maintaining a solid ethical underpinning, and knowing how to generate cash flow against all odds.

As we have noted, innovations outlined in this book may prove hard for mainstream businesses to adopt. Big companies content with producing more of what has proven successful may lack cutting-edge competencies, or may be unwilling to commit the initial capital necessary for a new approach. This is a major advantage for committed entrepreneurs. Basing their actions on solid science and their vision on social and emotional consciousness, they can implement and develop these innovations to create waves of change that infuse every business sector, shifting entire markets towards sustainability.

They will succeed by developing successful partnerships, taking advantage of institutional aggregation, and achieving market viability by garnering consumer support across a wide socioeconomic stratum. Market success will stem from the availability of better products that cost less than their competition.

A time of crisis, when market leaders are stressed, and some are even on the edge of survival, is perhaps the best moment for the young and the young at heart to set their minds on a new business model. Practically speaking, there are not too many careers available when millions of jobs have been lost and well-paid jobs for graduates are the exception rather than the rule. As well, and contrary to expectation, the barriers to market entry are actually lower in a downturn. In a relatively stable economy, innovations do not easily find their way to market. However, when the entire economic framework evidences turmoil, decision makers latch onto any object that seems stable or that stands out. A major firm may be disposed to accept products and methods with a fundamentally new or different approach.

The task of an entrepreneur is literally to coalesce something new into being, to be the carrying force that brings an idea into substance, the agent between thought and realization. Yet alone, even if well funded and passionate, you are just alone. Market success often depends on partnerships. One of the ways to succeed with the introduction of these innovations is to build partnerships with change agents who have the power to influence the market and tip the balance. Innovations do not necessarily flow into the market, nor are company executives and investment bankers the only players who shape the market. Often market breakthroughs are brought about by change agents. Though numerous innovative consortia exist (consider the role of media, grassroots activists, and NGOs), there are established ways to create pressure effectively.

For example, insurance companies have the pulse of today's market, tabulating trends in the world economy through the monies they must pay out. Insurance companies are an obvious pressure point for change in the market, especially when savings are substantial. They closely follow a wealth of statistics, which is one of their core competences. No one knows how to crunch numbers better. In fact, a decision on their part to object to business as usual is based entirely on the simple science of statistics. Insurance companies, along with consumers, institutional investors, local communities, and local governments, are the stakeholders who drive decisions that stimulate innovation beyond the steady pace and comfort zone of industry.

To illustrate this, let us consider how insurance companies earn money offering fire insurance policies. When infant death by fire became a concern based on statistical data, insurance companies and industry manufacturers lobbied for the adoption of requirements specifying the use of fire and flame retardants. The risk of fire damage statistically decreases when any fire and flame retardant is used. A lower incidence of fire means an increase in industry's profit. A few decades later, if their statistics indicate an increase in male infertility, allergies, or even cancer at young age, and these statistics can be scientifically linked to the fire and flame retardants in use, then the insurance industry could once again stimulate change by urging lawmakers to accept a new standard or a new solution, while restricting (even against the will of the industry) the agents suspected of causing such conditions.

Insurance companies and their expert statisticians know all too well that correlation does not prove cause and effect. Rather, it is the reversal of the burden of proof that changes the business model. To achieve a secure angle, the company must demonstrate that it has considered all options and has concluded that negative effects could never occur. For change agents, it offers another lever for securing faster acceptance of breakthrough innovations. In our case in point, consider that insurers could earn multiple revenues by selling product liability policies to the makers of toxic fire retardants. If emerging evidence were to link a particular chemical to a specific illness, the liability insurance premium would increase, perhaps to a point where cost pressures would spur management to change even faster than legal guidelines dictate. The cost of insurance and the reluctance of re-insurance companies to cover the risks would force the company into action.

Insurance companies could further augment their revenue potential by integrating data from each of their separate risk businesses. This would provide a formidable base of information with obvious pathways for shifts in industry, encouraging innovations on the recommendation of insurance companies. Health insurers could link toxicity beyond the Ames Test, which assesses the mutagenic potential of chemical compounds. They could rank the chemicals suspected to cause health problems, suggesting substitutes.

THREE LEVELS OF SUSTAINABILITY

All too often industry finds natural substitutes for effective but toxic products, then manufactures the natural replacements in the traditional "heat and beat" mode that is responsible for our excessive carbon footprint. When industry finds solutions in biology, it reverts to cloning and genetic manipulation to secure "predictable" results. Thus, the inspiration from nature to find substitute molecules for the market's standard bearers requires more than the simple shift from one molecule to another. The molecule and the manufacturing system must be inspired by natural processes to create the desired convergence toward sustainability. A Blue Economy offers a blueprint that follows physics and nature in materials selection and production methods. From this basis it initiates a generative and regenerative cascade of implementable innovations. We thus have sustainable product, sustainable manufacture, and sustainable whole systems. In terms of business and economic benefit, this creates competitive products, competitive processes, and competitive business models that go far beyond core business practice.

Nature works at ambient temperature and pressure. Even abalone shells, which are stronger than the bullet-proof ceramic Kevlar™, are methodically assembled layer by layer. The shells are made from calcium carbonate and proteins, materials that are completely locally sourced. The process is sustainable. The ceramics manufacturer could argue that nature produces too little, too slowly, and that industry standards require efficient, timely, and predictable results. It is true that the time needed to manufacture

ceramics in an oven at a temperature over 1000° is considerably less than the time needed by the abalone. However, a ceramics company purchases mined materials. These mines had to be discovered. A permit was needed to exploit the resources. These materials must be shipped around the world, processed (at high pressure and high temperature to speed and standardize operations and product output), and delivered in the appropriate format. When we take these factors into account, beginning with the search for the mine to the arrival of the calcium carbonate at the ceramic production facilities, the time and efficiency advantage is less obvious. It is worth noting that whenever mining is part of the production process, natural systems will perform faster and at a fraction of the energy cost.

ONE INNOVATION, MULTIPLE REVENUES

The innovations described herein clearly have the potential to generate multiple revenue streams. The market turns around money; money is thus a medium of exchange. Innovations that generate more market applications have greater appeal, and are thus most likely to be embraced by established businesses and entrepreneurs. The opportunity to generate multiple revenues is a very attractive phenomenon since it mobilizes parallel investments for several niche markets. This reduces the risk of innovation. Nonetheless, these are still high risk investments. The terms may not be appealing for the inventors but the need for cash may be so urgent that they accept an investment agreement.

In a downturn, cash is king. Those who have billions to invest can easily set the terms of the deal. The model of a core business with a single revenue stream is often preferred by investors who want management to focus on the single most promising application. Any investor will assess a new technology's chances for success. Entrepreneurial companies wishing to raise venture capital must reveal a very long list of "things that can go wrong." At the same time, hardened Silicon Valley venture capital companies will listen to a presentation of one innovation with dozens of possible applications. Without exception they will ask for the one application that guarantees to gross $100 million dollars within three years.

While risks are inherent to business, those associated with the majority of the innovations considered and reviewed this book have been calculated, mitigated, and are much lower than usual for the market. In fact, these innovations can reduce risk because they alter the business model at its core. The achievements of a platform technology where basic parameters have been successfully applied clearly reduces risk and offers potentially better returns than funding a narrowly defined niche. Such a vast potential for sales implies that investors reassess the risk in light of these multiple revenues. This is the key advantage to nearly all the top innovations we describe.

We need not look far to demonstrate this fact. For example, there are 37 known commercial applications for the vortex. There are over 20 for seaweed furanones that control the proliferation of biofilm by jamming bacterial communication (see Chapter 8). Savings are hard to miss in replacing a $50,000 surgery with a $500 non-surgical intervention that provides permanent heart monitoring without batteries and at a lower cost. Instead of selling a pacemaker one million times per year, the medical industry can sell monitoring patches a billion times a year.

The silk polymers developed by Oxford Biomaterials (see Chapter 7) are already under development in five different companies, each with separate financing. Pax Scientific has opted for the same approach, raising financing in five separate fields of application for its insights on how nature moves water and air with less friction. Biosignal, the Australian startup developing antibacterial applications for furanones (see Chapter 8), had a comparable strategy of spinning off potential applications for agriculture, consumer, industrial, medical equipment, and therapeutic markets before its technology portfolio was merged with another company. Each of these in turn might raise diverse funds for mobilizing niche solutions such as anti-corrosion in oil and gas, antiperspirants, or a potential cure for cystic fibrosis. All derive from the same platform technology. Watreco, the start-up company built around Curt Hallberg's mathematical interpretations of a vortex, brings solutions to the market as varied as saving energy in ice making, speeding percolation on golf greens, de-scaling pipes, and pumping air into fish farm tanks. These venture companies exemplify entrepreneurs who are ready to move businesses forward.

The power of these technologies to provide multiple cash flows through multiple applications reduces risk and dramatically increases the value of the intellectual property, potentially allowing inventors to sub-license technological applications and focus on what drives their interest and simulates their curiosity. The power to overcome obstacles requires partnerships. Although inventors and marketers have different goals, a winning coalition can begin with solid leading-edge science and build on the sharp competitive analysis of entrepreneurs. The world of risk capital is ready to finance people with good ideas. What is needed now is the capacity and willingness to bring innovations to the market.

Innovations with the potential to generate multiple revenues in diverse markets are attractive. If these cash flow generators change the business model, then businesses that develop these innovations not only meet an important need, they will be pursued as investment and entrepreneurial opportunities.

CASCADING RESOURCES IN A COMMUNITY

Such innovations can also empower communities to respond to their own needs, especially in societies under major stress. They offer the foundation and the means to grow initiatives into movements, achieving market share despite adverse conditions. Communities that have neither money to trade nor capital to invest are often regarded as less responsive to the introduction of new ideas. Yet the achievements of Father Godfrey Nzamujo in Benin, Chido Govero in Zimbabwe, and Paolo Lugari in Colombia demonstrate that this is not true. The design and implementation of these integrated biosystems have converted nonviable communities into economic successes where money flows and capital grows. Half of the world's human population lives in rural or agricultural settings. Developing nations with rural and agricultural populations can greatly benefit from integrated biosystems complemented with bio-refineries, such as the method of conversion used in Las Gaviotas for collecting resin from harvested trees, locally processed with renewable energies from the region into nine different products, with all waste from the process used in the production of construction materials. Integrated biosystems will also permit industrialized nations to dramatically reduce their ecological footprint and increase their material efficiency.

REAL OPPORTUNITIES, REAL SOLUTIONS

This shift in business model that is becoming more evident and necessary develops from our growing understanding of nature's MBA – how natural systems rely on the forces of physics, rather than consuming the resources of the planet and the very things needed to maintain survival. The impact is surprising. The results are compelling. There are vaccines that need no refrigeration, heart rhythm devices that need no surgery, vortex technologies that de-scale water pipes without chemicals, algae that defeat bacteria by deafness, or silk that cuts with razor-sharpness – the list is long! The replacement of something that is chemically toxic and clearly unsustainable with what is nothing more than a natural process may well help solve the biggest challenges of our time, while opening a window of opportunity for a portfolio of completely new products and services.

This opportunity to replace "something" with "nothing" – to replace a toxic or non-renewable material or process with one that relies merely on physics and natural processes – is particularly exciting. The capacity to reduce risk by generating more cash flow makes products and services competitive. This is where it will foster a new wave of entrepreneurship. This is how millions of sustainable jobs will be created, fundamentally shifting old model products and by-gone production methods to innovations and processes based on the scientific understanding of already benchmarked solutions that encourage the next generation to become innovators. The billions of years of experience accumulated in the evolution of ecosystems and species do count when it comes to perfecting solutions and providing

alternatives for different environments. These are proven solutions that evidence resilience and flexibility.

In past decades the goal of sustainability required everyone to pay more and invest more to save the environment or reduce pollution. Few were prepared or willing to adopt this means to effect that goal. Even government tax levies and fines for polluting practices did not noticeably promote stewardship. Now we can achieve better results and create multiple revenue sources while building social capital and community resilience. Those who profited in the past from poor choices can now rationalize investing in new solutions that will strengthen economies and communities from the roots upward. The driving force of success could well be thousands of entrepreneurs whose boundless enthusiasm and commitment more than compensate for any lack of capital or experience. Moreover, innovations with the greatest market success will be those that address basic needs. This is what management wizard Peter Drucker claimed in the 1980s: *"The needs of the poor are opportunities waiting for entrepreneurs."*

When manufacturers choose to replace a toxic process with a less toxic alternative, they are simply "doing less bad." That is the option taken when billions of dollars are poured into less toxic though longer lasting batteries. These batteries still rely on mining, smelting, and harsh chemistry with an overwhelming majority ending up in landfills that pollute the environment, poisoning ecosystems while posing a long-term health hazard to us all. Many will argue that a halfway measure is at least on the right track. Yet this is nothing short of a duplicitous moral standard. We all have the urge to do more good. Let us not accept that doing less bad is good enough.

Current scientific literature offers insights into thousands of possible breakthroughs inspired by ways that natural species have solved challenges to procurement and survival. Though fewer have revealed the entirety of their process, the possibilities remain and the mysteries can be solved. Time will permit us to understand and implement innovations that will dramatically shift our methods of production and consumption toward sustainability.

In the next chapters we will further explore the framework of the Blue Economy from the basis of existing contributions and solutions that are at work right now. A Blue Economy is what will apply the achievements of ecosystems to economic systems. Indeed, implementing a Blue Economy will ensure that human systems, in fact all living systems, can attain the stability and security that will safeguard and maintain their evolutionary and regenerative path.

CHAPTER SIX

CASCADING MODELS, MULTIPLE CASH FLOWS

Give me a place to stand, and I can move the Earth!

— ARCHIMEDES

In times of upheaval, positive minds look for solutions, wherever they can. There are always areas of growth even when the overall economy is considered to be in decline. Health care, food production, and pollution control are three areas where there is consensus that increased expenditures are certain even in rough times. Few markets better exemplify growth potential than the burgeoning worldwide demand for edible and medicinal mushrooms.

Ever since a middle class with purchasing power emerged in China, demand for the fruiting bodies of *shiitake (Lentinula edodes)* and other fungi has been explosive. Double-digit growth rates have been the norm for over two decades. Europe and North America are also discovering the unique nutritional and medicinal effects of several mushrooms with unfamiliar names like "Judas ear" *(Auricularia auricula)*, "enoki" *(Flamminula velutipes)*, "maitake" *(Grifola fondosa)*, or "reishi" *(Ganoderma lucidum)*. Soon these words may well become part of our daily vocabulary just like "expresso", "latte", "sushi," and "pizza."

Demand for fungi and the number of jobs required to meet that demand has risen ever since these delicacies could be produced at will. Wu Sangong, a 13th century farmer-scientist, initiated the Chinese foray into healthy protein from fungi, one of the five kingdoms of nature. The *shiitake* capital of the world is Qingyuan, located in the Pearl Delta of Guangdong, China.

Qingyuan is smaller than the San Francisco Bay Area, yet this region employs over 120,000 people farming *shiitake* mushrooms with a market value in the West of over one billion dollars. According to Prof. Shuting Chang, a mushroom expert at Chinese University of Hong Kong who has made major contributions to the international success of mushroom farming, the total export value of Chinese mushroom cultivation topped 17 billion dollars and supported 10 million jobs in 2007. Though for decades this has surprised Western food and population experts, fungi grown on rice straw clearly contribute to food security for China's large population.

Harvested remains of plants, fruits, and vegetables (Plant Kingdom) provide feed for chickens, ducks, pigs, and fish (Animal Kingdom). This food source is complemented by protein from mushrooms (Fungi Kingdom), which prodigiously converts plant waste, especially straw, to food. Bacteria (Monera Kingdom) are also mobilized in digesters to convert manure to a growth medium for algae (Protoctista Kingdom).

Annual US demand for tropical mushrooms is barely 175 grams per person per year. Consumption in Canada is already double that amount. Hong Kong reaches an amazing 30 pounds per person per year. If US consumers were to eat only as much fungi as Canadians, this would translate into an additional two billion dollars in revenue. If the US population were to shift its food habits to match those of Hong Kong, the tropical mushroom industry would top any other business in the world, even petroleum, at today's market prices for petroleum and mushrooms. The significance of this statistic is that mushrooms are traditionally farmed on agricultural waste, which is widely considered a nuisance and often simply burned.

The biomasses from plant husks, cobs, or straw on which mushrooms thrive contain no protein or polysaccharides of any importance, yet mushrooms are rich in protein. Based on dry weight, some varieties of oyster mushroom compete with meat for concentration of protein as well as all the essential amino acids. Interestingly, white button mushrooms *(Agaricus bisporus)* remain the most consumed species in the West, although they have the least protein and require pasteurized horse manure to grow. Some countries even import this waste from overseas to locally farm the white buttons. Imagine, we have world free-trade in horse manure to produce low quality protein! This is neither a sustainable nor a competitive business model for achieving the nutrient needs of an expanding world population.

The interplay of natural systems is capable of securing a cascade of protein from multiple sources, and is thus free of reliance on a single source. This offers insight into how we can provide worldwide food security with what is locally available. Mushrooms convert plant waste into edible fruiting bodies. The portion of the fungi that remains in the substrate after harvest is mycelium, which is highly nutritious for animals. Animals in turn generate manure which bacteria digest, enriching the soil so plants and microorganisms thrive. The cascading of nutrients from one species belonging to one kingdom to another species belonging to another kingdom is an ecosystems marvel. That is why there is neither starvation nor unemployment in an ecosystem. Everyone is busy contributing their best, gaining sustenance from something that was waste for another, and satisfying the basic needs of all.

The business model for the production of tropical mushrooms is simple. First, a fibrous biomass is sterilized under pressure and high temperature, although some know how to skip this process. Most of the time the growing medium is dead or dying biological matter. Next, mushroom spores are introduced in small quantities. Since bacteria have been largely eliminated by the sterilization process, the mycelium quickly expand into the substrate over a few weeks. Once the substrate is fully populated, a thermal or water shock is applied. This causes the fruiting bodies to emerge. Mushrooms typically reproduce quickly when their survival is threatened. What we refer to as "mushrooms." are the offspring – the fruiting bodies.

The Chinese reuse all straw waste to grow straw mushrooms (*Volvariella volvacea*). Unfortunately, several straw crops have been genetically modified, as is the case with rice, to have short stalks and thus much less straw.

Elsewhere in the world straw is burned, generating massive air pollution. Burning rice straw is a horrendous problem in Egypt, affecting upwards of 20 million people along the Nile Delta. Those who study massive population needs have yet to emulate the Chinese wisdom of converting straw into protein, and the mushroom substrate into animal feed. In fact, countries such as Egypt have adopted genetically modified short-straw rice, and at the same time have experienced a shortfall in food security, relying on imported wheat to make up the difference.

Current mushroom farming practices are not always sustainable. Where oak is used as the preferred growing medium, it is logged, shredded, and converted into a high quality growth substrate for *shiitake*, one of the priciest and healthiest mushrooms on the international market. The rapidly increasing demand for shiitake strains harvest capacity in oak forests throughout China.

Over the past 15 years, innovative and efficient farming of local and tropical mushrooms has evolved to a low cost, competitive, year-round business. The innovations are multiple and have led to the creation of a new business model for production and marketing. The model of mushroom farming inspired by the cascading of nutrients in ecosystems has been benchmarked in Africa and Latin America. An increased Western demand for exotic mushrooms, coupled with a price trend towards greater affordability, would be critical to securing widespread adoption of this cholesterol-free, fat-free food. Increased demand would spur cultivators to search for more abundant waste materials as a growing medium. Since mushroom farming is relatively more labor intensive, this waste-to-food chain would create thousands, even millions of jobs. Entrepreneurs working locally to realize this potential would create job opportunities, particularly in areas where accessing the employment market holds greater challenge.

THE BUZZ ABOUT COFFEE

At the turn of the 21st century, mushrooms overtook coffee as the second most widely traded commodity. Now a new opportunity emerges that will increase the value of both: mushrooms grown on coffee waste. There are two waste streams related to coffee. The bulk of the waste is generated on the farm and is known as "pulp." Brewing coffee produces a second waste stream known as "grounds." From the time the beans leave the farms to the moment they finish brewing in coffee pots, 99.8% ends as waste and only 0.2% is ingested. While this currently contributes mightily to the waste management issues we noted earlier, there is now a positive and creative approach that cascades waste streams generated by both farms and coffee shops into nutrient streams for mushrooms. This opens up an unparalleled opportunity. The farmer earns about one tenth of a cent on a coffee shop espresso that sells for three dollars, a mark-up factor of 3,000! Given that the annual world consumption of coffee in 2008 was 134 million bags (one bag is 60 kilograms), the total biomass that is left to rot is a shocking 23.5 million tons. If the value realized from the coffee bean can be replicated or even surpassed with the potential value of the waste from coffee harvest and production, it would be a genuine bonanza.

Mushrooms grow on ligno-cellulose. The massive waste generated in the process of converting coffee from a berry on a bush to a beverage in a cup is mainly ligno-cellulose. Better yet, coffee is a hardwood, like oak. In 1990, Prof. Shuting Chang, whom we introduced earlier, demonstrated that coffee is an ideal substrate for cultivating mushrooms, especially oyster and *shiitake*. Even the medicinal and highly prized *Ganoderma lucidum (reishi)* thrives on coffee grounds.

From farm, to roaster, to consumer, the coffee bean is a perfectly monitored crop. Seldom will you find any agricultural product that is subject to more stringent quality controls. When the coffee is brewed, hot water or steam at high temperature passes through and sterilizes the ground and roasted beans. All this is to great advantage for mushroom purposes, as it simplifies the production process of mushroom farming. The steamed and wetted grounds, returned to the packages of their arrival, could be directly inoculated with mushroom spores without the added necessity of sterilization. This would further reduce cost and readily supply local entrepreneurs.

Furthermore, since the caffeine stimulus in the coffee grounds encourages some mushrooms to fruit faster, using grounds would generate a better cash flow than the typical mushroom farm. This corresponds perfectly with our economic ideal: less investment, more cash flow; one initiative, multiple benefits. This translates to lower cost, faster output, higher customer loyalty, and better return on investment.

MULTIPLE BENEFITS OF THE PULP-TO-PROTEIN MODEL OF COFFEE WASTE TURNED MUSHROOM NUTRIENT (Helping to Meet the United Nations Millenium Development Goals)			
FOR THE CONSUMER AND THE PRODUCER		**FOR THE PLANET**	
RICHER	coffee provides the ideal nutrients and growing medium for mushrooms	LOW ENERGY	coffee grounds are sterilized, no further processing is necessary
CLEANER	both brewing and inoculation require only hot water	LESS METHANE	grounds used won't decompose in landfills so less greenhouse gas
FASTER	caffeine makes mushrooms grow faster	LESS GRAZING	post-harvest substrate is a high-quality animal feed
CHEAPER	raw materials are free	LESS LOGGING	coffee is also a hardwood and an ideal substitute for oak
HEALTHIER	mushrooms are protein-rich and cholesterol- and fat-free	LESS LANDFILL	coffee shops waste removal costs and contribute less to landfill waste
FOOD SECURITY	waste from the cash crop secures food for the region	FOOD SECURITY	waste from the cash crop secures food for the region

A venture that converts waste into a highly nutritious food that is cheaper and healthier for everyone is attractive in these challenging times. From a business perspective, the best message is that this method offers improved cash flow, which interests investors and bankers. After Prof. Chang undertook the first scientific studies, Carmenza Jaramillo spent six years studying the utilization of coffee waste to propagate fungi for CENICAFE, the research institute of the Colombian Federation of Coffee Farmers. She published more than 20 peer-reviewed scientific papers in international journals to report and document her findings. Dr. Ivanka Milenkovic at the University of Belgrade scientifically analyzed the use of the mushroom substrate as animal feed and found no loss of meat or milk production. Clearly this Pulp-to-Protein method has major economic benefits.

It is unfortunate that on the farms coffee pulp is simply left to rot, often with the excuse that it is good fertilizer. Annually, 16 million tons of organic waste left to decompose on coffee farms and in landfills produces millions of tons of greenhouse gas. The Pulp-to-Protein approach reduces the need to harvest wood. This allows trees, particularly the hardwoods such as oak, to continue to fix carbon, which slows the adverse effects of climate change. Feeding waste back into the nutrient cycle simplifies waste management and cuts methane gas emissions from rotting biomass. The integration of mushrooms and coffee leads to a dramatic reduction of every negative. In combination, two negatives become a positive.

PULP-TO-PROTEIN TO MITIGATE CLIMATE CHANGE	
IMPACT ON CLIMATE CHANGE	**PROGRESS TOWARDS MILLENNIUM GOALS**
Low energy use	Food Security
Preservation of forests	Empowerment of Women
Lower Transportation Energy Costs	Improved Childhood Health
No Landfill	Environmental Sustainability
No Methane Gas	Global Partnerships
Elimination of Charcoal Usage	Reduce HIV/AIDS
Cultivation of Slow Food	Learning Self-Sufficiency

When we look at coffee from the perspective of global development, we realize that the use of pulp on coffee farms would offer many advantages that would offset the negative impact that has tainted this cash-crop monoculture for decades. What we see in the current model is that coffee as a cash crop provides a living for farmers and their communities only when market prices are high. The moment the price drops below a certain threshold, farmers, their families, and their communities suffer. Significant declines in coffee prices result in the onset of poverty so severe that many *cafeteros* plow their coffee bushes into the soil, turning to subsistence farming with two cows per acre on their plot of land and little or no chance of ever making ends meet. Unable to feed his family and prepared to do anything to save them from hunger, the farmer moves with his family to a shantytown at the edge of an urban area, joining millions of others looking for jobs that pay little and offer only a bleak future.

At the end of the 20th century, Vietnam became the world's second largest exporter of coffee, creating economic havoc in many countries, particularly in Africa. However, as soon as coffee and mushrooms become a unified ecosystem, the dichotomy between cash crops and food security evaporates. We can envision a potential end to poverty in the coffee regions from a nutrient cascade involving plants, fungi, and animals. Each pound of farm waste generates at least half a pound of protein-rich food for the farming family. Because the mushroom substrate is an excellent (and free) animal feed, farmers will be able to afford and maintain livestock, which will further augment their nutrient needs and food security. It is a unique opportunity to observe how the waste of a cash crop like coffee can provide food security and many additional benefits. These farming techniques can resonate with the young, the unemployed, and the disadvantaged, as well as with hardened MBAs who see an opportunity to generate cash from nothing. A decade of field experience in Zimbabwe gives us a brilliant demonstration of these benefits.

The "Orphan Teaches Orphans" program, started by Chido Govero, herself orphaned a the age of 7, teaches other orphans how to grow mushrooms using locally available agricultural waste, including water hyacinth, an invasive species that proliferates throughout much of Africa. Water hyacinth has been named "Public Enemy Number One" in Zambia, and is fought with chemicals and non-native species like the weevil beetle. Yet one kilogram of water hyacinth can provide the nutrient base for up to two kilograms of mushrooms. Chido collects wild mushrooms during the rainy season and has mastered tissue culture techniques for the production of mushroom seed stock. With Chido's inspiration and guidance these orphan girls, who have suffered much, find the will and acquire the skills to build a future without abuse and provide for their livelihood and sustenance. Food security motivates many to think beyond food.

PULP TO LIVELIHOOD

Based on results in Colombia, each coffee farm undertaking mushroom cultivation could generate two new jobs. With an estimated 25 million coffee farms in 45 countries, this translates to an additional 50 million jobs worldwide, while providing food security not just for the workers but for their families as well. If we include other waste streams like straw, cobs, clippings, and water hyacinth, we are quickly edging towards truly amazing numbers. The capacity to provide local food for local populations increases farm income and farm stability. Instead of expending time and money to gather a subsistence diet with only the most basic nutrients, a considerable quantity of healthful and protein-rich food as well as animal feed can be derived from mushroom production.

This is only a tributary of the cascading model of the emerging Blue Economy. It provides an economic stimulus to generate jobs in rural areas. It has the potential to become one of the engines to re-launch the world economy. If there are jobs on the farms that pay, provide food, and insure that generations of expertise and tradition are used to their full potential, none will be tempted to leave for a bleak future in the slums of the nearest metropolis.

There are other tributaries: the creation of inner-city jobs. World-wide, coffee grounds are produced in more than 100 thousand inner-city coffee shops. From the Arab cities of the Middle East, to the *kohi shoppu* in Tokyo, to the traditional French cafés and the voracious American coffee culture, converting coffee grounds into mushrooms could mean a potential 100,000 additional jobs in urban zones. This pioneering effort has been tested in Berlin, Germany as well as in the San Francisco Bay area. It is not difficult. Knowing that orphans in Zimbabwe can do it with hardly anything but local waste, the assurance of success in the city is robust.

Jobs are only sustainable if income is generated. Income is only sustained when value is added. The core of this proposition is healthy food at a lower cost and greater availability. That part of the market will always grow because of its price elasticity – lower prices create proportionally more demand, sustaining the farmer's livelihood and growing the business. Calculations using research data and hands-on experience indicate that the income potential from cultivating mushrooms in a coffee ground substrate is vast. Considered together, and solely on the basis of coffee waste, the inner-city and farm-based production units could produce an estimated 16 million tons of additional nutrients for human consumption. This is half the protein provided by the entire world's fish farming. It is a secure revenue stream and a major resource for a global food market that is under severe stress from population explosion. Cascading nutrients and energy, not genetic modification, is what will allow us to respond to humanity's basic needs.

THE PULP-TO-PROTEIN MACHINE	
Jobs on the farm	1 acre farm = 2 jobs x 25 million coffee farms worldwide = 50 million jobs
Jobs in the inner-cities	10-15 coffee shops = 1 farming unit = 10 jobs x 21,000 coffee shops in the U.S. + 100,000 ~ worldwide = 1.2 million jobs
Results	16 million tons of fresh protein worldwide in +45 countries 5x sales increase 2000–2010 – worldwide 51.2 million jobs

Waste has always been unpopular. Aside from what we contribute to the "waste stream" on a personal basis, massive-scale disasters have turned our attention toward nuclear waste, petroleum spills, and chlorine pollution. The branding of waste has been universally negative. Imagine now a waste that generates jobs and healthy food. This is only good news. Since coffee pulp and coffee grounds make such an ideal substrate for mushrooms, and generate all the benefits just described, it should be touted and become part of coffee's image: *Coffee makes for healthy food and secure jobs.* Coffee could be associated with energy efficiency, sustainable livelihood, climate change mitigation, and even nourishing food at lower prices. The social capital would be substantial and widespread. Considering that it all started from something considered "waste," coffee can hardly be positioned more positively. Whose waste is it really?

It would be an admirable act of corporate social responsibility if the coffee traders of the world – from Neumann Kaffee Gruppe to Nestlé Foods – were to insure that all the farms they buy from convert all on-site waste to an ideal mushroom growing medium. It would create jobs and enhance food security. If the proponents of fair trade were to provide their farmers with the technical assistance necessary for converting waste to mushrooms, with whom would farmers prefer to trade? Cascading coffee waste could become a strategic tool for positioning long-term supply contracts with farmers, importers, and roasters.

To go one step further, traders and consumers who already support the organic and fair trade movements can be made aware that the real arena for fairness, the real opportunity for growth and development, can come from the 99.8% of the coffee harvest that has little value for those who harvest, purvey, and consume the bean. Such a viewpoint goes far beyond organic and fair trade. It permits the coffee trade to embrace sustainable development to the fullest extent anyone has ever imagined. The label "organic" only certifies the absence of chemical fertilizers and sprays. It does not say anything about resource efficiency. The label "Fair Trade" secures a fairer reimbursement for farmers, but does not secure the added value for the environment. Few coffee drinkers actually realize how little of the biomass generated at a coffee farm is consumed, or the wastefulness associated with their consumption habits. If the traders and distributors helped foster a Pulp-to-Protein model on the farms whose beans they market, such collaboration would bring about self-sustaining communities that experience food and livelihood security rather than malnourishment and despair. What incredible potential might be redirected for the benefit of the poor, the jobless, and the Earth!

The Pulp-to-Protein model is based on the power of ecosystems, and builds on worthy organic and fair trade initiatives. It creates value for 100% of the nutrients. If fully developed in all coffee-producing communities, by turning a waste stream into an income stream, this business model could generate a staggering 1.5 million times more revenue than coffee produces today. Imagine! 1.5 million *times* more revenue! It is in this fashion that entrepreneurs in the emerging Blue Economy will look at all waste streams, and succeed either by eliminating them or by converting them to tributaries that cascade livelihood, food security, and abundance for all.

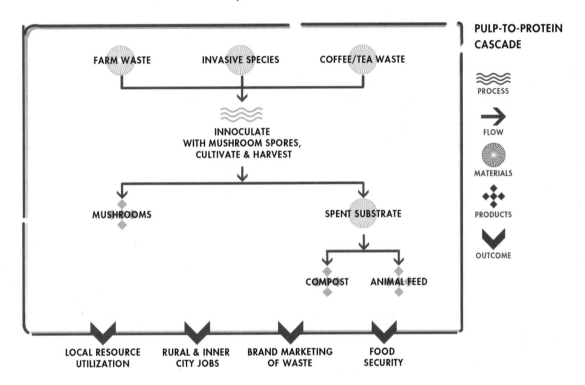

Imagine how much better that cup of coffee would taste to the well-to-do of the world when they realize that their purchase helped train another coffee farming community in how to achieve self-determination, sustainability, and food and livelihood security. The invigorating effect of the coffee would be enhanced with the flavor of satisfaction, and without further expense. The consumer has the power to channel what they pay to those who do it sustainably and equitably, using what is locally available, providing food for all, and empowering communities.

These mushroom cultivation programs have been field tested and fully realized from Colombia to Zimbabwe, from San Francisco to Germany. The Colombian state of El Huila has over a hundred coffee-to-mushroom companies and is rapidly replacing illegal crops with nutritious food. The conclusion of all contributors is that this works. The expertise is fully prepared and readily available.

The power of a just and sustainable economic model is that it generates greater value for all stakeholders. The Pulp-to-Protein business model is not about investing more to save money or to recover the additional expense, but about reducing costs for everyone while generating additional revenue. When waste becomes nutrient, it creates value that can be measured in jobs, cash flow, and profits. Green business and fair trade are stepping stones. Economies that cascade like ecosystems achieve the goal of providing multiple benefits for diverse partners.

FROM WASTE TO SUPERFOOD

Continuing to play with the potential of our Pulp-to-Protein model, let us imagine an entrepreneurial enterprise that makes coffee and coffee consumers healthier: an infusion of medicinal mushroom with that espresso or latte. Most mushrooms are rich in protein. *Reishi* and *shiitake* are prized nutritional varieties that are also medicinal marvels. In ancient times the wild red *reishi* was exclusively reserved for the Emperor of China. Although little is published in the way of clinical trials, the beneficial influence of these mushroom varieties for health conditions ranging from diabetes to hypertension is time-tested in traditional medicine. If the costs of these exotic mushrooms could be reduced using the production system just described, a bit of *Ganoderma* in that morning cup could be offered to customers wishing for an instant immune-system booster.

This arithmetic is attractive for all the parties involved. Beyond the first mileposts of employment, income, and nourishment, if Starbucks Coffee were to offer its worldwide customer base a healthy *Ganoderma* infusion for their coffee, it would initiate a massive increase in demand for the mushroom that in Japanese means "one thousands lives." If only a hundred customers each day at the 19,000 Starbucks coffee shops around the world were to order a fluff of *Ganoderma* in their espresso, macchiato, latte, or chai, at say $0.50 a serving, it would annualize to an impressive additional revenue of $365 million dollars.

Consider further that were Starbucks to help develop the Pulp-to-Protein program on the coffee farms and in urban areas, it could easily donate 10% of their increase in revenue, or $36.5 million dollars per year, to fund the effort. This would handily pay for itself in terms of social capital and tax-deductible expense, to say nothing of the employment, income, and nourishment made possible from a market consuming approximately two tons of *Ganoderma* per day. Such a sum represents $25 dollars per pound of mushrooms for the coffee farmer. Where the cash transfer of the total value in *coffee* itself is one to the farmer, and 2,999 to everyone else, for *Ganoderma* the terms of trade could tilt towards one for the farmer and ten for everyone else. This would generate a net cash infusion into rural and inner-city economies that would effectively stimulate supply and demand, build consumer confidence and social capital, and provide opportunities for jobs and education seldom seen or mentioned today.

Negative branding of waste through publicizing blacklists of the worst polluters in the world has caught the attention of the public at large. With the Pulp-to-Protein model we have nothing less than a complete re-branding of waste. A product negatively associated with exploitation and poverty could be transformed into a means to eradicate injustice and generate livelihood security. The chance for such a positive accomplishment comes at an opportune moment. Positive branding marks a shift in the focus of the business model. Entrepreneurs who are prepared to take up these business models can play a critical role in society by empowering their clients to speak with their purchasing power.

Tea as well could quickly engender a Pulp-to-Protein initiative of its own. The amount of tea biomass that is ultimately consumed in a cup of tea is only half of what is consumed from coffee, a mere one tenth of one percent. Fruit tree clippings are another possibility for exceptional mushroom growth medium. These hardwood species lack the added stimulus of caffeinated coffee grounds. They are nonetheless a quality wood that should not be incinerated as is the current practice. Ivanka Milenkovic from the University of Belgrade tested apple orchard clippings as a growth substrate for mushroom cultivation. Not even the coldness of winter weather seemed to slow mushroom growth. In the field tests, goats were partaking of the mushroom substrate residue at harvest, even before scientists could establish the amino acid content. As noted earlier, bison herds in New Mexico share that appetite.

There are endless possibilities and resources. The key is simply to uncover value in waste. Water hyacinth is an ornamental plant from Latin America that creates havoc in tropical lakes, rivers, and dams, proliferating on the massive flow of nutrients from soil erosion and excessively utilized fertilizers that accumulate in water bodies. Instead of trying to obliterate this invasive aquatic plant, it could be harvested and converted to a growing medium for mushrooms. Whereas foraging ruminants would not eat the water hyacinth itself, the mushroom substrate remaining after harvest would make an ideal feed. Merely with the waste from coffee, tea, hardwood clippings, water hyacinth, and straw, astronomical volumes of nutrients can be derived.

Ecosystems inspire us to look beyond conventional models to cascading models, where waste of one becomes raw material for another. Generating multiple benefits for diverse partners is a fair and positive Blue Economy model that evolves towards ever greater levels of efficiency with ever more diversity. This is how rainforests regenerate from depleted savannahs. This is how a cash crop like coffee could not only provide food security and meet basic needs for clean water, fresh air, and healthy soil, but could also substantially augment local income and increase social capital. Thus while 10,000 jobs today may be considered a success, there are 25 million coffee farms that could benefit from this model. Given the magnitude of the possibilities, perhaps even Nestlé, a giant in the coffee trade business, might reconsider its rejection of an undertaking that seemed too far outside its core business definition. With a little vision, perhaps the greater goal of profitability along with food security and environmental stewardship would be enough.

CHAPTER SEVEN

SPINNING A SILKEN TALE

When one tugs at a single thing in nature,
he finds it attached to the rest of the world.

— JOHN MUIR

TOPSOIL ON THE CUTTING EDGE

Centuries ago, the Chinese confronted a growing demand for food and a limit of fertile soil. As they searched for ways to acquire additional arable farmland by regenerating topsoil, they observed and reflected on the materials and processes that natural systems used to make arid land fertile. They noted in turn how farming and animal husbandry often failed to maintain the flow of contributory elements, causing fertile land to degrade and become barren, arid soil. What they discovered and the strategy they devised not only changed the course of their civilization but may well enable us to use an ecosystems approach to change an economic model and thus business strategies for modern products as diverse as airplanes and razors.

The mulberry tree *(Morus alba)* thrives in most of China's typically arid soil. The mulberry leaves are eaten by the wild moth caterpillar *(Bombyx mori)* – more commonly known as the silkworm. The silkworm's droppings fall to the ground, attracting bacteria and micro-organisms and quickly producing nutrients that build the soil. Over years, then centuries, and even millennia, the density of newly-created, healthy topsoil increases about one millimeter each year. This equates to the annual formation of 15 to 25 tons per acre of organically enriched topsoil.

This natural symbiosis of caterpillars and trees and the contribution to soil fertility promised food security for an expanding population. China undertook a large-scale planting scheme. As dynasties rose and fell, soil fertility was regenerated and maintained. Previously infertile land became productive without tilling, plowing, or irrigation. Farmers intercropped with cowpeas and groundnuts. Throughout history, Middle Eastern and European countries also planted mulberry trees, and benefited from the positive effect on soil fertility and erosion control. The Italians planted vineyard borderlands with mulberry trees to stem erosion on vineyard slopes, as did the Turks.

These natural methods to generate topsoil were eventually forgotten as attention diverted from the practices of sustainable farming to commercial monoculture. A lucrative industry and enormous wealth emerged from producing one of the legendary artifacts of human culture: silk, the natural polymer spun from the silkworm's castings.

According to Chinese legend, the idea to use caterpillar castings as silk thread is attributed to Chinese Empress Si-Ling-Chi (Lady of the Silkworm). One afternoon, as she sat under a mulberry tree to sip her tea, a cocoon fell into her cup. She noticed the strong, smooth threads of the cocoon uncoiling, and began pulling them from her cup. She was fascinated and enthralled as a thread over a thousand feet long emerged. It is said that Empress Si-Ling-Chi first developed the uses of silk for clothing and for wrapping fruits and vegetables – a proven preservation technique. Her husband, Emperor Huang Di (the famous Yellow Emperor), has been credited with the invention of methods for raising silk worms and spinning silk thread. Emperor Huang Di is also said to have taught humankind to fabricate with wood, ceramics, and metal, and to have ordered the construction of the first boats and wheeled vehicles.

As the legend implies, silk is a serendipitous discovery. It is a by-product that originally had no value compared to the strategic long-term importance of soil regeneration and the fertilization of arid land. More recently, the introduction of synthetic polymer textiles made from petrochemicals not only replaced a renewable (silk) with a non-renewable (petroleum), it deprived intercropped farmland of millions of tons of fertilizer. The popularity of stronger and cheaper synthetic polymers decimated silk production. Consequently, the planting and care of mulberry trees became obsolete. The millennia-long tradition of regenerating topsoil fell into oblivion since its by-product could not compete in the modern market. Worse, while plastics and polymers made inroads into every stratum of consumption, the land not only lost its source for nutrient and soil replenishment but also required petrochemical fertilizers to boost levels of food production. This increased the energy input needed to achieve a harvest, and furthered dependency on fossil fuels while increasing greenhouse gas emissions.

A loss of topsoil today represents one of the greatest challenges to food security for the world's future population. Ethiopia, a mountainous country with highly eroded soils on steeply sloping land, loses an estimated one billion tons of topsoil a year, carried away by rain and wind. This is one reason Ethiopia always seems to be on the verge of famine, never able to accumulate enough grain reserves to provide a meaningful measure of food security. In dust storms alone, two to three billion tons of fine soil particles leave Africa each year, inexorably draining the continent of its fertility and biological productivity, while depositing enough dust in the Caribbean seas to cloud the waters and impact coral reefs. The farming practices brought to Africa by European colonizers are not adapted to the continent's climatic conditions.

Some farmers build the soil they sow. Most, however, simply rely on chemical fertilizers, pesticides, and intensive irrigation. Using modern farming practices, from one to ten tons of topsoil per acre are lost annually. However, soil losses of as much as 125 to 250 tons per acre are common. Losses of 750 to 1800 tons per acre due to soil runoff from a single rainfall have been recorded. When all these factors take their toll, farmers are persuaded by the promise of higher yields to look to petrochemical fertilizers and genetically modified seeds, although such promises are often short-lived or misleading.

Over a five year period Prof. George Chan extensively studied integrated farming systems around the millennia-old Chinese tradition of using mulberry trees and silkworms. He assisted farming communities in more than 70 countries to realize the practice of nutrient cascading by planting mulberry trees and introducing silkworms to build topsoil. The application of Prof. Chan's topsoil-generating techniques has inspired agriculturally based industries in Namibia, Germany, Japan, Fiji, and the US to adopt their own nutrient-cascading strategies. Thus an ancient Chinese tradition is now transforming the modern food production industry.

SILK FOR CARBON CAPTURE

Natural silk contains upwards of 30% carbon. Replacement by petrochemical fibers ends carbon fixation from silk production and from the growth of mulberry trees. As well, it ends the associated topsoil regeneration. Just this one case demonstrates that petroleum emissions are only half of the problem. The substitution of a renewable (silk) by a non-renewable (petroleum) eliminates natural carbon sinks. The ecosystem then looses efficiency since it is incapable of replenishing soil nutrients. It therefore requires additional input in the form of fertilizers. This releases more greenhouse gases, especially since nitrogen-based fertilizers are one of the biggest sources of nitrous oxide (N_2O).

According to the Intergovernmental Panel on Climate Change (IPCC), even though this gas is released in small quantities, its impact is huge. The emission of one ton of N_2O equals the emission of 310 tons of CO_2. Traditional farming techniques work in harmony with the delicate interconnections that characterize an ecosystem. With silk production we see a stunning example of how these positive cycles unwind when replaced by monoculture and synthetics. The fertilizers and plastics proffered as symbols of modernity are in reality case studies of how production and consumption systems devolve from sustainable to unsustainable.

Wallace Carothers, the chemical engineer who invented nylon for Dupont, could have had no idea that his petroleum-derived fiber would unravel a web of life that had harmoniously enfolded industrial production in a nutrient cascade benefiting land and agricultural cultivation over five millennia. It is fair to say that in our quest for modernity we have demonstrated considerable ignorance concerning the impact of our inventions. How can we now expect that government and industry will be able to solve the challenge of climate change unless they gain an understanding of the thousands of connections that can be destroyed through facile ignorance? Once we grasp the elegant interplay of physics and biochemistry in ecosystems, we can model more breakthrough innovations that open ever more possibilities for progress and sufficiency. It is up to all of us to see the opportunities.

THE GEOMETRY OF SILK

Recognition of the problem is also a key to its solution. There are hundreds of species that produce silk. Ants, wasps, bees, mussels, and spiders are among them. Only one, the Chinese silkworm, has been domesticated. Sophisticated instrumentation makes it possible to analyze at the nano-level all the different silks produced. Scientists are beginning to see how these natural polymers can outperform some of their synthetic counterparts and even some metals, such as titanium, which is considered to have the highest strength-to-weight ratio of any metal. If we can learn how to manufacture biocompatible polymers as these other species do, under ambient conditions, with available nutrients, it opens a new world of possibilities and a potentially virtuous cycle of soil regeneration and climate stabilization.

While on a Smithsonian mission in Central America, Oxford Professor Fritz Vollrath encountered a species of golden silk orb weaver spider, *Nephila clavipes*, that spins a one-meter diameter web of a beautiful golden color. He was fascinated by experimental evidence suggesting that the color served a dual purpose, both attracting prey and providing disguise. After decades of research he came to understand silk and its remarkable qualities of resilience, strength, and flexibility. He realized that the extraordinary performance of the spider's silk is due to its geometry at the nanoscale. Geometry is part of mathematics. In this case Vollrath used it to determine how the crystalline and non-crystalline structure of silk creates variations of strength that often out-compete metals and designer plastics. By merely controlling pressure and humidity in the rear abdomen at the moment of its spinning, the golden orb spider is capable of producing seven different types of silk.

The *Nephila clavipes* web outperforms many others in terms of tensile strength and versatility under changing conditions. The extreme toughness of spider silk stems from the controlled folding during spinning of all the proteins that compose the silk. This protein folding is largely dependent on the precise extraction of water accomplished with no more than the pressure in the spider's abdomen. Professor Vollrath's comparisons between spider and insect spinning provided further insights into the extrusion processes.

Spiders have a remarkable capacity to recycle their web, reconditioning it to meet new requirements. They ingest the portions of their web that they wish to renew, converting the polymers into their original amino acids. How could we not be impressed by this performance? It models one of the best recycling programs ever designed for a polymer! How does this compare to the "disposable" plastics of our modern life that continue to accumulate in a massive floating continent of fine pebble-size plastic waste in the Pacific Ocean, toxifying the surrounding ocean life?

However, it is challenging to domesticate spiders. The species are aggressive. Even if such defensive behavior were overcome, their productive output is low. They simply recycle too much, reprocessing their web into a new variety of silk adapted to the changed circumstances, with little need for additional production. These limitations compelled Vollrath to compare the structure of silk spun by the mulberry silkworm with the structure of silk spun by the golden orb spider. Using the basic amino acids as building blocks, he and his Oxford team replicated the spider's recipe to structure silk from the silkworm to match that of the silk from the spider. The processed polymer they developed is a silk with the properties identical to those that make the spider's version unique.

Professor Vollrath is engaged in the design of a systemic approach to the production of biocompatible polymers from renewable resources, very much along the lines of the original Chinese strategy for regenerating topsoil. Building on his visionary research, Vollrath has established business entities that are manufacturing these polymers and identifying markets where these biocompatible products can outperform and underprice petroleum-based polymers and expensive metal alloys. Instead of generating collateral damage, as is the case with products that spread greenhouse gases, these products can help reconnect our economy to the original purpose of China's silk production: regeneration, renewal, and abundance – of soil fertility, harvest capacity, and carbon capture.

Over a century ago, the annual output of raw silk hovered around one million tons. Current production fluctuates in a range below 100,000 tons per year. With the exception of luxury fabrics such as those made by Hermès, the future market for silk will not be textile or clothing manufacture. It cannot compete in price with brand-name petrochemical synthetic polymers that hold greater market share in the textile industry. However, it notably outperforms (by a factor of six in price and performance) expensive metals such as stainless steel and titanium. Titanium has become the standard structural material for jet engines, spacecraft, desalination plants, medical prostheses, orthopedic implants, dental implants, sporting goods, and mobile phones. Although the aerospace industry uses up the largest portion of processed titanium, consumer goods increasingly include titanium in stainless steel manufacture, as well as many products ranging from bicycle frames and jewelry to implants and prostheses.

It is here that we can spot a potential strategic shift in the business concept that could give rise to a new economic development model. The production of titanium from metal ore consumes large quantities of magnesium, chlorine, and argon gas. Titanium must be welded in an inert atmosphere to protect it from contamination with oxygen, nitrogen, or hydrogen. Both the energy inputs and the use of scarce and mined resources are significant, so that the end products have high price tags. Processed and cured titanium has a high tensile strength-to-density ratio and high resistance to oxygen and seawater corrosion. Because of these desirable qualities, customers pay more and ignore the collateral damage to the environment. When we contrast a life cycle analysis of titanium with the simplicity of mulberry leaves transformed into silk, at relatively ambient temperature, pressure, and moisture, silk clearly emerges on the positive side of the sustainability index. We quickly understand how we can move these industries towards sustainability. Companies willing to take advantage of Vollrath's nanoscale insights for controlling silk's geometry will find that these biocompatible silk polymers are an ideal substitute for high-performance metals.

A CLOSE SHAVE

An ubiquitous example of our unsustainable consumption is the razor we use to remove hair. There are few activities more banal than shaving. Hair grows inexorably, year in, year out. Cave paintings show that even prehistorically men scraped off unwanted hair using implements such as stones and clam shells. During the Bronze Age, humans developed the ability to forge simple metals and began to make razors from iron and bronze. Early Egyptians shaved both their beards and heads, a custom eventually adopted by the Greeks and Romans, particularly soldiers facing hand-to-hand combat: a lack of locks meant one less handhold for an enemy.

A modern shaving blade manufactured in the early 21st century uses almost 20 times less metal than the first disposable ones introduced by King C. Gillette over a century ago. While this confirms the drive towards material efficiency, lowered cost and thus greater affordability result in less incentive to extend a product's useful life. As Gillette's strong research team increased profitability and market share, the overall volume of individual razors as well as the total weight of metal waste increased dramatically. An estimated 10 billion throw-away razors annually contribute 250 thousand tons of valuable metal as waste to our landfill volume. Most unfortunately, the latest models have increased the number of blades from two to five or even six. Here we witness a rebound effect that undoes the material efficiency gains of the past 50 years.

Razor blades are exposed to high levels of moisture and must therefore be made from a special corrosion resistant steel alloy or titanium. The grade of steel must be hard enough for the blade to hold its shape, yet flexible enough for it to be processed. Carbide steel is preferred because it is made using carbon, silicon, manganese, chromium, and molybdenum, with the remainder being iron and a finishing layer of titanium. The steel is heated to temperatures of 2012° F, then hardened by quenching in water to a temperature around -94° F. The steel is tempered at 662° F. The blades are then stamped to form the appropriate cutting edge at a rate of 800-1,200 per minute. Because the blade is so small, a special metal and plastic support structure is required to hold it inside the cartridge. Just like titanium, stainless steel is part of a production and consumption pattern that makes life unsustainable. This whole process offers only a few clean shaves and then the razor ends up in a landfill.

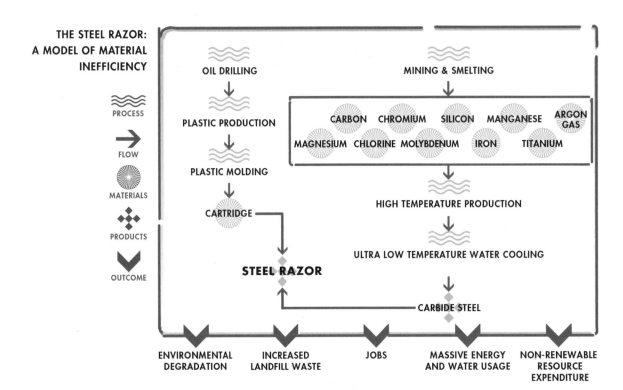

THE STEEL RAZOR:
A MODEL OF MATERIAL
INEFFICIENCY

The shaving industry now has a choice. Rather than market growth by volume, they can turn the razor business into something that contributes to solving the environmental and employment crisis while offering something better and cheaper. A razor made of silk will cut through keratin (hair) but will not slice the skin since it rolls hundreds of fine threads over the surface of the skin, in effect a miniature version of a hand-pushed grass mower. The technology is here. Its fine-tuning and production are just a matter of time and money. The fact that silk can be substituted for mined ores, dramatically reducing carbon emissions and even sequestering carbon, reveals an ideal cost/benefit structure. At $100 per pound for processed silk, each silk-blade razor would cost less than a dollar, yet its performance and feel would be equal to the latest industry versions.

SMOOTH AS SILK

Because the manufacturing is a trade secret, another use of unsustainable polymers has escaped consumers' attention – cosmetics. After water, polymers represent the second largest category of ingredients in cosmetics and personal care products. A diverse range of polymers are used as film-formers, fixatives, thickeners, emulsifiers, stimuli-responsive agents, conditioners, foam stabilizers, skin-feel benefiting agents, and antimicrobials. The market value of synthetic polymers is currently $15 billion dollars and steadily growing. They have replaced many cosmetic ingredients formerly derived from natural sources. While it may be difficult to visualize how silk can replace stainless steel in razors and airplanes, our tactile association with the softness of silk makes it much easier to imagine how silk could be a main component of skin and hair care products. Using silk nano-technology products as substitutes for synthetic polymers could be a most promising and highly profitable direction for the cosmetic industry.

It will take only one market leader like Clarins or Shiseido shifting from synthetic to natural polymers to gather the attention of all the major players in the market. The first application would likely be sunscreen products,

since silk could provide a dual functionality. Silk polymers would give structure to the cream and dissipate ultraviolet rays. Silk could also be a biocompatible replacement for titanium in the expensive titanium oxide creams that are marketed to protect against ultraviolet exposure.

The hair coloring market is a second area where naturally produced silk nanostructures could quickly gain market share. Greeks and Romans used highly alkaline soap, boiled walnuts, and henna to create different shades. Although such color tinting products are kinder to our body, they do not retain their coloring over time. The coloring products made from harsh chemical polymers provide more permanent hair color. Yet published research linking cancer to the prolonged use of hair dyes has prompted the US Food and Drug Administration to study the potential toxicity of these coloring agents. Fortunately, new insights on silk polymers have made it possible to develop biocompatible products that can obtain and hold a desired color. Silk polymers and other biologically derived renewable raw materials could handily replace toxic hair dyes and at the same time release a cascade of positive health and ecological effects.

BIOCOMPATIBLE MEDICAL USES

Silk thread has been used worldwide for many years as a suture in intricate surgical and ophthalmological operations. It is suitable for this purpose because of its fine, soft fibers and tensile strength. It is also easy to tie yet difficult to untie. Its protein composition makes it compatible with the human body, eliminating the need for surgical removal. Other medical applications have been commercialized: anti-hay fever masks, gauze pads, and bandages for dermatological disorders are made from silk. The development of technology to dissolve silk fibers and make film from silk protein has opened the way for research and development for use in artificial skin, blood vessels, tendons, and nerve regeneration, as well as contact lenses, catheters for surgical procedures, and anticoagulants. All these applications exploit silk's biocompatibility and permeability.

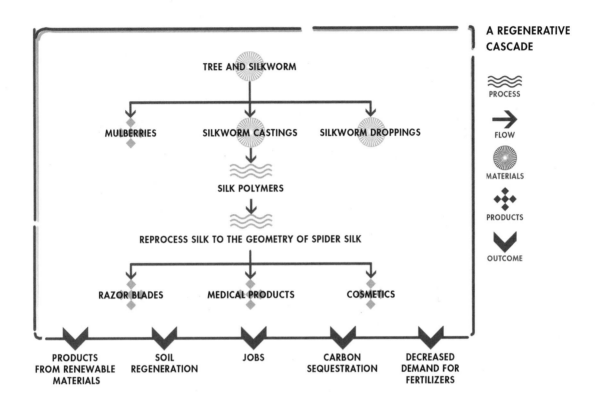

A **REGENERATIVE**
CASCADE

〰〰 PROCESS

→ FLOW

⊛ MATERIALS

◆◆ PRODUCTS

∨ OUTCOME

TREE AND SILKWORM

MULBERRIES   SILKWORM CASTINGS   SILKWORM DROPPINGS

SILK POLYMERS

REPROCESS SILK TO THE GEOMETRY OF SPIDER SILK

RAZOR BLADES   MEDICAL PRODUCTS   COSMETICS

PRODUCTS FROM RENEWABLE MATERIALS   SOIL REGENERATION   JOBS   CARBON SEQUESTRATION   DECREASED DEMAND FOR FERTILIZERS

Today when knee or spine tissue cartilage is damaged and cannot regenerate, an artificial knee made of titanium is surgically implanted. Another product being developed by Professor Vollrath and his team is a porous silk scaffold with mechanical properties that nearly match those of human fibro-cartilage. The silk scaffold is inserted in place of damaged cartilage and stimulates cell growth on its porous biocompatible surface, regenerating the cartilage using the body's immune response. A natural system with biocompatible components can successfully strengthen an existing structure, as opposed to a system with expensive and incompatible components that require immunosuppressants to overcome rejection. The world market for biocompatible devices already approaches $20 billion annually, with an annual growth rate of over 10%. Silk sutures will soon be complemented by silk-based wound dressing, replacement joints, and orthopedic implants, all stemming from insights into how natural systems perform.

THE REWARDS OF SUSTAINABILITY – A DECADE OF REMARKABLE ACCOMPLISHMENTS
100,000 metric tons of silk convert 6.25 million acres of arid land to fertile land.
1 kg of raw silk generates 9 kg of pure fertilizer (caterpillar droppings), generating 9 million tons overall each year.
A decade of producing silk will produce sufficient topsoil to start intercropping around the mulberry trees.
The production process will fix 300 million tons of CO_2 equivalents, in trees, soil, and silk, by avoiding mining and ore processing and the use of N_2O from unnecessary fertilizers. It will reduce emissions on the order of magnitude of one billion tons of CO_2, while generating on average 2.4 jobs per acre, creating 15 million jobs … in one decade.

The demand for medical devices made from silk offers a high-end proof of concept that these products are financially viable even under present economic conditions. Professor Vollrath and his team have succeeded in bringing silk-based products to market. The opportunities for these technologies to become available worldwide will substantially stimulate the demand for silk. If the research is done for products as complex as these, making razors or cosmetic ingredients from silk polymers will be easy. It is just a matter of putting our minds to it! And who will do that? Will Schick, Gillette, or a consortium of entrepreneurs transform a surprisingly unsustainable consumer product into a quality product that sequesters carbon and is as smooth as silk in performance? At it's peak, 100 years ago, the annual volume of silk production had reached one million tons. If the demand for silk to make razors and cosmetics were to reach just 100,000 tons over the next 10 years, imagine the beneficial effect this would have for increased soil fertility.

The added appeal of this approach is that it does not eliminate any industry jobs. It merely reduces demand for mined ore and dramatically cuts the amount of energy used, which we may all consider as a positive contribution. The number of jobs potentially lost in the energy and mining sectors will be far outnumbered by the number of new jobs created – a total of fifteen million jobs for each 100,000 tons of additional silk harvested. Applying a sustainable model that uses silk instead of plastic is more competitive, has greater marketing appeal, generates topsoil, and cuts carbon emissions. This is the Blue Economy we seek to bring to the center stage of modern society.

CHAPTER EIGHT

FROM THE MIGHTY TO
THE MINISCULE

The sun, with all the planets
revolving around it and depending on it,
can still ripen a bunch of grapes
as if it had nothing else in the universe to do.

— GALILEO GALILEI

ONLY A HEARTBEAT AWAY

While we rightly worry about human-induced climate change, humanity is hovering between two killing fields: children dying of malnutrition from shortages of the most basic nutrients, and adults dying of malnutrition from excesses of the wrong foods. Our artificial and refined diet and our lack of exercise combine to create a terrain that lessens our quality of life and shortens our lifespan. The unconscionable truth is that we know it. Until this pattern shifts, monitoring heart disease is a foregone necessity.

Heart disease takes a higher toll of lives than any other single malady. Medical researchers have tried to address this for decades and have found ways to apply technology to beneficial effect in helping correct heart malfunction. Dr. Jorge Reynolds is one of these researchers. Having studied electronic engineering at Cambridge University and graduating in 1953, he devised a way to correct an irregular heartbeat by modulating an electric current that was sourced and transformed from a car battery and attached to two diodes connected to the heart.

Between 1954 and 1964, Professor Reynolds developed a prototype version of a pacemaker that could be placed into the heart to correct heart function by keeping it beating. Even though the device was the size of a car battery on wheels and required continuous connection to the post-surgical patient, over 1,700 patients were aided by his invention. In fact, in 2009 seven of these patients were still alive. His prototype pacemaker is on display at the Museum of Science and Industry in London. In the 1960s Reynolds transferred all his patents and protocols to a third party for further development and dedicated the rest of his life to research. He was looking for a better way to get the human heart to keep working. His curiosity and research led him to study the heart functioning of other mammals. When he began to study the whale's heart and circulatory mechanism, his fascination was complete.

Energy from Whales

Long ago, the whale was a land mammal who returned to the sea, evolving into the largest and most intelligent animal living on Earth. In the 18th century the whale was sought after for its blubber. Whale oil, rendered from whale blubber, was globally harvested and traded. Its uses ranged from nighttime illumination to cooking oil. Whales were hunted to near extinction. It took another 250 years of human development for us to realize that the real marvel of the whale is not its blubber but rather its capacity to generate six to twelve volts of electric power merely from potassium, sodium, and calcium. This is remarkable since whales rely solely on krill and small fishes for their nutrition and energy. This biochemical capacity to generate electricity is a phenomenon that has been studied by Reynolds, who has non-invasively monitored the whale's heartbeat for over three decades.

Reynolds wondered how the heart of this magnificently large mammal adapted throughout the whale's remarkable physical and physiological transformations. With each pulse, over a lifespan of approximately 80 years, and without any maintenance or intervention, the whale's heart, bathed in blubber, flows 250 gallons of blood along 100 million miles of arteries and veins. While the muscles, the valves, the veins, and the arteries evolved throughout time, Reynolds pondered how the whale was able to distribute electric current to its massive physique and coordinate the pulsing rhythms at a scale one thousand times greater than the heart of its dog-like ancestor. There are no known cases of cardiac arrest among whales. Yet if our heart were to lie in so much fat, it would simply stop working.

Reynolds posed these key questions: What do we learn from this? What clues are there? No one could offer answers. He embarked on an intensive quest to learn everything he could about whale and other mammalian hearts. Wishing to record and graph the whale's heart, he designed an EKG recorder to attach to a whale and transmit heartbeat data via satellite to his research center in Bogotá. Though we might imagine the difficulty of designing and fabricating the machinery, and setting up electronic data transmission, the real feat was how the attachment was made. Reynolds did it by hand, one whale at a time, working from an open boat in the ocean waters. This was science on the edge!

Reynolds' career in heart research spans five decades but his fascination is not limited to whales. He recorded EKGs from over 200 animals, some as small as a fly, as elusive as a pink dolphin in the Amazon, or as curious as a grazing iguana in the Galapagos. Today, Reynolds and his team have compiled over 10,000 whale EKGs. They used advanced sound filtration systems, originally designed for military eavesdropping, as underwater audiophones. This greatly facilitated the research, as it eliminated the need to physically attach the equipment to a whale. The team eventually gathered so much data that Reynolds could accurately map the functioning of a whale's heart. Further remarkable data was revealed from medical dissections performed on expired beached whales. Scientists postulate that the whale has channels of cells that appear solely dedicated to guiding electric currents in and around the heart. These currents coordinate its flow and are capable of adjusting their pathways to bypass damaged tissue.

Reynolds' curiosity drove his research far beyond observations of heartbeat. To comprehend at the molecular level how potassium, sodium, and calcium combine to power electric currents without either metals or batteries, he studied the entire genesis and transformation of the whale heart beginning with its embryonic materialization at the time of conception. He mapped his findings onto a three-dimensional virtual heart. Using off-the-shelf AutoDesk engineering software, he gave other scientists and cardiologists access to open source information that could be mapped before their eyes.

His observations made him rethink pacemaker fundamentals. By now a practically ubiquitous device prolonging millions of lives, the pacemaker replaces the natural capacity to generate electric currents with a battery-powered device that connects into the depths of the heart. Yet defects in the hundreds of thousands began to plague these devices. This pushed Reynolds to think beyond the obvious. He hesitated at first because of the simplicity of his idea. Inspired by the whale, he thought that he could recreate these cell-thin tubes to improve the distribution of current throughout the heart. He envisioned replacing the existing device he had helped invent with a nano-scale carbon tube having the same power as a pacemaker. Instead of replacing the natural function of the heart, the tiny carbon coil would simply channel the current from healthy tissue to damaged tissue. That was a revolutionary thought: build on the existing power generation capacity, and just improve conductivity.

The second revolutionary concept was based on his realization that the whale, all other mammals, and even the fly generate and conduct current with neither battery nor wiring. Our planet's diverse living species have learned to generate the electrical power they need using a quite extensive collection of energy sources: gravity, temperature differential, pH differential, kinetic energy from muscle movement, piezo-electrical energy from movement of the heart and blood, energy derived from CO_2, and bodily biometals. Reynolds' studies concluded that all these species' applications work and have in fact been proven over millions of years.

He designed a series of new medical devices that operate like everything else in nature – that is, without cables or a battery. He focused on how whales generate a continuous flow of electric pulses from the minuscule supply and fine coordination of chemical reactions produced with a combination of potassium, sodium, and calcium. The medical devices and bodily monitoring systems he produces, offered by the start-up company CoroCare, rely only on the sources of energy that exist in and around the body.

The first such application Reynolds designed, the nano-pacemaker, is a minute device of just 700 nanometers (700 millionths of a millimeter) in length that is controlled by the latest microprocessors. It takes its inspiration from the whale's conductivity channels and has proven its viability in the laboratory. However, the argument that this works successfully in whales is unconvincing for the Food and Drug Administration. The cost to develop this prototype into an FDA-approved medical device is in the range of one hundred million to five hundred million dollars. Although Reynolds has limited seed money available, he currently banks on anticipated sales of subsequent inventions to fund the required clinical trials.

It is easy to understand why the market leaders in pacemaker sales like Medtronic, Johnson & Johnson, and Boston Scientific, who now have their market securely captured for decades to come, would object to this innovation. They are earning royalties on each surgery, in conjunction with the pharmaceutical industry that will supply medicine for the rest of the patient's life. How would the leading pacemaker manufacturers react to an innovation that eliminates a guaranteed income of at least $50,000 for each patient diagnosed with a treatable cardiac arrhythmia problem, and another average of $50,000 for a lifetime supply of medicine? All this expense could be reduced to a $500 procedure. Placement of the nano-wire is done with a catheter and requires no general anesthesia. Since patients are not likely to require any continuing medication, the total cost for insurance companies drops by a factor of 2,000. Insurance companies should be keenly receptive to this application.

HEALTHY, BATTERY-FREE ELECTRICAL CURRENT

Our industrial system is oriented to immense size and power. Thus it is not surprising that the minuscule electrical charges generated by natural systems are dismissed as trivial. Self-winding watches and flashing lights in children's shoe soles are on a short list of familiar commercial applications. Yet our heart and brain function with such microcurrents. No one is wired or carries a battery, except when a pacemaker has been surgically implanted or a hearing aid is fit into the ear. Simple, naturally generated current is powerful enough to continuously regulate the flow of blood through our heart each day. Over a single lifetime, the energy the body produces, sourced from the core elements in food, is sufficient to lift a 40-foot shipping container from the harbor in Mumbai (India) to the top of Mt. Everest!

Reynolds' research and subsequent innovations may well herald the end to our dependence on chemical batteries that load our landfills and pollute our environment. By eliminating the need for a battery, we would also be eliminating pollution and toxic waste. Batteries offer convenience, but they are a major source of demand for mined materials, and are seldom fully recycled. It is no secret that metals from batteries pollute and are health hazards. There are over 40 billion batteries manufactured and sold each year. The vast majority of smaller "disposable" batteries just become waste. Worse, this trend is accelerating. It is one of the double-digit growth segments of the market. Even Sweden and Germany, two countries with great societal discipline, do not recycle half of what is used. Because their low cost, availability, and size make recycling them easy to dismiss, these smaller batteries most often collect in landfills. It is another daily tragedy that we fail to realize the adverse impact such a tiny device has on the health of our planet and ultimately on our own health. The metals it contains are indiscriminately dispersed into the ecosystem on which we depend for critical resources like drinking water and fertile soil.

We also fail to consider the high energy cost of battery power. If we compare the cost per kilowatt hour of a battery to the cost of the same energy from a socket at home, most of us would be surprised to discover that we are paying 100 to 500 times more for battery power than we pay for electricity in our homes. Industry analysts who have come to this realization are now avidly searching for the most efficient battery. Billions are being spent by governments and private investors to find the longest-lasting and least-polluting battery that will give consumers the convenience and flexibility of electricity when they need it. While huge amounts of money are expended, we seem to have collectively forgotten that any battery made of metals (heavy metals) is taxing our Earth's resources beyond the capacity to sustain future demand. Worse, it increases mining and the unregulated dispersal of metals into the environment. Batteries may be a convenient source of energy but the economic and environmental costs are beyond reason.

HEALTH DATA ONLINE

Reynolds' nano-pacemaker was his first innovation, inspired by observing natural sources of electric current. Another of his inventions, the CoroPatch, is a thin-film patch that can be taped to the skin to measure and transmit body temperature and heart data without batteries or wires. It is charged by the body itself and available physical forces. Some sophisticated applications come to mind.

Charting the pattern of temperature variation is a simple but effective time-sensitive indication of fertility. A woman has a lower body temperature before and a higher body temperature at ovulation. Furthermore, an elevated temperature for 18 consecutive days indicates, with a high degree of certainty, that conception has been successful. A thin-film patch could measure temperature to within 0.3 to 0.5 degrees of accuracy without batteries or wires. It could communicate this data to a personalized website or even send a cell phone message, which would offer women greater precision and autonomy in their reproductive choices.

In the realm of heart monitoring, where a visit to the hospital for an EKG is indispensable to an accurate diagnosis, subsequent check-ups could be undertaken using a thin-film patch placed on the chest. Three to six contact points could send critical data to a personal website, or send a registered image to a cell phone. It could confirm health status, recommend a follow-up visit to the cardiologist, or, in an emergency, automatically call for aid, providing an exact location from the GPS position of a cell phone. The cost of a hospital visit for an EKG easily surpasses $750 dollars. The patch could cost as little as $20 dollars. Even if a patient were to require a patch ten times a year, it would still cost less than one extra visit to the hospital. Yet its revenue potential is substantially greater, as the lowered cost would make the application available to many more individuals. This is exactly the business model that makes an effective tool for economic revival at a time of need: multiple applications and revenue streams for a successful platform technology.

A thin-film application such as the CoroPatch would eliminate the recording and analysis of routine EKGs and would require attention only when a monitored reading diverted from an established pattern. This would free cardiologists and their staff to attend to more substantive revenue-generating work, resulting in a net gain for medical professionals, for hospitals, and for insurance companies. The patch could accumulate an amazing data set on the functioning of the heart in the most diverse conditions, both from normal patients and individuals at higher risk. The amount of data available from one patch-based check-up is 14,000 times greater than from a two-minute hospital reading. In sum, the net benefits are that more data would be available, real-time monitoring would be cost-effective, per-patient costs would be considerably reduced, and the time savings would contribute to other revenue-generating tasks – all without the use of any batteries.

At the same time, the increase in mobility and flexibility goes hand-in-hand with a reduction in the use of metals. Batteries are replaced by no batteries, eliminating the need for costly investments in research and development to find a new, less toxic battery. Mining demands would be reduced, as would overall carbon emissions, since metal processing is unavoidably energy intensive. This is a technology that is good for our health, good for skyrocketing medical costs, and good for the Earth. When Reynolds' company calculates its first profits, part will be reserved for the preservation of whale habitat. The financing of ecosystem conservation inspires us to make our world less dependent on batteries and metals, and capable of drawing upon existing locally-available energy sources as part of an emerging new financial and economic framework.

COST COMPARISON ANALYSIS FOR **EKG** VS **CoroPatch**		
DELIVERY	HOSPITAL	THIN FILM PATCH
Cost	Min $750	Max $20
Power	Grid or battery	Self-powered
Data	2 minute sampling	24 hour monitoring
Carbon footprint	Drive to hospital	Wherever you are
Ecology	Batteries to landfills	100% recyclable
Analysis	Cardiologist only	Cardiologist when urgent
Data transmission	Automated emergency call-in	Web-based two-way monitoring
Data mining	Back office processing	Cell phone data Real-time health monitoring
Jobs	Same service	20 jobs for every 1,000,000 patches
Revenue	More of the same	One billion patches and unlimited portfolio of new services

How many jobs does this technology generate? Though it is still in a developmental stage, the picture that emerges is rather attractive. While no one in medical services, from nurses to cardiologists, will lose their jobs, a multitude of data will be accumulated. This would be attractive to the very lucrative field of data mining, one of the most profitable income streams for companies like Google and Yahoo. The detailed statistics and demographics derived from data mining could fine-tune studies on how food and medicine and even lifestyle affect health. It would support therapeutic design, management, and measurement.

Over the next decade, the newly created thin-film patch industry could generate an additional 20,000 to 50,000 jobs. The services around this could well create a multitude of entrepreneurial employment opportunities.

Perhaps a new wave of economic activities would emerge similar to the arrival of cell phones. However, the first ones likely to quickly adopt this unique service are top athletes, such as Tour de France competitors, mountaineers scaling imposing elevations, or marathon runners testing the limits of their perseverance. There is a bright future indeed for something based on nothing.

A COOLER WAY TO COOL

For decades medical researchers have had great success in developing vaccines to eliminate serious diseases. Unfortunately the vaccine delivery mechanisms have not been as successful. According to estimates by the World Health Organization, only 50% of all vaccines produced and sold are actually successfully administered. Furthermore, the lack of refrigeration at out-of-the-way points of administration means that only 50% of at-risk children can be reached.

Thus the key challenge for vaccines is preserving the cold chain. There are an estimated 6,000 solar medical refrigerators installed at medical delivery sites in developing nations. Their purpose is to keep vaccines at reliably cold temperatures. At an average cost of $5,000 to $7,000 per refrigeration unit, this represents a total investment in excess of $30 million dollars. Although photovoltaic energy is arguably a more reliable energy supply than is kerosene, there is another alternative: a nature-based delivery mechanism that substitutes both fossil and clean fuel refrigeration with *no refrigeration at all.*

Typically, when water evaporates, cells dry out. The cell membranes rupture, making reconstitution impossible. However, scientists have identified and studied a host of micro-organisms as well as other simple plant and animal species that can completely dehydrate and appear to be dead, yet can survive and be restored to full biological function in less than two hours merely by contact with water. Two of these species – one a microscopic water-dwelling animal known as the "water bear" or "tardigrade" *(Hypsibius dujardini)*, and the other a species of creeping fern native to Africa and the Americas known as the "resurrection fern" *(Polypodium polypodioides)* – are organisms that survive by producing high sugar concentrations in their tissues. As water is lost these special sugars solidify as if they were glass, preserving cells and tissue. When water is once again available, the glass-like sugars dissolve, allowing the cell's normal biological functioning to resume.

Bruce Roser worked with the UK firm Cambridge Biostability Ltd. to engineer this natural process for the stabilization of pharmaceutical products. Roser's application not only eliminates the need for vaccine refrigeration but overcomes the challenge of supplying syringes by delivering a complete vaccination package system requiring neither cooling, nor a local water source, nor any further handling. This means a dramatically improved delivery of functional vaccines at much lower cost. The World Health Organization estimates that potential monetary savings for the developing world are in the range of $200 to $300 million per year. The humanitarian savings are even greater.

Not only can this technology eliminate the cold-chain delivery mechanism for vaccines, other applications using this no-refrigeration innovation may herald the end of the supermarket frozen food department (perhaps not the ice cream!). All that is needed is the research that can devise a way to phase out dependency on perfluorocarbons (PFCs), a greenhouse gas that is currently used to suspend micro-particles in vaccines. We often forget to consider why we freeze food. It is to preserve it longer without loss of taste or texture. Thus, the application of this technology potentially reaches into high-value markets like baby food, frozen foods, and functional foods. Even perishable products derived from coffee, tea, fruits, and meats could be brought to market using a method that has been tested in the most challenging of circumstances: delivery of viable vaccines to developing countries.

How many jobs might be created by substituting "refrigeration" with "no refrigeration"? In the field of health services, the fact that several hundreds of millions of dollars will not be wasted on expensive energy to power refrigeration means that uncountable millions can be used to finance other budget priorities. Estimates are that some 40,000 to 60,000 additional health care positions in developing countries could be funded with the savings, a very welcome prospect.

Direct and indirect emissions from refrigeration systems worldwide account for approximately 20% of the greenhouse effect. Though the refrigeration of vaccines is only a minor component, Roser's preservation technique, teamed with other existing industrial technologies, demonstrates that an innovation inspired by tardigrades and ferns can achieve more than getting vaccines to the children who need them most. It helps reduce carbon emissions along the way. We can be inspired by these multiple benefits.

(DID YOU HEAR?) THE FUROR OVER FURANONES

The first living species on Earth were bacteria. Photosynthesis by bacteria emerged at least 2.8 billion years ago, well before plants existed. While scientists call them *"monera,"* we call these single celled organisms "germs," "bacteria," or even "bugs." Bacteria are everywhere and just about everything we know finds its origin in bacteria. Our eyes, nose, ears, and tastebuds are all associated with these first living creatures. Few of us seem to recognize that we are in symbiosis with bacteria. While we like to think that our ancestors were apes, we are really nothing more than the great-great-great-great grandchildren of bacteria! Knowing that we cannot digest food without them makes it even more curious that we want to obliterate them all.

Ever since microscopes permitted us to see these nucleus-free single cell organisms, and science and industry convinced us of their evil intentions, we have been on a quest to exterminate them. If we are so determined to kill them, using the harshest versions of chemistry and antibiotics (originally based on the biology of the fungus), then we find ourselves … killing ourselves. We "cleanse" our bathrooms and kitchens with chemicals that are not conducive to life. Assuming that we brush our teeth twice a day, there are still probably more bacteria living in our mouth than there are people living on Earth. Our preoccupation with killing bacteria is one campaign that is certain to fail. Bacteria are basic and ubiquitous forms of life that actually comprise almost 10% of our bodies by weight.

Failure is certainly the result we are likely to achieve with our excessive use of bactericides. Not only are many of these chemicals linked to a higher incidence of cancer and an array of unhealthful and physiologically disruptive side-effects, our desire to eliminate these microorganisms in fact spurs them to mutate faster. Bacteria pursue genetic modifications at will since they have neither nucleus nor DNA. This chemically loaded killing spree has put these tiny but mighty organisms on the evolutionary path towards super bacteria. Our immune systems, already continuously stressed by coping with increasingly ineffective chemical bactericides, and functioning without the benefit of the helpful bacteria eliminated by the same chemical overload, cannot keep up. The double whammy of chemical attack and depleted natural defense mechanisms exhausts our body's ability to respond effectively.

Since trying to kill bacteria may in fact kill us, it is worth observing how the second form of life on Earth – microalgae, or *protoctista*, ancestor of seaweeds – adapted to bacteria, the first form of life. Considering that the ocean, from which life emerged, is literally a soup of bacteria, killing bacteria did not make sense for the newer microalgae. Had the *protoctista* developed a poison potent enough to kill all bacteria, it would have annihilated every other form of life, including itself.

As seaweeds started populating the oceans, they quickly found their surfaces colonized by bacteria. Bacteria slowly build a biofilm just like those that line our digestive system, cover our scalp, and populate our tongue. If the colony gets out of control and bacteria sense they have a quorum, they may decide to take over the host.

How did the seaweeds then cope with the need to compete and the challenge to survival? To survive as a recently arrived species, seaweeds needed to become better at mastering their environment. The *Delicea pulchra*, the red seaweed found between Tasmania and Japan, perfected a way to jam communication among bacteria. Instead of endangering their own long-term future and attempting (ineffectively) to eradicate bacteria, *Delicea pulchra* simply learned to make the bacteria temporarily deaf. It creates a small molecule, named a "furanone," which occupies a bacteria's receptor and makes it impossible for the bacteria to "hear" other bacteria of the same genus.

This is a brilliantly effective solution. Bacteria use chemicals to talk to each other. If they do not receive specific molecules, because the necessary receptors are already blocked – by a molecule from seaweed – bacteria do not have a clue where other family members are. Under these conditions it is difficult for bacteria to form a dominant biofilm. Better even, existing biofilms disintegrate when there is no communication to coordinate joint action. If there is no biofilm, there is no danger of infection.

Scientists Peter Steinberg and his colleague Staffan Kjelleberg, who conducted breakthrough research of the *Delicea pulchra* at the University of New South Wales in Sydney, Australia, quickly understood the value of their discovery: human-induced superbug mutations could be replaced by seaweed-inspired bacterial controls! The potential applications they envision give them many choices of where to start.

Yet industry roadblocks are daunting. Because it applies to controlling the spread of bacteria, a broad range of industries, including private housing, commercial buildings, transport, agriculture, consumer products, medical devices, and pharmaceuticals could benefit. But a naturally occurring substance that deafens bacteria and thereby eliminates their proliferation threatens Big Pharma's antibiotic cash cows, which seem to be prescribed at will for just about any health inconvenience. Moreover, the financial investment and approval procedures are such that actually bringing a new medical innovation to market can take years, if not decades. If it were not for lengthy and complicated government approval procedures, furanones might have replaced antibiotics and bactericides by now.

Meanwhile, other fields less burdened with approval processes are readily apparent. Consumer goods and industrial and agricultural applications represent vast potential for this significant platform technology. Consider deodorants, currently manufactured with questionably safe ingredients including titanium and zinc. Body odor is caused by bacteria feeding on perspiration. A furanone-based deodorant would result in fewer bacteria and consequently less odor.

Then there is tooth brushing, part of our daily routine. The amount of bacteria in our mouths is impressive. Although bacteria contribute to the digestive process and to our ability to taste food, bad breath and tooth decay are also caused by bacteria that feed on food residues in the mouth. If furanones were present, no bacteria-laden biofilm could form. Thus a furanone rinse would have a major refreshing effect.

Agriculture is likewise affected by biofilms. Seeds could be protected from bacterial contamination by simply dipping them in a furanone bath. Cut flowers, which decay under a bacterial onslaught, would remain fresher longer when held in furanone-infused water.

Heating and cooling systems in buildings are at risk for the creation of biofilms including the worrisome accretion of *Legionalla*. This bacterium is tough to eliminate because it lives in a host. The doses needed to kill the host expose the building's occupants to an excessive chemical burden. The alternative is to install filters and replace the filters regularly, further increasing handling costs and downtime. In all these applications furanones offer a remarkable alternative to the toxic chemistry in widespread use today.

British Petroleum made the headlines in 2006 because their Alaskan pipelines leaked. Few people realize that the corrosion commonly affecting pipelines that transport oil, gas, or water is induced by bacteria. Every two weeks, the entire pipeline is shut down and flushed with acidic chemicals to kill the accumulation of bacterial biofilm on the interior. Since it is known that even these measures are not powerful enough to remove all the corrosion-causing microorganisms, a pigging machine is used to scrape the surface and remove these accumulations. Perhaps furanones trickled into the pipelines could simply and safely deal with this problem.

Reverse osmosis production of fresh water from seawater is adversely affected by the accumulation of biofilm on the membrane filters. This reduces their effectiveness by more than 50%. Today, just as is the case with oil and gas pipelines, entire water purification systems must be shut down to kill bacteria with chlorine. The drawback is that excessive use of chlorine chemically degrades the osmosis membranes, reducing the life of a system and increasing costs.

SOME POSSIBLE USES OF FURANONES	
Housing and Building	Air conditioning, Water supply
Agriculture	Fish farming, Food preservation
Industry	Food processing, Micro-electronics
Transportation	Oil and gas
Pharmaceutical	Cystic fibrosis, Tuberculosis
Medical Devices	Urinary catheters, syringes
Consumer Products	Deodorants, Mouth and tooth hygiene, skin care

This handful of applications is only a fraction of the possibilities. The real future of furanone use, and Peter Steinberg's core fascination, has always been the application of his insights to pharmaceutical and medical devices. Cystic fibrosis and tuberculosis are two biofilm-based illnesses where a colony of bacteria slowly and steadily overwhelms the host, eventually fatally. As soon as the bacterial biofilm is formed, antibiotics attain far less effectiveness. A thousand-fold dosage increase is sometimes required. Imagine the impact of a seaweed-inspired synthetic analogue. As bacteria in the biofilm are rendered deaf by the furanones, individual bacteria dissipate and disintegrate since they do not sense a quorum. Ultimately the supra-structure becomes nonfunctional and the individual bacteria can be more readily eliminated by the body's natural maintenance processes.

The understanding that furanones do not obliterate but rather functionally impair detrimental bacteria offers in itself a fresh insight as to how we could improve health and treat illness without stimulating the evolution of superbugs that defy our own immune system. If Steinberg's medical applications ever reach the market, perhaps through Biosignal's new patent portfolio holder, Venturepharma (VPL) (listed on the Hong Kong Stock Exchange), it will break ground for hundreds of different applications. The reasoning is impeccable, the performance is demonstrable, and the cost of production is likely to be competitive, since effective concentrations of furanones appear to be just tens per billion.

If we take an educated guess at evaluating the net job potential, we must consider that the production of furanones will replace the volume production of chemicals that are proven occupational and health hazards. Thus, employment in the manufacturing sector would have neither loss nor gain. Improved material efficiency can be estimated at 20-25%; for example, reverse osmosis membranes and pipelines would function longer, more efficiently, and with lower maintenance costs. However, the most important job generation will likely come from exploring the bacteria-defeating product possibilities of a remarkable species silently at work.

MIRACULOUS MAGGOTS

The spread of AIDS, malaria, and IDD (iodine deficiency disorders) throughout Africa have caught the attention of Western health experts. A number of philanthropic US foundations are aggressively funding the quest for solutions. Yet overlooked is the reality that more Africans are adversely affected by a lack of basic wound care than by these debilitating diseases. Poor wound care leads to infections, gangrene, and amputations, all precursors to social marginalization and shortened life expectancy. If a basic treatment were more widely available, especially in rural villages, subsequent larger problems would be avoided. Though it sounds incongruous, one surprising (and successful) wound care technique comes from insights into how maggots insure hygiene.

In nature, when an animal dies and begins to decompose, flies arrive in swarms. They feast, then lay their eggs. The maggots that hatch quickly consume the rotting flesh. With the flesh consumed, there is no opportunity for bacteria to proliferate. The maggots either grow into flies, or are devoured by birds, fish, or other species having the highly acidic digestion needed to quickly absorb the 80% protein content of the maggots.

The use of maggots in delicate wound treatment is historically well-documented. Healers in ancient Mayan culture and Australian aboriginal tribes regularly used maggots for wound healing. Napoleon's Surgeon General, Baron Dominique Larrey, reported the use of maggot treatment for wounds during France's Egyptian campaign in 1799. Hygienic conditions in war campaigns certainly left much to be desired. Maggots were an important and effective field therapy. The widespread use of maggots for wound therapy prior to World War II diminished following Alexander Fleming's discovery of penicillin in 1928.

More recently, with the acknowledged dangers of antibiotic-resistant bacteria, medical doctors have sought to re-introduce maggot therapy. Worldwide, over 4,000 therapists in 20 countries use maggot wound therapy. Prof. Dr. Stephen Britland from the University of Leeds pioneered research into the healing capacity of maggots. Advanced Gel Technologies (AGT) aims to complement the products developed by ZooBiotic Ltd., based in Wales, which started as a government services provider and is now the world's largest supplier of live maggots for wound therapy. His research found that maggots do more than simply clean wounds. Maggots produce enzymes that stimulate cell-growth through the release of slight electrical charges. For the maggots, even antibiotic-resistant bacteria are nothing more than competitors for food. Left to do what they do best, maggots perform very well indeed.

However, modern hospital conditions require sterile conditions, and maggots are not traditionally associated with bacteria-free hygiene (though the same is often said of modern hospital settings). One of Britland's innovations has been to devise a way to collect the active wound-healing ingredients that maggots produce without collecting the maggots. This procedure is quite simple and not much different than what happens when we take a few gulps of salt water when swimming in the ocean – we regurgitate. Maggots are collected then immersed in salt water to induce disgorgement. The procedure is fast, cheap, and easy. This scheme, as proposed by Advanced Gel Technologies, would allow wound therapy to be accomplished using only the enzyme-rich regurgitated matter, without the disconcerting sight and sensation of maggots consuming necrotic bacteria-laden tissue.

Maggot therapy favorably compares with vacuum treatments, where leg ulcers are locally isolated in a low pressure environment to facilitate cell growth. The use of maggots for wound therapy eliminates the need for antibiotics, as no bacteria remain once the maggots eliminate the dead tissue. Antibiotic resistance thus becomes a non-factor. Clinical trial results demonstrate that maggot treatment is at par in performance with the strongest antibiotic regimens, in itself a remarkable testament.

Aside from the key benefit of healing with a low risk of infection, another major advantage is hospital cost savings for patients who are not critically ill but nonetheless require nursing care to protect them from infection. This is of particular importance for burns or ulcers contracted by diabetic patients. When Britland's research team received funding from the British government to develop and commercialize this therapy, it was because the medical records clearly demonstrated a dramatic Health Services savings for wound care treatment. Money is saved by reducing the length of hospital stays from an average of 72 to only 14 days, heretofore often prolonged because of unhealed leg ulcers requiring amputation. The biggest expense is rearing maggots, as they dine high on the food chain, being fed meat. Fortunately, they are not particular, and will dine on any portion of carcass or slaughterhouse waste available to them.

Considered in the context of Africa's health care challenges, maggot therapy could greatly contribute to the successful treatment of wounds. It is a lack of treatment that causes major health problems. When wounds are not treated, ulcers remain. The World Health Organization estimates that the lack of wound care in Africa generates as many fatalities each year as malaria. It seems this problem should be easy to resolve. However, the cost of delivering the necessary products to remote areas is high and therefore ineffective. A cascading model that utilized inexpensive raw materials, delivered output, and generated cash flow and jobs could easily be configured. In fact, the system benchmarked at the Songhai Center in Benin (introduced in Chapter Two) demonstrates how this can be accomplished. Maggot wound therapy could become a major health care initiative, while simultaneously generating massive numbers of jobs without imported material and equipment.

The country of Benin in Africa is a small former French colony bordering Nigeria. It has a rich history as a part of the Songhai Kingdom, which stretched across Benin and Nigeria before the French and the British imposed boundaries that severed culture and tradition. In 1985 Father Godfrey Nzamujo, a native Nigerian, undertook an ambitious plan to create an integrated farming and livestock operation that would provide food security for the people of the region. Earlier we described how he started the Songhai Center in Porto Novo, Benin. Like any farming program that includes animal husbandry and an abattoir or slaughterhouse, maintaining a high level of hygiene was a major challenge. What to do with the offal and the carcass portions that are not readily processed into meat and sausage? When mad cow disease swept Europe in the last decade, it was attributed to the use of animal waste as feed. European slaughterhouses were forced to incinerate all their waste. Father Nzamujo planned a different approach: feed it to the flies, as happens in nature – but in a controlled environment.

Father Nzamujo's strategy exemplifies a Chinese farming principle: if you have pests, give them the foods that they really like. Reserve a plot of land to grow their favorite nutrients and the pests will leave your crops in peace. The same applies to flies, which are always a nuisance in any food processing project. Killing flies with chemicals is like killing bacteria; it is not very effective. Their ecological function guarantees ample presence and supply.

Father Nzamujo allocated a remote site on the Songhai Center property where all slaughterhouse waste is deposited in small, square containers covered with bird nets to discourage feasting by vultures. The flies arrive and leave their eggs; the maggots hatch and grow. Harvesting is done by filling the containers with water, which causes the maggots to float to the top of the water to reach the air necessary for them to breathe. From there they are easily scooped off each day and fed to quails. The quails flourish and the eggs they produce are air-exported to France where quail eggs are a highly sought-after delicacy. A portion of the maggot harvest is also used to feed fish, which in turn are netted for local consumption, and the remains contribute to soil amendments that nourish the chemical-free food crops. The Songhai Center generates organic food. According to Father Nzamujo, *"That is easy in Africa, since fertilizers and pesticides are difficult to come by, and even if available they are too expensive."*

Feeding maggots to fish and quail generates a lucrative return on many levels. However, regurgitated maggot enzymes that can be easily harvested and used for medical wound care generate a value that is a multiple of the whole system. It does not take a mathematician to do the arithmetic in terms of income and jobs. Considering that Africa imports most of its medical wound care supplies, the ability to utilize a locally produced resource represents a huge savings. At Songhai Center, although no more than 60 pounds of enzyme could be collected on a monthly basis, their model holds promise as a major opportunity to lessen Africa's need for imported wound care materials and to make this ideal application broadly and inexpensively available to those in urgent need of treatment.

There are an estimated 15,000 abattoirs in Africa. Additionally, many animals are slaughtered in small villages. An estimated 200,000 villages locally process slaughtered livestock. If every abattoir in Africa were to complement their operation with a maggot farm, a fish farm, and a poultry farm (chickens, turkeys, quails), it would create an estimated 300 thousand to 500 thousand jobs in the production of maggots to provide protein-rich livestock feed and better, cheaper wound care. There would be no additional expense for raw materials. Only what is currently wasted, or what takes additional energy and effort to dispose, would be used. It would also eliminate the health risks associated with handling slaughterhouse waste. Maggot enzyme collection at this scale would be sufficient even for export. Such more extensive use would translate into unprecedented medical savings and tremendous benefit to wound care patients, who would regain health and mobility more quickly and reliably.

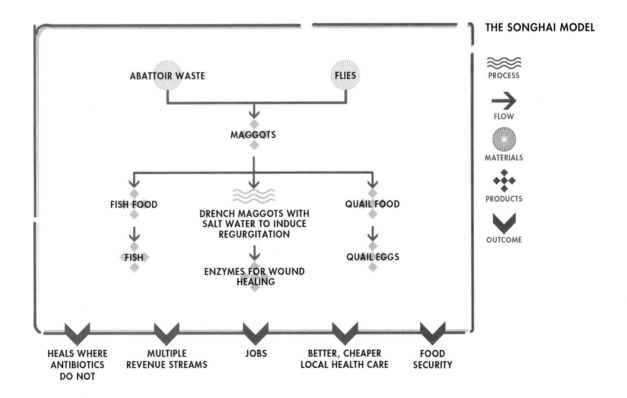

PAINLESS INJECTIONS

If maggots offered you a bit of inspiration and perhaps garnered a little of your respect, let us move on to the mosquito, another creature on most short lists of irksome pests. For some, a mosquito bite is nothing more than the cause of a bothersome itch, a micro-massage, or perhaps a nuisance. But for Tetsuya Oyauchi from Terumo, a large Japanese medical instrumentation company, and Masayuki Okano, president of a small metal-pressing company, the painless bite from a mosquito was an accomplishment that piqued their curiosity. Okano wondered, *"Why do our syringes cause such pain, when mosquitoes are perfectly capable of extracting blood without any pain?"*

Most people have an aversion to injections. They hurt. Anticipating the injection causes an anxiety that is almost unavoidable. A few patients will even faint. When the Terumo engineers and researchers learned what it was that allowed mosquitoes to painlessly draw their sustenance, and what it was that caused painful injections, they were stunned by the mechanical simplicity. It was about sizes and cone-shapes. The mosquito's proboscis is finer at the tip and gradually widens along its length. It was once thought that a needle's inside and outside diameters should be kept constant to transfuse medication. Making the tip diameter smaller was thought to make it harder to inject medical solutions, thus limiting how small the tip of a needle could be. But it is the cylinder-like shape of needles that causes pain.

Okano-san is known in Japan as the "metalwork magician." Starting with a super-thin sheet of stainless steel, Okano rolled it into a tiny tapered cylindrical cone, sealing it by welding the seam. Oyauchi used his medical engineering expertise to refine and develop what he names the "Nanopass 33 Syringe." Its tip diameter is only 0.2 millimeters, 20% less than previous needles. Rolling the metal into a cone with a specific contour gives the needle point its fineness. The tip can be superfine and gradually become wider, just like the shape of the mosquito's proboscis. The problem was solved.

Terumo's patent application for a tapered "injection needle and liquid-introducing implement" was granted in 2004. Today hypodermic needles by Terumo are the standard for diabetic patients' daily needs. In Japan alone, there are some 600 thousand diabetic patients who require daily insulin injections. Nearly eight percent of the American population suffers from diabetes, some 23.6 million people. Thus the Terumo needle meets the needs of a large and appreciative customer base. Since it uses less metal there is also a net gain in material efficiency.

The Nanopass 33 needle received the Grand Good Design Award from the Japan Industrial Design Promotion Conference in 2005. Upon accepting the award, Okano commented, *"It is fun to make something that doesn't exist in the world, and accomplish something people think can't be done."* Like the case of silk, this is another example of how geometry borrowed from nature shapes products and helps solve our needs. While the Terumo needle cannot claim to have generated jobs, it has substantially reduced the pain suffered by patients needing medical injections This puts it far ahead of the many disruptive technologies we thoughtlessly condone.

GASLESS PROPULSION

In nature, ecosystems first use the powers of physics without recourse to chemistry. The value of this is once more demonstrated by a significant potential application: propulsion gases. University of California researcher Mario Molina, who with Sherwood Rowland received the Nobel Prize for their original work first published in 1974, identified propulsion gases as the cause of the drastic ozone layer deterioration we now endure. Their work led to banning the infamous CFC gas and its derivates under the Montreal Protocol. Though industry offered a few new variations on propulsion gases, their use exemplifies how doing less harm is still very harmful.

Propulsion gases are commonly used for consumer applications including misting devices for medical dosing of antihistamine or bactericide, and for cleaning and hairspray products. Mist spray technology enables droplet size, temperature, and velocity to be closely controlled. Thus it has other applications such as in the fuel-injection systems of automobile engines. More recently the use of this chemistry has been replaced in some cases, such as hairspray, by a high pressure atomizing dispenser. It is another of the fine examples demonstrating how the chemical industry found a solution that moved in the right direction but failed to eliminate the unwanted and unplanned side effects caused by inhaling designer chemicals. (We could note as well that patients suffering from cystic fibrosis or tuberculosis might better eliminate the biofilm of a detrimental bacteria when a seaweed-inspired furanone is effectively blended with air and inhaled.)

Even though the French philosopher Voltaire once declared, *"The perfect should not stand in the way of the good,"* it is timely to make a fundamental distinction between the good and the "less bad." The search for a perfect solution should not stop anyone from implementing a good solution, but the search for total risk elimination should remain high on the agenda. In the case of propulsion gases, total risk elimination becomes a practical reality with the help of the bombardier beetle. It has an ability that may help improve delivery of aerosolized respiratory medicines, greater automobile fuel efficiency, reduced emissions from fuel-injection systems, and even lowered risk of explosions in mines.

In nature, much has to do with nutrients and defense, or predator and prey. The bombardier beetle *(Brachinus carabidae)* is a rare evolutionary survivor. This amazing little insect has the ability to spray a stinging 100°C (212°F) liquid irritant over a distance 10 times its own length. This captivated the mind of Andy McIntosh, Professor of Thermodynamics and Combustion Theory at Leeds University, who was introduced to the bombardier's remarkable feats by Cornell University entymologist Tom Eisner.

Just two centimeters long, the bombardier beetle uses its exothermic spray to defend itself against ants. The bombardier creates its spray by reacting hydroquinone with hydrogen peroxide stored in its fuel glands, producing a blast of steamy liquid. The beetle's one centimeter (0.4 in) diameter "combustion chamber" works rather like a pressure cooker. Once more, it is about pressure – physics – more than chemistry. The liquid in the chamber is held under pressure, a valve is opened, and flash evaporation occurs. The valve closes, the chamber refills, and the liquid heats to above the atmospheric boiling point when the chamber valve is again opened. The beetle does this quickly and efficiently, spraying at 400 to 500 cycles per second. *"Essentially, it is a high-force steam cavitation explosion,"* explains McIntosh.

This ingenious mechanical propulsion system that perfectly distributes a substance into the air at a particle size of no more than two nanometers has been modeled by scientists, who can reproduce its action at 20 cycles per second with the same throw ratio. Because the bubbles in the chemical reaction of hydroquinone with hydrogen peroxide are so small, the ratio of the surface area to the volume administered is greatly increased, thus likewise increasing efficiency.

Says McIntosh, *"No one had ever studied the bombardier beetle from a physics and engineering perspective. At first, we did not appreciate how much we would learn from it."* His new discovery has the potential to eliminate the impact of propulsion gases on the ozone layer while increasing dispensary performance. The Swedish entrepreneur Lars Uno Larsson was enthused by this innovation and is taking it from concept, to pilot, to potential commercialization. The innovation has found its entrepreneur. Once benchmarked, it can inspire others to pursue a wide range of applications.

BUNDLING INNOVATIONS

What possibilities emerge from this examination of just a few innovations is that the combination of several of these technologies could potentially allow us to reconfigure our approach to health care. If one technology motivates us, bundling several innovations may encourage the design of a system that can impel our world towards true sustainability, and eliminate our dependency on the false comfort of chemistry that relies on non-renewable resources with unforeseen and detrimental effects. It suggests that we might rethink our approach to health and health care, to seek out and promote solutions that substitute "something" with "nothing," that take inspiration from the physics of the natural world.

To achieve this, to even work towards this goal, more contributions are needed. If the bacteria-suppressing furanones from seaweed or enzymes from maggots can be administered using a mechanical misting device inspired by the bombardier beetle, then we are truly achieving a new era of health care delivery. We will not be depositing residues and waste materials with undesirable side effects into the ecosphere and its inhabitants. Instead, we can borrow components perfected over millions of years to achieve a functional, integrated system. The real power of evolution is not just that one species survived but that a collaboration emerged. Multiple species fine-tuned their processes to reach symbiosis, achieving their needs and enhancing their survival.

This implies that the opportunity for entrepreneurs is not just creating new batteries or antibiotics but in bundling innovations into sustainable systems. For businesses, for the economy itself, the employment opportunities the Blue Economy heralds point to a solid evolutionary path. The innovations of many will combine to achieve a greater whole.

What we have explored only scratches the surface of the potential. In less than a hundred years of "modern" scientific and technologic invention and application, we have achieved diminishing success in conquering viral and bacterial pathogens and the dangers we perceive in our surrounding biota. Yet any number of nature's time-tested solutions can inform our ability to overcome bacteria and viruses. Earthworms and barberries are producers of potent antibiotics and have resisted bacterial mutation for millions of years. The bombardier beetle, in surviving against armies of ants, deserves admiration and emulation for its exceptional capacity to outwit a species known for its superior swarm intelligence. This alone should further inspire us to respect biodiversity and ecosystems. It should motivate us to go beyond preservation of biodiversity toward insuring that ecosystems continue to evolve without human-induced species loss. It offers a compelling logic for humanity to collaborate with evolution towards ever more cohesive and adaptive ecosystems.

BIODIVERSITY AND HEALTH

With the loss of biodiversity comes the loss of the chance to learn from our fellow sentient species and to adapt the solutions they have invented. This is particularly the case for the gastric brooding frog or platypus frog *(Rheobatrachus silus)*. Unfortunately, this species, native to Australia, did not survive excessive exposure to pesticides, herbicides, and the release of non-native species into its habitat. It could have taught us much about promoting healthy digestion and controlling bacteria. Once the mother frog conceived, she swallowed the offspring, brooding them in her stomach until they were ready to be released into the world. This is possible through control and eradication of acidophilic bacteria and the delicate pH management of the stomach environment. The first phases of the tiny frogs' life occur in an alkaline environment. If the typical gastric acidity persisted and acidophilic bacteria remained competitive, the offspring could not survive.

Our digestive health could have taken great inspiration from the *Rheobatrachus silus*. Stomach ulcers and gastric cancer have been poorly understood for decades. Extreme acidophilic bacteria were not considered the cause of these stomach diseases. Scientists Marshall and Robin Warren nonetheless identified ulcer- and cancer-causing bacteria so that the design of an appropriate cure and even a preventive treatment for high risk patients could be formulated. In 2005 both scientists were awarded the Nobel Prize in chemistry for their work. Had we the opportunity to further study the gastric brooding frog, we might have learned how to avoid the health hazards of excessive stomach acidity altogether. This knowledge was lost because we were ignorant or dismissive of the impact of our flawed systems on the life around us, which allow waste to be wasted and to end up as pollution. Thousands of species are now threatened by just this ignorance.

Our beautiful blue planet Earth, endlessly cycling in the embrace of dark cosmos and brilliant sunshine, provides us the living conditions on which we depend not only for survival but also for happiness. It is time to actively and consciously link our health to the health of the Earth. It is time to reassess the contributions and genius of our ecosystems, and find ways to adapt natural processes and whole systems solutions to secure our livelihoods, our survival, and our planet. In so doing we will discover, as has every other species through millions, perhaps even billions of years, new models for survivability, sustainability, and abundance; models based on a Blue Economy – an economy of support and exchange – that provides more with less, and that is conducive to all life.

CHAPTER NINE

A RAINBOW OF
POSSIBILITIES:
REMAKING COLORATION
AND COSMETICS

The eye is the primary means whereby
our understanding may most fully
and abundantly appreciate
the infinite works of Nature.

— LEONARDO DA VINCI

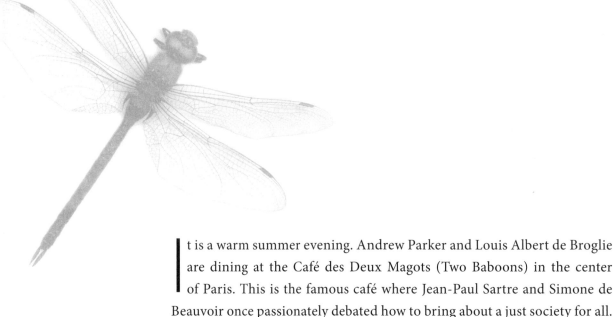

t is a warm summer evening. Andrew Parker and Louis Albert de Broglie are dining at the Café des Deux Magots (Two Baboons) in the center of Paris. This is the famous café where Jean-Paul Sartre and Simone de Beauvoir once passionately debated how to bring about a just society for all. Interestingly, Parker and de Broglie are talking tomatoes.

Louis Albert de Broglie farms 630 varieties of tomatoes at his Bourdaisiere castle along the Loire. He has dedicated his career to the rediscovery and renewal of plant biodiversity. Andrew Parker is a research scientist at Oxford University and at the London Natural History Museum. From his years of study and research he has discovered much about how species perceive color and develop vision. Much of his recent work has focused on developing ways to produce color applications without using chemical pigmentation, which is primarily how it is done today.

The dinner conversation has turned to a discussion of which tomato might boast the best biological system to reduce excessive exposure to ultraviolet light. What, might you ask, do tomatoes have to do with ultraviolet protection? To answer that, let us first explore how we perceive light itself.

LIGHT PERCEPTION

Visible light is made up of photons, which are packets of electromagnetic radiation that travel in straight lines, reflecting off objects then passing through the transparent, curved cornea into the eye. As the photons pass through the cornea and the lens, they transition from traveling through air to traveling through liquid. This liquid contains proteins with refractive properties, causing the photons to change direction and further bend to focus onto the retina, which is essentially a sheet of light-sensitive cells. This process is enhanced by the adjustment of the pupil diameter to admit the right quantity of light. Specialized muscles adjust the shape of the lens to improve focus and visual flexibility. Meanwhile, muscles attached outside the eye work to keep the same focal point and to scan back and forth in a coordinated manner. Photons strike a retinal molecule, a modified form of vitamin A. Contact with an incoming photon causes the retina to react by initiating a complex biochemical cascade within the cell that ultimately generates an electrical signal sent to the brain. There, the information from millions of retinal photoreceptors is combined to provide details about contrast and color. The upside-down images formed on both retinas are mentally combined and inverted and the resulting images are interpreted – in this case, as the words on this page.

Lenses are a key component of the art of light. These refract light, converting or diverting the beam. The earliest mechanical lenses were devised in Assyria some 3,000 years ago. However, several of nature's fauna developed lenses hundreds of millions of years ago. The octopus created thin film lenses. The brittle star produced distortion-free lenses. These two marvels of lens technology are indications that our scientific understanding of optics still has a long way to go, and that there is a huge potential for commercial application.

New applications do find their way to the market in a most surprising manner. In Japan, dragonflies represent lightness and joy. They remind us that we are light and, if we choose to do so, we can reflect that light

in powerful ways. The dragonfly's ability to generate energy through the concentration of light has garnered the attention of renewable energy researchers. Concentrated solar power (CSP) is an emerging and benchmarked industry. In the desert of southern Spain, over 1,000 mirrors have been positioned that reflect sunlight to superheat water in a central tower, a development and investment of Abengoa. It uses mirrors to focus sunlight onto the water much as the dragonfly does. By 2050, the solar power harvested using CSP is expected to eliminate the atmospheric release of 2.1 billion tons of CO_2. Annual CSP investments could exceed \$100 billion and create almost two million jobs.

ULTRAVIOLET: LIGHT HUMANS DO NOT SEE

Light does not always bring color. There is also light from the sun that we do not see at all. Light has different wavelengths. Ultraviolet light has shorter wavelengths than visible light, having a frequency higher than what we identify as "violet" – hence its name. Ultraviolet light emanates at a higher frequency than the human eye can distinguish. The potentially beneficial effects of UV light exposure are well documented. It can address many skin diseases such as psoriasis. It stimulates the production of vitamin D, which helps the body absorb calcium to maintain bone strength and lower cancer risk. It provides a natural control mechanism for mites in carpets, rugs, and upholstery. Ultraviolet light treats the water in swimming pools to control bacteria, replacing the use of chlorine, that ubiquitous (and toxic) germ killer.

There are also well-known negatives to excessive UV exposure. It may lead to skin cancer, especially since our protective ozone layer has been damaged by propulsion gases like CFC (chlorofluorocarbon), which, as we recently learned from the bombardier beetle, need not have been used in the first place. Consumer product marketers promote a variety of protection schemes to counter the perceived risks of excessive UV exposure. These include designer chemicals like oxybenzone, a compound that absorbs UV but is now a suspected photo-carcinogen. In the laboratory this chemical

may have low reactivity, but when illuminated by light, it gets excited and is potentially harmful to biological tissue. Zinc and titanium oxide, organic particles that reflect, scatter, and absorb UV rays, were marketed for their UV-protective properties. But recent research at the University of California Riverside indicates that these sunscreens must be reapplied every two hours to remain effective. Otherwise, they unleash free radicals that can cause skin cell damage that may be worse than the UV exposure!

In nature many species have adapted to prolonged exposure to ultraviolet light and are able to neutralize its effects. Of course, plants must have sunlight to drive photosynthesis. Being rooted, they cannot move into available shade when the sun is too bright. They must create protection. Many animals are also vulnerable to prolonged UV exposure. The mechanisms evolved by plants and animals to protect against these negative effects can give us resources, insight, and inspiration.

The edelweiss, the unofficial national flower of Austria, has been studied in detail by the Belgian scholar Jean Pol Vigneron. The edelweiss does not reflect UV but rather absorbs it in thousands of little hairs, avoiding tissue penetration that destroys living cells. Many lichen and fungi exist in high arctic, antarctic, or desert areas where UV exposure is extremely high. As a result they tend to have absorbing pigments. For instance, a novel photo-protective mycosporine has been isolated from the fungi living in symbiosis with *Collema cristatum*, a microalgae-forming lichen. The pure isolated compound prevents UV-induced skin cell destruction when applied prior to irradiation. Certainly, some lichens show better protective traits than others. Yet this field of research is most promising because it offers simple protection, replaces toxic applications, and eliminates reliance on mined materials that require massive energy to extract and process.

Certain fruits such as apples and tomatoes are notably sensitive to ultraviolet radiation and must protect themselves. They offer a biochemical recipe that provides better protection than titanium oxide. The tomato skin is rich in lycopene, a carotenoid in the same family as beta-carotene. Lycopene has powerful antioxidant properties and provides a high level of UV protection. In fact, as the two colleagues at Café des Deux Magots now discuss, some tomatoes even do better than others in generating this protective shield.

THE EVOLUTION OF COLOR AND PERCEPTION

The optical mechanisms for vision first developed some 540 million years ago during the period called the Cambrian Explosion. Suddenly – in less than one million years, a short span in evolutionary terms – and for no obvious reason, a broad range and diversity of life began to flourish. Creatures took on hard body parts, shells and spines, and shapes and colors of every description. The ability to perceive and visually distinguish surrounding phenomena became a dominant force of evolution. Vision was a survival advantage for both predator and prey. Food could be more easily identified, predators could be recognized, and mates could be located. Some species evolved bright colorations and intricate patterning to blend with their environment, to warn of their power to defend, or to impress mates.

Cambrian decendants – birds, mammals, reptiles, fish, mollusks, and wonderfully iridescent beetles – have all created their own way of seeing, as well their own way of producing color. Poison dart frogs use conspicuous color to tell predators that they are not good to eat. Venomous coral snakes sport rings of bright color to advertise that they are not to be messed with. A white milk snake, which isn't poisonous and could be quite safely eaten, benefits from the coral snake's reputation simply by copying its colorations. A cuttlefish changes color to match its background in a millisecond. A chameleon camouflaged with stripes and spots can stalk its prey without being seen.

Dr. Hopi Hoekstra, Loeb Associate Professor of Natural Sciences at Harvard University, studies the genetic mechanisms at work in a species of mouse that adapts to its environment by being sand-colored if it lives at the beach and dark if it lives inland. Parrotfish are able to change their sex and appearance from female to male. Females in a group are much less colorful

than the dominant male. If the male fish gets eaten, the dominant female changes her sex – and puts on the brilliant colors of the male. Parrots, the birds, see ultraviolet light. They look flamboyant to each other, even when we only see monochromatic feathers.

Pigments are chemical substances produced by living organisms that appear as colors because they selectively absorb and reflect certain wavelengths of light. Pigments can never add to but only subtract wavelengths from a light source. A frog is green not because it has green pigment, but because it reflects blue light from yellow pigment. The white hairs of a polar bear or an arctic fox's winter coat are actually clear. There are neither pigments to absorb nor structures to reflect certain wavelengths. Thus, they reflect the entire spectrum, making the animal appear white.

The *Cyphochilus* beetle and other beetles have a highly unusual brilliantly white shell. The *cyphochilus* has evolved its superb whiteness on scales that are just five micrometers thick, ten times thinner than a human hair. The random surface structure on its scales simultaneously absorbs and scatters every color. Industrial mineral coatings, such as those used on high-quality paper, plastics, and some paints, need to be twice as thick to be as white. According to measures for whiteness and brightness, beetles are whiter and brighter than milk or the average human tooth, both of which are considerably thicker.

Many animals acquire their coloration through pigments that they metabolize. Others take in pigments through what they eat, displaying those pigments through their skin. For example, the pink coloration of the scarlet ibis comes from its diet of crabs and shrimp that consume red algae. (Imagine if humans could generate colors simply from what we eat!) Nearly all the blue hues we see in the animal world, including the colors of the blue damselfly *(Enallagma civile)*, are produced not by blue pigment but by blue light reflected from tiny tissue structures that scatter light and often enhance it. Some species produce color not by pigmentation but by microstructures in fur, feathers, scales, petals, or other features that reflect only certain wavelengths of light. In animals, the building material is often keratin.

Birds-of-paradise and hummingbirds have feathers that possess a stunning iridescence, a metallic sheen that is perhaps the most spectacular color effect of all. The color effects of the Egyptian scarab and the rainforest beetle have been copied in jewelry for millennia, but have never been industrially reproduced. Some orchids enhance their visual attractiveness by the combination and spacing of gold and silver flecks in their otherwise chemically pigmented petals. A similar effect is found in African violets. Through millions of years of trial-and-error many organisms have perfected methods to enhance attractiveness using metallic color effects, although no metals are involved. The underlying structures that generate these colorations vary widely from species to species. One exceptional color producer identified and described by Andrew Parker is the sea mouse, *Polychaeta aphroditidae*. This marine animal is covered with iridescent hairs and the effect is sheer beauty.

COLOR PIGMENTATION AS COMMODITY

The earliest known pigments used by humans were minerals. Natural iron oxides produce a range of colors and are still discernible in cave paintings after 20 millennia or more. As early as the Middle Ages, the search for permanent and stable colors drove industry towards complex chemistry and created highly profitable businesses. Two of the first synthetic pigments were white and blue. White was made by combining lead with vinegar in the presence of CO_2. Blue pigment, known as "blue frit," was made with a calcium copper silicate derived from crushed glass colored with a copper ore such as malachite.

In the merchandizing world of today, like the Cambrian Age of pre-history, coloration still serves as an attractant. In the contemporary case, however, bright colors and unique patterns are displayed more in the hopes of attracting a buyer than a mate. The marketing, selling, and even consumption of products such as paint, ink, fabric, plastics, cosmetics, and food, rely on coloration to stand out. The demand for color is vast and growing. In 2008, total world pigment consumption reached nearly

eight million tons, good for a turnover of more than $17 billion dollars. This means that the average price for a ton of color was more than $2,000 dollars. This is four times the price for cellulose for paper-making, or palm oil for biofuels. From a business standpoint, color pigments are a high-end product with solid margins.

It is remarkable that humans are prepared to adorn themselves with clothing and cosmetics without ever asking about the ingredients and methods used to create these accessories. Today color pigmentation is created by cadmium, chromium, cobalt, lead, mercury, titanium, and zinc. In short, it depends on mining practices and ore processing that are far from a model of sustainability. Furthermore, the application and use of color pigments is now highly regulated, since many have been shown to be potential health hazards. Yet none of the modern industry standards require biodegradable pigments. Nor are regulations to be found when it comes to disposing cast-off goods and their metal oxide color components. Along with batteries, color pigments are probably responsible for the majority of heavy metal pollution in landfills. Since these pigments were designed to last and not to fade, thus not to degrade, they can concentrate at dangerous levels of contamination. When indiscriminately dispersed into the environment, they often pollute entire ecosystems.

Color is beautiful but it is a dirty business. From a business standpoint, the most desirable color is white. Optical brighteners such as chlorine bleach and benzene, the market standards for "brightening" fabric, paper, and plastics, effectively produce visible white because they have very strong light absorption capabilities. These optical brighteners convert the yellowish color from oxidation to an effect perceived by the eye as white, giving the impression of cleanliness. Clean or not, the impression is what we value. However, these optical brighteners are suspected allergens and are highly toxic. While pigments and optical brighteners may be the best we have, how can we manage this differently than the way our industrial society has done? The hope is that once we grasp how light and color shaped evolution in the past we may be able to use nature's solutions to shape the industries of tomorrow.

Andrew Parker has identified the simple structure responsible for the iridescent coloration of species such as hummingbirds and beetles, and understands how to produce metallic iridescent color the way nature achieved it millions of years ago. He has challenged himself to formulate iridescent colors that can be manufactured on a commercially viable scale and produce a desirable visual effect while emulating the creative ways nature has produced color. He rightly contends that if these vibrant and attractive colorations can be formulated using the physics and biochemistry adapted by animals and plants, it not only represents an important breakthrough, it offers a strong marketing message that resonates with the growing segment of manufacturers and consumers who are looking for nontoxic and non-polluting alternatives. His goal is to establish the technical research base for a portfolio of innovations that could find applications in multiple industries. Photonic engineering may soon provide coloration results without cadmium, lead, or chromium!

The manufacturing technique may be as simple as the production of glass. If the concept proves successful, the potential is vast. The preliminary trials are convincing. The first application is for cosmetics, a sector with a unique interest in generating colors beyond those offered on the market today. Since cosmetics are more than beauty and also embrace skin health, Parker's work has multiple facets. Companies looking to differentiate themselves with a "fresh and natural" angle in their marketing strategies will be interested in this innovative approach. Parker's research efforts may well be a milestone in industrial development and a platform for the creation of new industries that are in true harmony with ecosystems. The only challenge remaining is organizing supply.

Beyond cosmetics there are applications such as a chemical-free coating for glassware and crystal, which have traditionally relied on lead. A novel crystal figure could be produced, if a piece of glass containing the appropriate microstructure was invisibly inserted into a crystal statue of the whole animal. It would feature spectacular flashes of color in a much

more effective way than can be achieved with glass prisms. This would not only have the same visual effect as the living animal, but the effect would be based on an optical device identical to what the animal uses.

WASTE FOR ONE, RESOURCE FOR ANOTHER

The dinner conversation at Café des Deux Magots is animated. De Broglie has remarked on the incredible volume of biowaste in the tomato processing industry, all of which, he notes, could become the raw materials for cosmetics and sunscreen products.

The location of a tomato processing plant is carefully chosen to minimize transportation from the farm, so that as quickly as fresh tomatoes arrive, they can be converted to tomato paste. Unilever, the world's largest processor of tomatoes, averages 1.65 million tons a year. With a high volume of tomatoes to process, there are factory waste streams for everything that is not processed and packed. The tomato skin waste generated from this volume of tomatoes amounts to some 30,000 tons a year. If the Unilever factories were to add a subsidiary operation that produced a lycopene-based sunscreen from tomato skin waste, then today's titanium-based UV protection agents would be instantly under-priced and outmoded. The renewable available raw material would be free, and using it would actually save the tomato paste factory the expense of waste "disposal."

It is true that compared to coffee, tomatoes generate much less waste. Still, the processing residue is expelled through the wastewater treatment system, using thousands of cubic meters of water. Of the remaining solids, some three percent ends up as landfill. This goes unnoticed, since supply chain managers and corporate policy focus on short-term gain, and do not search for any value from waste. To us, however, these few percentage points should be interesting indeed. In business there is a saying that a penny saved on each product is a million added to the bottom line. However it is a logic that is not applied once an output is considered waste. This is where ecosystems offer solid inspiration, since nature finds value in waste.

What nature's whole systems teach us is that achieving material efficiency isn't accomplished by just one process. There are always multiple functions, as tomato skins superbly illustrate. Tomato skins diverted from the waste stream are not only good as an antioxidant and for ultraviolet sunlight protection, they are the source of a naturally derived, food-safe red coloring that could be utilized in many frozen food products ranging from packaged salmon, to strawberries, to ice cream. Thus if tomatoes were the core business, the spin-offs in health (UV protection), personal care (cosmetics), fisheries (protein food) and ice cream (dessert) would fit them into a cascading model. Iron oxides and synthetic color pigments derived from petroleum and mined metals are only offering one product and an unaccountable waste stream. Lycopenes are part of a cluster of utilizable materials that can be rescued from biowaste. Red lipstick made from tomato skins would have a cachet of its own. In fact, if women knew the ingredients presently used for lipstick manufacture, the tomato skin version would become irresistible.

An entrepreneurial business plan would involve developing lycopene extraction and processing technologies; knowing the lycopene extraction potential from the skins; assessing the volume of UV-protection products the market consumes and at what price; and determining the volume and price of red pigment purchased by the food industry. A tomato skin processing plant established near a tomato processing factory could sell extracted lycopene at a competitive industry price to be manufactured into food-safe pigment dyes and UV sunscreen products. This transformation of waste management to accelerated innovation would profitably generate local jobs, provide lower consumer prices for higher quality products, replace unsustainable business practices, and help secure health and reduce toxin exposure. Such an environmentally sound and financially secure business model can succeed on many levels.

From the viewpoint of cost analysis, it is considered too expensive to extract lycopenes from tomatoes for the lycopenes alone. Yet this conclusion implies that we would waste the rest of the tomato and that would not make sense, although this is exactly the way industry rationalizes today. In such a narrow economic analysis, Parker's proposal to derive both coloration and ultraviolet protection from the tomato could never compete with titanium oxide in sunscreen lotions. On the other hand, if the raw material for both is from tomato waste, then we are in business. The generation of two value-adding derivatives (UV protection and color pigment) from one waste stream is a much improved business proposal altogether. This logic is not taught in the world's best academic businesses schools where core business–core competence strategy is locked in with discounted cash flow analysis. Double revenue streams generated from free materials results in a much higher integrated cash flow than what the processing of tomatoes alone could ever achieve.

Thus the entrepreneurial business model could also incorporate use of the tomato seed waste as well as the skin. Tomato seeds from the larger volume paste processors are either dumped in landfills or sold cheaply to cattle farmers. The nutritional value of the seeds for cattle feed is low – it is a filler, rather than a feeder. However, tomato seeds are rich in health-boosting trace elements and emolliating monounsaturated and polyunsaturated fatty acids. Thus a better match of materials to market would be to turn these seeds into products that soothe our skin or nourish our bodies.

The world demand for processed tomato products – boiled, sliced and diced, canned, bottled, dried, in all its many international flavors – could also meet the demand for safe UV-protection products, cosmetic products, and pigment dyes from the unused tomato peels and seeds. Cascading materials in this fashion offers unique opportunities to develop promising markets, create successful applications, and achieve busy factories. If these derivative processing facilities were located near the primary tomato processing center, the transport costs would be minimal. This clustering of businesses contributes to cash flow, reduces costs, and generates jobs.

THE BIOREFINERY OF THE FUTURE

Imagining ways to reintegrate waste streams into nutrient streams brings into focus the outline of a biorefinery. The concept of a biorefinery was originally developed by Prof. Dr. Carl-Göran Hedén, member of the Club of Rome and of the Royal Swedish Academy of Sciences. Hedén's idea of a biorefinery involved the capacity to generate more with what has already been harvested or processed. Envisioning a cascading of nutrients and materials, he devised a demonstration facility where all chemicals and catalysts were processed in a closed loop. Lignin, hemicellulose, cellulose, lipids, and essential oils were extracted from one tree. Revenues were tripled merely by eliminating waste.

In the case of the tomato, we might calculate how many jobs could be generated using the biorefinery concept. The net job generation of this initiative may be larger than expected. The Food and Agricultural Organization of the United Nations (FAO) reports that the worldwide area utilized for tomato farming is nine million acres. The world output is just less than 100 million tons. The USA alone produces 10 million tons. Considered entrepreneurially, we would say that the world wastes around two million tons of potential additive, pigment, and oil sources. This amount is impressive and allows us to realize that it is possible to replace metal-based pigments and UV-protectors without ever stressing the Earth to produce alternatives, and without competing for food as is the case for corn grown to produce fuel or plastics. The Earth is already producing all we need; we only need to use what is available.

At present one ton of color pigment costs an average of $2,000 dollars. Tomato-derived natural pigment sources could be made available for roughly $1,000 dollars per ton, as the materials are from spent product that is available for free or for the cost of local transportation. Inexpensive raw materials would make it possible to produce the pigment at a lower base cost. This new business opportunity would factor out at about two billion dollars. That is the value of what is wasted today, dumped in landfills, devoured by cattle that cannot digest it, and off-gassing methane pollution in the process. In Brazil (where Unilever currently has its newest processing plant), factory workers live comfortably on $10,000 dollars per year. We could safely state that a turnover of two billion dollars in a country like Brazil could generate possibly 100 thousand jobs.

These numbers give rise to a broader debate. Prior to embarking on a guesstimate, it is important to remind ourselves of the market dynamics. If something is expensive yet desirable, demand will remain low. As the price decreases, demand will increase. Price elasticity studies show that lowering the price of highly desirable products generates a greater than proportional increase in demand. If tomato-based biochemistry were available at half the price of what is used today, then it would undercut the dominant products on the market and stimulate demand. Where part of the increase would be the replacement of the non-sustainable options now available, the overall demand would also grow. Apple press cake (the residue from juice extraction) and grape pomace (the skins and seeds from pressing) represent another wealth of raw materials that could be utilized in similar fashion.

Worldwide, two million tons of tomato waste equates to only 12% of the world's coffee waste. Yet thanks to our appetite for ketchup, salsa, and spaghetti sauce, this waste stream could supply every lipstick manufacturer in the world with all the color pigments they might need. Color pigments from tomato waste would provide cheaper, better, natural, and proven UV protection while helping the women of the world enhance their beauty. Nor does this lipstick taste like tomatoes! This is the basis of the new economy that we see emerging. While it is already more than an idea, imagine what would happen if everything produced were to follow this logic. Here again is our Blue Economy, working with what we have, responding to basic needs, accomplishing greater sustainability than we ever envisioned, generating jobs, and building social capital while competing successfully in the market.

As we might imagine, the two friends dining at Les Deux Magots had much to discuss – perhaps we could say a most fruitful conversation. If Heinz and Unilever – the giant tomato processors of the world – neglect these opportunities, then entrepreneurial partnerships will emerge that take the science and the cash flow to the next level: profit derived from responding to the basic needs of all – including a healthy blue planet on which to live.

CHAPTER TEN

ENVISIONING NEW
ENERGY OPTIONS

*If you do not change direction,
you may end up where you are headed.*

— CHINESE PROVERB

The class of fourth grade children in Yokohama, Japan, is excited: they are getting a banana they can eat during class, and the aroma is as pleasing as the taste. The teacher also gives each of them a hardboiled egg. They are instructed to cut the banana peel into little pieces with scissors and to pulverize the eggshell. The two are mixed and a little water added. Next, the probes of a digital voltmeter are inserted into the eggshell-banana peel paste. Everyone exclaims and claps their hands: the voltmeter registers an electrical flow!

The reaction in Japan is no different in Curitiba, Brazil, or Stellenbosch, South Africa: adults are surprised and children are excited. Everyone wonders how it is possible. We are only familiar with modern sources of energy such as steam generators, nuclear power stations, coal-fired electrical power plants, hydroelectric generators, and photovoltaic solar panels. Yet these forms of energy are all recent arrivals on Earth. For the previous four billion years no one relied on any of these human engineering marvels. As a result of this ingenuity we struggle with climate change due to excessive CO_2 and face long-term societal costs for storage and containment of nuclear waste.

While we are busy getting electricity from the grid, we are unaware that our heart requires just 0.2 volts, built up by the combination of 70 millivolt charges, to regulate the daily flow of roughly 2000 gallons of blood through all four chambers of the heart. Its power supply consists of nothing more than the biochemistry of potassium, sodium, and calcium. There are no batteries and nothing is wired. No metals are needed. Indeed, thanks to a selective diet evolved over millennia, we ingest a blend of molecules that, amongst other functions, provides a regular supply of biochemicals to make our heart, brain, and nervous system work without maintenance – hopefully measured for decades, or even longer. No power station designed by man supplies energy as reliably as the simple biochemical reactions performed within our body.

Amory Lovins, cofounder of the Rocky Mountain Institute, is among the world's most creative thinkers on energy. He has often shown that our society's centralized energy production, consisting of huge power stations with masses of wires and cables reaching like tentacles into every home, is not the ideal way to achieve a sustainable electrical supply. If we were to take time to observe how natural systems have secured a continuous supply of energy for millennia, we would realize that none of our mainstream power generators apply those principles. Indeed, the collateral damage created by our present energy scheme risks destroying the very life support systems on which we depend.

Today, it is the means of providing energy that tilts the supply equation towards trouble. The massive output of three gases – carbon dioxide (CO_2), methane (CH_4), and nitrous oxide (N_2O) – has had a pervasive impact on the thin band of breathable atmosphere that surrounds our planet. The delicately balanced atmosphere that envelops the Earth is the result of millions of years of interactions with its forest cover. Since less than 30% of the original forests remains, unless we embark on massive regeneration of forests in all climates, the basis by which the atmosphere is maintained is shifting beyond repair. The sources are known. The carbon dioxide comes mainly from burning fossil fuels, the methane from animal waste, and the nitrous oxide from applying petroleum-derived fertilizers to our agricultural crops. We have created a system much like a huge tanker ship on autopilot. It is hard to stop, takes time to change course, and has no one to make the quick decisions required to avoid collision.

The drive towards energy efficiency only started in earnest after the first petroleum crisis in 1974. The Club of Rome had warned about the vicious cycle of population explosion, increased industrial output, rising energy demand, and excessive pollution. Yet nearly all the current alternatives to fossil fuel have major drawbacks. None are inspired by how natural systems have resolved the issue of energy security through millions of years. Worse, most of the options being considered make no economic sense. Ultimately we must go beyond temporary and intermediate options such as nuclear, photovoltaic, hydrogen, and wind power, and embrace solutions proven in ecosystems that continuously renew and refresh air and water.

Nations that have opted for nuclear power as their back-up energy source have committed their citizens to cover the risks, often without asking permission. Nuclear proponents should ask the world's leading insurance companies if they are prepared to cover the risks without a taxpayer-funded guarantee. What they will discover is that no insurer is willing to write a policy for a nuclear energy site unless the government agrees to accept full risk, forever! This generates neither jobs nor value.

RETHINKING DEMAND-SIDE ENERGY POLICIES

In nature, most species meet their basic needs using the resources available to them. How can we model this for our energy generation and consumption? If we consider how natural systems efficiently generate energy, as they have successfully done for millions of years, we might discover the means to cut demand by a factor of 10 or even 20 while offering greater accessibility. The idea emerges of a consumption system that requires much less external energy, that significantly reduces the need for mining, and that dramatically cuts the pollution from carbon dioxide, methane, and nitrous oxide. The new business model we envision will actually undo some of the collateral damage that has been tacitly tolerated. This is the new approach to demand-side management: intervention on the supply side. If we make better use of what is available, if we retool to achieve greater efficiency, if we learn how to produce sustainably, it will mean that we have learned physics. We will at last be achieving best use of our physical universe. Replacing something with nothing, and reusing waste as raw material, means we need less, and have more.

Over time every species has adapted to refine and conserve the energy it needs to naturally heat, cool, transport, or transform. Bottlenose dolphins and whales know how to reduce drag, bluefin tuna know how to conserve heat. The boxfish inspires car design with its superb efficiency. Antifreeze is naturally made by yellow mealworm beetles; the abalone produces ceramics in cold water. We can include the cold light made by squid, the hibernation chemistry of bears, solid-state energy produced by lichens, frictionless sliding accomplished by the Arabian sand lizard, water harvesting by desert beetles, and the heating and cooling systems perfected by termites. Each adaptation convincingly demonstrates that species can evolve ways to achieve maximal energy efficiency. When the contributions of each are woven into ecosystems that cascade nutrients and energy, we cannot but be in awe of their elegance and precision. Energy is never an objective on its own, it is a means to an end. Most of the time energy brings food and water, creates housing, facilitates transport (to get food or mates) and promotes health. Ecosystems generate energy far more efficiently than our manufactured approaches. Nature teaches us that replacing "something" with "nothing" can bring us the surprising solutions we need for sustainability, and create the industries of the future.

That is the concept: replace something with nothing, or with something so tiny and different, that it has no resemblance at all to the system replaced. This is a radically different way to solve our energy problems. It also underscores the business model shift that is required to reduce our dependency on oil and the mined materials that are refined by burning additional fossil fuels.

Recall Jorge Reynolds' CoroPatch, which monitors temperature, heartbeat, blood sugar levels, and heart function continuously without the need for cables or batteries. It saves money and provides more real-time data. The same technology could be used to channel electric current from healthy energy-conducting tissue to damaged tissue, replacing the pacemaker. Ultimately, it may lead us to the point where all batteries and wires could be eliminated, a truly massive savings of materials and energy. The billions of small batteries manufactured and ultimately discarded today rely on high performance metals; those metals would no longer be mined.

Recall Fritz Vollrath's silk nano-engineering. Where designer polymers – plastics – have replaced metals over the past 50 years, they have increased demand for petroleum, the raw material for these plastics. Here again is the opportunity to use benchmarked, tested, developed technology that mirrors nature's methods and 40 centuries of farmers' wisdom. Replacing titanium with silk would realize a dramatic reduction in the demand for steel and high performance metals, as well as reduce the need for mining and energy consumption. Chelating bacteria are also being researched that can meet demand by recovering metals from end-of-life batteries. Instead of employing smelters that evaporate metals, chelation recovery is done at ambient temperature, using less energy.

Recall Bruce Roser's innovation using natural processes to stabilize temperature-dependent pharmaceutical products that would otherwise perish. Eliminate the need for vaccine refrigeration and we can shave $300 million dollars off the cost of heath care delivery in developing nations. Such a portfolio of "replacing something with nothing" technologies, applied to our health care delivery system and our food production systems, will further reduce energy consumption. The energy savings would be truly massive, counted not just in what would be preserved but also by what would be reused.

Recall Curt Hallberg's vortex technology. The greatest and most reliable source of energy on Earth comes from gravity. We cannot neglect the vast opportunities offered by a force that works 24 hours a day, not merely when there is sunlight. Just about every living species has adapted to this very predictable force, and uses it to optimally meet its needs. A vortex is reliably generated by gravity, and has the potential to provide potable water with a minimal expense of energy. The swirling force of the vortex, used in applications that would remove bacteria and air from water, would eliminate the need for bactericides and cut energy consumption.

UNLOCKING NEW ENERGY OPTIONS

It is curious that what we often describe as invention is merely what the ecosystems of our living Earth have been doing for countless eons. When Thomas Edison created the first light bulbs, his original filament was bamboo, rich in naturally occurring iron. A hundred years later, these original light bulbs still work. However, contrary to common misconception, Edison did not invent electricity. It has been used in cells for billions of years. Minute differences in pH (potential hydrogen) on opposite sides of a cell membrane generate minuscule currents, often too small to measure. Electric current in natural systems never relies on mined and smelted metals, yet achieves conductivity with practically no resistance. Energy that flows through concentrated metals in a battery requires mining and generates massive pollution both in processing and post-consumption. Bamboo and whales are two species that have much to teach us about electricity and conductivity.

Nature draws on six main sources of electricity: heat, light, friction, pressure, magnetism, and biochemistry. Magnetism contributes the largest portion of electrical production worldwide. Power generators, whether hydroelectric, coal, oil, methane gas, or nuclear, all use magnetism as the actual means of electrical generation. Light acting on solar panels is slowly making headway but at high cost. Electricity is generated by spinning a coil within a magnetic field. Smaller less powerful electrical current can be generated directly by heat, pressure, and friction. Chemical reaction in the form of batteries is both the oldest means of producing electrical current and has had the greatest impact on our modern way of life. Biochemistry is a major source of bodily electric current and the supply basically comes along with the nutrient intake of the particular species – yet it is given no major industrial attention. The biochemical system as perfected by the electric fish is a marvel of engineering, not the least in its use of insulation.

Natural systems do not rely on any of the extreme methods that humanity has devised. In nature, fire and incineration are the exception rather than the rule. Even a 50% dry matter content is not handled by burning. Humans easily resort to burning everything considered waste, even water. It is a policy dominant in agriculture, in industry, and in municipal refuse disposal. Whenever we do not know what to do with something, we burn it. Lately experts have invented the argument that pyrolysis (chemical decomposition by heating) recovers the energy embedded in complex materials. There are even companies promoting the burning of water! Surprisingly, after funding years of study, Nestlé – the largest instant coffee processing company in the world – concluded that burning coffee waste (composed of over 80% water) was the best environmental option!

The exercise of observing natural sources of energy is inspiring. Though we may fully comprehend the law of gravity, few of us pause to question how the constituents that become apples – before these acquire form and submit themselves to the law of gravity – first defy it. It is this fresh look at the forces at work in ecosystems that provides the right state of mind to search for lasting solutions to our energy predicament.

How does the coconut fill with water? There is no pump, neither does it absorb rainwater. How do trees erect their massive structures? Where does osmosis in plants derive the power to trump gravitational forces, pushing nutrient-filled sap upward through their capillary network? Of course, there is interplay with surface tension and the powerful draw of the moon. It is responsible for tidal ebb and flow, another steadily predictable force in the physics of our universe. There are many forces exploited by natural systems, in great detail and at minute levels, giving all manner of life the energetic resources they have uniquely developed for their needs. This stands in stark contrast with the industrial solutions we have invented and financed. Modern solutions seem straightforward, yet their inherent inefficiencies are vast compared to clusters of natural energy sources. This is why we waste so much energy, and this is why we now ask, "Where are the real opportunities?"

ELECTRICITY FROM pH

While humans debate the values of nuclear, solar, coal, wind and photovoltaic generation, natural systems cascade their energy requirements among all contributors based on differences in pH. A tree generates electric currents from the difference between the pH of the soil and the tree. Potential hydrogen is an important factor in the natural energy equation because it controls the speed of biochemical reactions. It does this by controlling the intensity of enzyme activity, as well as the speed that electricity moves through our bodies. A higher pH means a substance or solution has greater alkalinity and a greater electrical resistance. Therefore, electricity travels slower with a higher pH. If something is acidic (lower pH), the current runs faster. A car battery is acidic. On cold days, a properly acidic battery quickly starts your car. Biochemically, what is alkaline is slow. Compare the lead-acid car battery to an alkaline flashlight battery. The flashlight battery discharges more slowly. Natural systems use this interplay constantly, without ever resorting to lead (car battery) or lithium (flashlight battery). In living species, membranes are the gates for these flows. Sometimes membranes let electrons pass rapidly, sometimes slowly; it is the management of the differential in pH levels that determines the current.

ELECTRICITY FROM TEMPERATURE DIFFERENTIAL

Thermoelectricity is the conversion of temperature differential to electricity. In our new energy model, electronic equipment could draw power from the warmth of the human body. In Germany, the Fraunhofer Institute for Physical Measurement Techniques has developed a way of harnessing electricity from natural body heat. Imagine! The difference between the temperature of the human body and its surrounding hot or cold environment is enough to generate electricity. Normally, a difference of several tens of degrees is considered necessary to generate enough electricity to nominally power electronic equipment, but the differences between the body's surface temperature and its immediate environment is only a few degrees. "Only low voltages can be produced from differences like these," explains Peter Spies, project manager at the Fraunhofer Institute. This ambient body heat differential capture device delivers roughly 200 millivolts. Electronic devices require at least one or two volts; an LED light will shine with about one volt.

Yet the Fraunhofer Institute engineers have found a solution. Instead of searching for ways to create more power – the standard way industry thinks – the Fraunhofer Institute engineers cleverly created circuits needing less energy – just 200 millivolts. They have built entire electronic systems that require neither an internal battery nor a connection to the grid. The system draws energy from body heat alone. Peter Spies is confident that in the future, when further improvements have been made to the switching systems, a temperature difference of only 0.5° will be sufficient to generate enough electricity to power a cell phone. This is exactly how natural systems evolved, with ever smaller currents achieving ever more until everything they needed was accomplished without waiting for a massive surge such as a lighting strike to make things happen. The first potential application, the nano-channel pacemaker inspired by Jorge Reynolds' work with whales, was described earlier. Peter Spies' breakthrough allows us to seriously consider how to liberate ourselves from the burden of the battery, metals, mining, and the massive energy required in commercial manufacture to produce a consumer product that will shortly occupy a landfill. In a Blue Economy, many instruments could be reconfigured to work without power from a battery or a wall socket. Nature offers endless inspiration.

Seiko, the Japanese watchmaker, marketed 500 units of the first watch powered by body temperature in 1999. Once fully charged, it operated for ten months. It became one of the most sought-after watches ever made. The power-generating capacity depends on the air temperature and individual differences of body temperature. When worn on the wrist, the watch absorbs heat through the back case and dissipates it from the front of the watch, generating power with its thermal converter. As the difference between the air temperature and the surface temperature increases, the power generation increases. As the difference decreases, the power generation also decreases. Ideally this is the way we will be working with energy in the future.

ELECTRICITY FROM GRAVITY AND PRESSURE

Pressure, or technically speaking, piezoelectricity, is another abundant natural source of electricity. "Piezo" is a root word from Greek that means "stress." The main source of compression is of course the pressure of gravity. The weight of a tree can generate electricity from the gravitational stress on rocks in the soil. As a source of energy, stress or pressure works most efficiently with materials that have a crystalline structure. In the past, obvious resources like quartz and diamonds were utilized. Rochelle salt (made from sodium bicarbonate and potassium bitartrate) was the first material used to demonstrate piezoelectric generation. Notably, the molecular composition of salt consists of potassium and sodium, the two key biochemical components powering our heartbeat. Recent insights into piezoelectrical generation added common products like cane sugar, dry bones, silk, and even wood. As cutting edge research explores yet uncharted paths, more sources of piezoelectricity will be discovered.

Whereas industrial uses are still undeveloped in much of the world, Japanese industry has given the commercial applications of piezoelectricity a vote of confidence. Numerous applications have nestled themselves into our daily lives without us ever realizing that they operate with energy from pressure. The original television remote controls used quartz technology to convert a button pressure into an electric current. The echo-location device in cars is also based on this energy source, as is the engine that powers the autofocus of reflex cameras. Simple pressure on the small lever of a cigarette lighter is enough to create an electric spark to light the fuel. Robert Bosch, the German car parts maker, developed the first piezoelectric fuel injection system. This is one of the factors that made the Volkswagen Jetta a very fuel efficient car. It outperforms the Toyota Prius, which gained fame in the USA merely by generating electric power from braking and recovering waste power from burning gasoline.

As our understanding of piezoelectricity broadens, a new vision emerges for the design of buildings that could produce electricity using the pressure the structure exerts upon the floor. A pilot project is under way in Torino, Italy, the city voted the 2008 Design Capital of the World. Quartz crystals are ubiquitous in the European Alps, and could be placed under pillars on each floor of a building, generating electrical power exactly where it was most needed. In fact, this application is a direct conversion of the power of gravity. The pressure exerted by the structure is easily calculated based on gravitational force. The potential is huge because the immense weight of a building pressuring crystals could generate several megavolts, certainly enough to power at least the building's elevator.

Gravity is our best hope for moving our societies in general and our buildings in particular towards sustainability. Using the electrical potential of pressure is the means to realize a completely different vision of energy-emancipated houses and buildings. Recall the description of how a design based on the same principles as the Namibian beetle's water collection method could produce water on a roof and how a vortex would clean that water as gravity pulled it from floor to floor. To this we can add electricity generated not from thin-film solar cells that power carbon fibers, but from the structure's gravitational force generating thousands of volts of piezoelectricity. Let our engineers focus on achieving this vision!

These energy insights offer ways that could draw down or eliminate the explosive demand for small batteries for hearing aids, toys, mobile and miniature devices, and cell phones. Where venture capitalists have invested billions in funding research for less polluting "disposable" batteries, the real investment return will be in tapping energy sources that integrate harmoniously with nature and eliminate dependency on metal extraction.

Another potential source of piezoelectricity is vibration, in particular the vibrations we call "sound." Although it is a level of sound that humans do not perceive as such, scientists have long known that seismic communication is common in small animals, including spiders, scorpions, insects, and a few vertebrate species, such as white-lipped frogs, kangaroo rats, and golden moles. Seismic sensitivity has been observed in elephant seals – huge marine mammals. Testimonials concerning elephants clearly sensing an upcoming tsunami, breaking their chains, and running to safety, drew scientists' attention. In 1997, Caitlin O'Connell-Rodwell, a research associate at the Stanford University School of Medicine, discovered that elephants can communicate over long distances with low-pitched sounds that are barely audible to humans. She charted a bold new research direction by proposing that low-frequency elephant calls generate powerful vibrations in the ground – seismic signals that elephants can feel, and even interpret, via their sensitive trunks, knees, and feet. According to O'Connell-Rodwell, the elephants communicate through the ground, and are able to discriminate very subtle vibrations through their feet.

She has conducted observations of elephant herds at the Etosha National Park in Namibia, and is applying the data collected on animal seismic sensitivity to the problem of hearing loss in humans. People with hearing impairments often develop the capacity for much greater tactile sensitivity in the auditory cortex of their brain than do people with normal hearing. *"We want to investigate the possibility that newborns with severe hearing loss could have their hearing improved by exposure to vibrational stimulation shortly after birth,"* states O'Connell-Rodwell. Elephants and hearing aids are both stimulated by sensing vibrations. Here again is one of the basic principles of physics at work – vibrations – helping to meet the changing needs of a species – creating cells in the brain to compensate for hearing impairment and sensitizing a nervous system to vibrations through hands or feet.

The most promising version of a piezoelectric power source is where the pressure created by a voice (yes! even sound creates pressure!) generates electricity. If the piezoelectric unit that converts sound pressure to electricity were in contact with your skin, both piezoelectricity and thermal electricity could power your phone. This means the more you talk the longer you can call. We might further imagine the look and design of a hearing aid powered by the wearer's voice to which it connects, supplemented by electricity powered by body temperature. Combining these proven power sources would quickly make the lithium battery and solar cell charger obsolete. They would establish the basis for a wide array of new energy applications.

Energy from Movement (Kinetic Energy)

Another variation of pressure is the kinetic energy generated by movement. Again the watch industry has taken the lead on this technology. Rolex commercialized the first gravity-operated watch in 1931. It contained a small semi-circular metal device that wound the watch simply by freely moving. More recently Seiko has introduced hundreds of variations on this theme and uses it as one of its main watch designs.

While this use of energy from movement has found a favorable market, how biological systems use kinetic energy elicits our greater curiosity. Flowing blood has mass and velocity, thus it has kinetic energy. The flow of blood through our vessels would be a simple resource that could be utilized immediately. Furthermore, as the blood flows inside a vein or artery, pressure exerted against the walls of the vessel can also generate piezoelectric energy. The total energy of blood flowing within our vessels is the sum of the energies from movement and pressure. Experts might argue that such minute amounts of energy are insufficient to make a dent in the world's demand for electricity. We are reminded of the Dutch proverb, *"Wie het kleine niet deert is het grote niet weerd"* – if you do not appreciate the small, you do not deserve the large. Surely advances in nanotechnology will find a way to convert these two pressures to electricity.

Even as limited funding has been made available for solar research and massive amounts of venture capital are invested in developing new types of batteries, research and development of pressure- and temperature-driven electrical generation has received no support from governments, private investors, or venture capitalists. Investors seem uninterested in exploring ideas for renewable energy sources that do not require heavy metals and energy storage. The Max Planck and Frauenhofer Research Institutes are pioneering the field of renewable energy beyond the mainstream. There are as well innovators like Alan Heeger, who discovered that thin-film polymers are highly electrically conductive and can replace batteries on just about everything; and Michael Graetzel, who is pioneering ideas to produce electricity the way a leaf achieves photosynthesis.

As the February 2008 article in the *Harvard Business Review* noted, were we to cover the Golden Gate Bridge with thin-film solar cells, not only would it eliminate the necessity of anti-corrosion chemical applications, it would generate enough electricity to power much of local municipal requirements. Here again is a multi-tiered approach that takes advantage of an economy of physics and natural temperature variations to capture electricity (revenue from renewable energy) and eliminate chemical use (anti-corrosion application cost). Such approaches move us closer to zero-waste models.

Physicists and farmers alike easily recognize the power of pressure and temperature. Yet these forces are neglected in our modern debates about energy efficiency. It is for this reason that innovative energy sources open a vast trove of entrepreneurial opportunities. These technological options permit generating small amounts of energy with limited investment. Potential applications are wide open and new markets are accessed everywhere and all the time. Even greater opportunity is open to those who bundle multiple technologies just as natural systems do, providing a reliable energy system that consistently performs with what is locally available. At this critical juncture, instead of losing focus in a debate over oil or nuclear sources, exploring innovative energy sources is a quest that should fully engage us.

CO_2 AS A SOURCE OF ENERGY

It is impossible to conclude a chapter on innovations in energy without discussing the societal potential of CO_2. While out-of-control CO_2 emissions are roundly excoriated for contributing to climate change, we need to consider the potential of CO_2 as a valuable input to our industrial society, helping to meet basic needs. Oxygen was originally a toxin that became a pre-condition to all life. In the same sense, if we turn our mental switch from "problem" to "opportunity," CO_2 could well become a major contributor to a sustainable society. "How?" you may ask. One answer lies with algae.

Having lived on Earth for a billion years, algae are among the earliest of photosynthetic organisms. These single-celled species were the first to develop a nucleus and to carry the memory of life known as DNA. Algae require only CO_2, water, nutrients, and sunlight to produce their own food and chemical energy through photosynthesis. Oxygen, the by-product of this photosynthesis, is abundantly released into the air and into the waters of the world's lakes, oceans, and rivers. Algae are not plants, belonging rather to the kingdom of protoctista. They are tremendously efficient at capturing the power of light, and consequently are the fastest-growing species on the planet. They grow ten times faster than sugar cane and compete with bacteria in output and proliferation. Managing algal proliferation would be like needing to mow your lawn three times a day, instead of only once every other week.

This capacity for growth renders algae an important contributor to managing climate change. Its virtues are that it gives off oxygen as it grows, it is high in oil content, and it contains high nutrient levels. The University of Minnesota Center for Biorefining has estimated that algae produce 5,000 gallons of oil per acre per year. The Brazilian team directed by Jorge Alberto Vieira Costa handily cultivates spirulina at low cost, generating 2,000 gallons of oil per acre per year. By comparison, corn yields 18 gallons, soybeans produce 48 gallons, and palm trees yield 635 gallons per acre per year. This is a result that is hard to dismiss. One of algae's other great virtues is that unlike corn-based ethanol, many strains can be grown in salt water on marginal land and can even take up carbon emissions from coal-fired power stations.

All oil and gas extraction processes generate brackish water, an unwanted waste product. The water is often left in retention basins that leach over time into surrounding soil, rendering the land toxic and infertile for centuries. Because warm water affects the habitat of aquatic life in rivers and oceans, coal-fired power stations also have retention basins for cooling water prior to discharge. These retention basins have been mandated by law, ostensibly to mitigate collateral damage to the environment. It takes only a little imagination to see that algae could be profitably farmed in these basins, thereby converting an unproductive waste receptacle into a system that attenuates CO_2, replenishes oxygen, and produces low-cost and renewable biofuel. Depending on the type of algae farmed, up to one third is lipids, oils from which fuels derive. What we envision is one more simple yet effective way to reduce our legacy of environmental damage by returning waste to the nutrient stream, learning how to utilize available infrastructure for productive outputs. In a Blue Economy, we will solve our current challenges by doing more with what we have. Farming algae for food and biofuel is an admirable example.

The National Renewable Energy Laboratory in Colorado undertook trials to document a portfolio of 300 protein-, carbohydrate-, and oil-rich algae that could produce biodiesel in the desert wastelands of New Mexico. In 1996 Jorge Alberto Vieira Costa from the Federal University of Rio Grande do Sul in Brazil adapted this research to help establish a project aimed at achieving food security at Mangueira Lake. Biodiesel was not the focus of his attention. The food security focus came from the needs of rice farmers in Southern Brazil who were challenged to compete on the world market without fertilizer subsidies. Joining Vieira Costa in his algae project was Professor Lucio Brusch da Fraga, a physicist by training but with a special degree in quality management.

It was a remarkable partnership. Mangueira Lake is one of the most alkaline lakes in the world; a far cry from qualifying as an environmental asset. Vieira Costa and Brusch da Fraga set out to demonstrate that it is possible to farm algae everywhere, including temperate climate zones like Southern Brazil. Once they mastered the production of algae around rice paddies in Vittoria do Palmar, on the southern tip of Brazil bordering Uruguay, they harvested the algae. It contained a high concentrate of micronutrients – what in the

US is called "super blue-green algae." They distributed this nutritional food source to the local underserved population around the city of Rio Grande. The social and medical delivery services, the schools, and the media lauded their success in alleviating hunger and malnutrition. Following this, they quickly realized that algae production in retention basins could accomplish more than food security. An extension of the program was explored: algae for biodiesel.

Even though Brazil only has five coal-fired power stations, compared to 3,000 in the US, they were able to run a series of industrial trials using coal-fired CO_2 exhaust in combination with algae farming to produce biofuel. Building from the ground up, Vieira Costa initiated a process similar to the Brazilian development economics that earned international acclaim for producing ethanol from sugar cane. Instead of rushing into business, Professor Vieira Costa established a research institute that undertook scientific inquiry into the typical ecosystem conditions found in Southern Brazil. He recruited a group of eager students who were progressing through undergraduate, masters, and ultimately doctoral degrees. From this institute came a strong portfolio of patents.

Vieira Costa and his team went from strength to strength, working with local biodiversity, local ecosystems, and local field experience. Their projects using Lagoa Mangueira and Laguna Morin as huge natural retention basins for algae farming have provided experience on how to evolve from the micro scale of a rice paddy to the industrial scale of retention basins at energy generation facilities. In essence, what we see is physics supporting biology. The residues left after extracting food, biodiesel, and esters (the latter for polymers usable for cosmetics) from the algae can be converted to ethanol. Thus, what we see is a substantial increase in productivity when conjoined with other complementary technologies.

Other opportunities for harvesting CO_2 are tremendous. Research has looked for inspiration in nature and the Brazilian team is not alone. Since 1998, CO_2 Solutions, the Canadian company introduced earlier, has produced standardized enzymes that fix CO_2 so it can be reprocessed into industrial quality carbonic gases and even into calcium carbonate for construction. They have proven their model on a semi-industrial scale. A research team headed by May-Britt Hägg from the Norwegian University of Science and Technology in Oslo studied how to purify gases and how to capture CO_2 just as our lungs do. Geoffrey Coates of Cornell University has developed the technology to convert both carbon dioxide and carbon monoxide into plastics and marketable chemicals by isolating the enzyme that converts CO_2 to polymers. Unilever and DSM, two Dutch companies that have placed sustainability high in their strategic options, decided to invest in this pioneering approach.

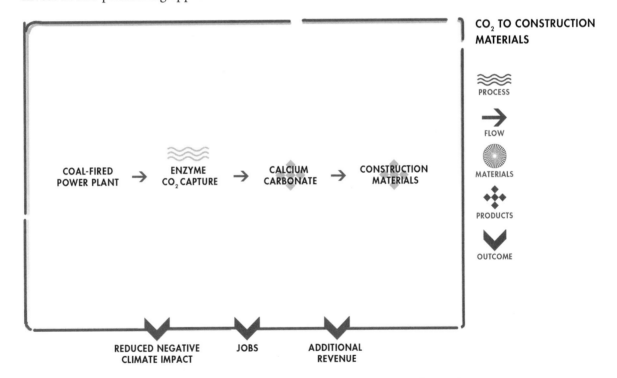

Algae and carbon dioxide live in symbiosis. Algae grow fastest with a rich supply of CO_2 and absorb this greenhouse gas like a sponge. Scaling up the industrial processes for using CO_2 to supply the algae requires blending more carbonic gases into water so that the algae are more productive, while maximizing sunlight exposure and avoiding shade. The present technique for mixing air with water is like killing a fly with a sledgehammer; the effort and force is used for a small result in output. Such inefficient processes help explain why the resultant products are too expensive. Worse, the producers typically settle for the core business model – in this case, the biofuel – and discard everything else. It is no wonder that the present techniques are not commercially viable even with petroleum prices on the rise.

If we assess how to best blend air into water, we would wisely look to nature. Natural systems never use pumps or air blowers. Nature relies on the vortex. Early estimates indicate that water pressurized with air containing up to 13% CO_2 could absorb up to four times more air if a vortex were used. Under the cap-and-trade scheme legislated for greenhouse gases, this is equal to generating four times more revenue with the same capital infrastructure simply by using gravitational forces! However, this is only the first improvement. The second is perhaps even more important.

Air bubbles containing carbonic gases can be distributed into the water and made available to the algae at a size that fits the algal membranes. Air bubbles that are ten times larger, and in some bioreactors even 10,000 times larger, than the pores in the algae's membranes, renders the process inefficient and uncompetitive. The oversized bubbles remain unused and end up as turbulence on the surface of the water. Vortex technology permits the production of micro-bubbles tailored to membrane openings. Why eat dinner with an excavator, when forks, knives, and spoons will do? The proof that the air bubbles are small in size is that the water body acquires a milky appearance. The catalyst for the whole process is water and the energy source relies on the most dependable force on Earth: gravity. These insights permit us to design sustainable and competitive solutions.

The power of algae is that the output is not limited to lipids that can be converted to biodiesel. Once the oil is extracted, what remains is high-protein micronutrient-rich matter suitable for human as well as livestock consumption, as Professor Vieira Costa imagined from the outset. His students even discovered that the residual algal membranes are composed of pure esters, and can be converted to natural polyesters. Thus we return to the concept of an entire biorefinery, or, as the Brazilian team would name it, "a whole photo-biorefinery" – one that renewably produces as long as the sun shines, gravity works, and CO_2 is emitted. Given the low risk that any of these three factors will cease to manifest, the odds are good.

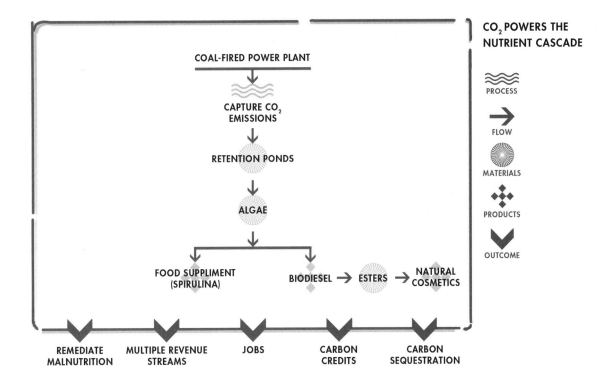

This bundle of discoveries and innovations can help mitigate climate change, while providing energy and food, using water as the catalyst. We wonder why anyone would propose "sequestering" CO_2 by pumping it deep into the oceans. Such a capital-intensive venture would earn nothing for the investors. It completely lacks economic sense, unless of course governments provide subsidies without reason. Nor would it earn profit on the sustainability ledger. "Out of sight, out of mind" is old thinking. It gives us superfund sites, overflowing landfills, recreation parks atop nuclear waste storage, and other shortsighted "protection by separation" follies that often result in irremediable loss and crippling damage.

With food and energy as the by-products to a process that transforms algae, CO_2, water, and sunlight into biofuel, what we have is an efficient symbiosis. To crown the benefits, the process generates jobs. How many jobs? The biggest CO_2 emitters are power plants and cement factories. If 10,000 power plants from the US, Europe, China, and the developing world were to apply these technologies, they would on average require 100 jobs per facility, in sum one million jobs. This would be a marriage of the old and the new, a bridge between fossil fuel, mainly coal and renewables. The investment required to build these facilities equals the cost of ten nuclear power stations at $10 billion dollars each. Would ten nuclear power stations generate a million jobs? No! How much time would it take to put these ten new nuclear facilities on line? At least a decade!

If we take a dispassionate look at the economic and social impact of one set of solutions versus another, if our debate concerns the economics, the average cost of investment, the potential jobs, and the generation of multiple benefits from health and employment from renewable fuels and natural polymers, it is clear that a nuclear power solution is unfeasible. The option of nuclear power has never been utilized by any ecosystem that promotes life. Economic and business models must now change focus to enhance life. Surely enhancing life should be the starting point of any activity humanity engages.

It is surprising that our engineers seem to ignore many potential energy sources, even though these are the real power sources for all the creatures with whom we share this planet. Discoveries for how we can respond differently to our needs for energy never seem to reach the antennae of corporate policy makers and strategists who believe that bigger is better, and who are risk-adverse even in times of plenty. To those industry professionals who would be quick to argue that no "alternative" technologies will ever power the grid, we offer the words of Maria, a young student from Curitiba, Brazil, who heard engineers say that the power generated by banana peels and egg shells would never compete with that of nuclear fission or burning coal. Maria listened patiently and respectfully to the petroleum company director, then responded, "Well, in 25 years – when I am old – I will prove you wrong." There is nothing better for a society than when the next generation is eager and motivated to make a difference.

CHAPTER ELEVEN

TRUE GOLD: MINES AS PLATFORMS OF HEALING

One generation plants the trees,
another gets the shade.

— CHINESE PROVERB

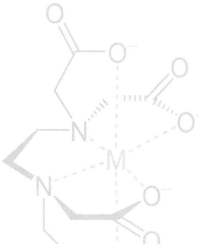

HOW TO RESTORE ERRORS OF THE PAST

Picture yourself at the end of a 45-minute ride outside Johannesburg, the industrial capital of all Africa. The desolate, moon-like landscape that now surrounds you could provide a perfect backdrop for the latest sci-fi movie. You are standing atop a mountain of mine tailings, rich in uranium and containing half a gram of gold per ton. You are imagining a straight line extending four kilometers (12,000 feet) upward into the air and sense the scope of the deepest mines on Earth, extending four kilometers beneath your feet. While we decry the environmental havoc, we must also marvel at the engineering handiwork. Deep in the Earth's crust, the natural heat reaches nearly 130° F. Imagine the expertise it took to solve the challenge of providing air and temperate conditions to 20,000 miners working as much as 4,000 meters below the surface. Ice-making machines in the belly of the Earth are used to make the working environment tolerable. Consider again, the biggest ice-making machines in the world, powered in the heated depths of the Earth to cool the air.

The question comes immediately to mind: "Could this ever be sustainable?" Could mining companies ever conduct their operations and leave the local community better off than when they arrived? Lichens are great miners, capable of extracting specific inorganic molecules like magnesium from rocks and sharing these with all other life in the ecosystem. Bacteria selectively separate metals through chelation, but mankind alone uses brute force and harsh toxins including mercury and cyanide to acquire desirable ores. Though we may lack the knowledge and skill to undo the errors of the past, it is within our ability to do better in the future. We may not currently be capable of transforming mining into a benign operation, yet we can at least design a strategy that assuages the environmental and social pain that mining inflicts.

From atop our mountain of tailings we are surveying one of humanity's most aggressive conceits. Armed with dynamite and consuming massive amounts of water and energy, mining operations extract minute concentrations of gold from deep within the Earth. The miners who toil in the shafts endure abject and barely tolerable living and working conditions, sending their meager earnings home to provide for their often far away families. No one knows how many will still be alive, much less on the job, in a decade.

Mining is a risky enterprise in more ways than one. Even with the world market price for gold reaching record levels, there is no guarantee that the extraction of this precious metal will remain profitable in the years to come, especially if all the external and remediation costs that burden the local communities surrounding the mines were fully covered from the mining companies' existing revenue streams. When gold ore reaches the surface from deep within the South African earth, it sometimes comes with a natural complement of uranium. The tailings – what is left once the ore is extracted – are dumped above ground, forming a stark line across the horizon. The magnificent view of the surroundings is clouded, not by pollution from the city nearby, but by dust released from the uranium-laced tailings. The uranium leaches into the air and the water, exposing all animate life to potentially lethal cancers. A few watchdog organizations decry this contamination and have repeatedly pressured management to find ways to abate these high levels of risk. Sadly, because shareholders prefer a steadily upward progression of capital gains, any plan or cost directed towards complete abatement does not even reach the Board.

Picture the richest concentrations of gold layered beneath huge water reserves amassed on a bed of dolomite. At an energy cost of $1.5 million dollars per day, water and air must be pumped into the shafts to provide a tolerable environment for the workers. Now, realize that the air vented from the mineshafts releases approximately 100,000 tons of methane per year. As fresh shafts are explored, the volume may even double year by year for a few decades. Apart from the impact of its effect on the atmosphere, methane is a tremendous risk factor for explosions. That is why every mining tool is expensive. They are made of copper, titanium, or beryllium because these metals do not produce sparks.

Mining entails health risks and major occupational hazards. Johannesburg – "Jo-burg," as it is known to the locals – is perhaps the only major industrial city in the world that is not located alongside a river or in a coastal zone. Rather, it is built around mining sites. The massive pumping of underground water and the diversion of a river into a 30-kilometer pipeline severed local agriculture's lifeline to water. What was once the vegetable garden for the Jo-burg megalopolis is now scarred by mine shafts and miles of tailings. The water that is available has questionable levels of pollution that will render the soil unsuitable for food production for at least a generation, if not more. Any form of farming, especially cattle ranching in and around the mines, cannot be recommended.

Geologists and biologists are learning more and more about the ways toxins are assimilated by water, air, and soil. Broadleaf plants accumulate toxins in their tissues. This creates health risks, particularly the irradiation and contamination of the animal life that consumes them for food. Because there is scant research and monitoring data, the statistics are unclear. Neither management nor government can obtain a full picture or a complete understanding of this complex process. As a result, anecdotal stories and brief scientific reports performed by outsiders are often based on little more than speculation.

These environmental and social realities are not the only reasons mines are under stress. While the world market price for gold has never been higher, the cost of operation likewise has never been so exorbitant. To make matters worse, the South African electricity grid is heavily stressed: ESKOM has informed the mining industry of its inability to meet demand due to a lack of investment in capacity expansion. Thus, rising energy prices for pumping air and water are exacerbated by an uncertain electrical supply. This forces the mines to make huge investments in back-up diesel generators to secure the safety of the underground workers and provide a habitable zone by cooling the horizontal shafts to a depth of several thousand meters. Simultaneously, energy is required to move ore from 12,000 feet below to the surface for processing. When the electricity is unavailable, the mines are forced to close for a day or two of the week.

A thorough inventory of mining's adverse impacts would necessarily include the ore-processing rubble gathered in mounds on porous soil, the uranium-filled dust clouds rising from the tailings, the desertification of land from the continuous pumping of water, the sink holes caused by the same process, and the accumulation of uranium in the waterways and soil. Nor could we exclude the social havoc associated with mine-site hostels for workers that are an open invitation to HIV infection and other sexually transmitted diseases. After visiting these deep mines and seeing the reality of mining life first hand, it would be easy to despair at the extent of the societal and environmental degradation that is everywhere evident. Yet to find solutions it helps to have a positive mindset, to learn creatively, and to act decisively. In South Africa, truth and reconciliation surmounted tremendous difficulties. The way forward is not about culpability, it is about acknowledging shortcomings and designing a new business model that can simultaneously please stockholders and remediate local conditions. Advocates such as Mark Cutifani, the CEO of Anglo Gold Ashanti, are committed to pioneering a new way forward.

BINDING THE WOUND TO HEAL

Operating a mine should be considered an intervention into the Earth's crust comparable to a surgical intervention in a human body. Even if we consider it a necessary procedure, we must bind the wound to heal. The past two centuries of mining has left many tragic legacies, some documented and some still to surface because disclosure and restoration take time. The advent of improved instrumentation and better understanding means that less invasive and more sustainable practices can and should be introduced.

From a core business management point of view, an economic crisis requires cost reductions at every level. Realizing the limitations of continuing business as usual, management must search for ways to lower expenditures. However, if we were to redefine these core business principles, if we were to turn our thinking around, we could identify applicable technologies and energy-saving solutions that would lower costs and strengthen cash flow at the same time. Innovation can generate new revenues and create social capital that will support the local communities even after the mines are exhausted. If we can save more, generate more income, remediate environmental damage, and create more value while investing less, everyone benefits. All that is required is that we think outside the box of current practice.

A METHOD FOR METHANE CAPTURE

Quite a few mines are massive producers of methane, a greenhouse gas that dramatically contributes to climate change. The volume of methane from one mine shaft is the energy equivalent of at least 30 megawatts of electrical power. Currently, it is pumped from the mine shafts into the atmosphere because it is erroneously thought that no technology can capture it at concentrations below 0.2 percent. If this "waste" were captured, it could generate the power that the mine must otherwise buy at 18 cents or more per kilowatt hour. Proprietary access to this naturally-occurring gas could augment a large portion of the electricity supplied by ESKOM, the highly stressed South African national energy supplier. Although nearly all methane gas from mines is lost into the atmosphere, signatories to the Kyoto Protocol can be compensated with carbon credits for methane capture or even just flaring methane at the source. The first carbon credits for flaring mine methane were issued to the South African Beatrix Mine owned by Gold Fields.

Methane is approximately 21 times more polluting than CO_2 and carbon credits are expressed in CO_2 equivalents. As such, these credits could generate $10 million dollars in four years, with very little investment and significant improvement of the working conditions for those underground. The payback period on the cost of installing pipes to capture and channel the methane is less than a year. Clearly, climate change protocols need not hurt your competitive market strength.

Carbon credits could be a quick addition to the bottom line that could tilt a marginally producing shaft toward profitability while contributing to social stability in the region and justifying additional safety investments within an open market. However, flaring of methane gas for carbon credits in a country that is facing energy blackouts seems an anachronism that merely scratches the surface potential. The mines have more to offer the energy market than just carbon credits.

Even at an average concentration of just 0.1%, the total volume of methane released is minimally estimated at three million tons per year. For all the shafts near Johannesburg it could be upward of six million tons for each mine over the next 25 years. Present air purification technologies require a concentration greater than half a percent. At least a few shafts have been identified that meet this concentration level. In fact, the concentration of methane in the air escaping the mine is often kept below 0.5 percent by blending higher and lower concentrations. Creative engineers will surely go beyond today's market standard to make air purification effective even for much lower concentrations of methane.

A methane concentration averaging one-tenth of a percent would make air purification potentially only marginally profitable. Even though the Clean Development Mechanism (CDM) under the Kyoto Protocol exists to create additional cash flow to finance such less attractive investments, a combined program that put in place vortex technology, wind turbines, heat exchangers, and potable water accessibility would provide the revenue strength necessary to carry over the air purification strategy.

MEGTEC Systems AB, a Swedish supplier of air purification technology, has installed systems that efficiently abate methane concentrations as low as 0.1% without adding energy to the oxidation process. In 1983 Australia's West Cliff Collier Power Plant constructed a 1.2 megawatt power generation plant, and a second larger 12.5 megawatt plant in 1985, to utilize the methane gas content in the ventilation air. At the heart of the technology is a system capable of efficiently oxidizing the extremely low methane content, while handling extremely large volumes of air – a combination typical of mine ventilation. It is important to take into account that the methane concentration is below one percent and the project only utilizes one fifth of the entire air volume from the shaft. With the production of just six megawatts of electricity, the power plant reduces methane emissions equivalent to 200,000 tons of CO_2 per year.

This model demonstrates exactly how nature works with what is locally available, gathering what is useful for the task. Beneficial use can be made of even minute amounts of methane. If the giant mines outside Johannesburg were to utilize the MEGTEC or similar technology to capture the escaping methane, they could potentially operate a 90 to 180 megawatt facility. This is as much as 50% of their present energy needs. Even though these are merely estimates, the basic numbers are attractive enough to warrant follow-up. Many mines could pursue this strategy, yet none do since management simply cannot break through their core business blockade. Surely someone will see the sense in capturing the methane in exchange for carbon credits, profitability, and planetary survival. It's another great opportunity waiting to be seized.

CONVERTING WATER FROM COST TO REVENUE

Pure, clear fissure water, devoid of bacteria and exposed to the highly positive energy emitted by gold, is drawn from cracks in the deep. It is currently used to dilute highly polluted processing water to meet wastewater quality standards. We are hard put to think of any more wasteful use of pure water: to blend it with toxic water so that "on average" it meets minimum safety standards? South Africa is suffering from a critical water shortage on top of an energy shortage. The projections for the shortfall between demand and supply are dramatic. While water for Johannesburg is pumped at great cost through pipelines from Lesotho, gold mines like the Driefontein and Kloof siphon away 100,000 cubic meters of water every day.

Rather than diluting and polluting pure water, chelating bacteria or vortex technology could easily and inexpensively separate toxins and impurities from the processed water to meet discharge standards. Spending R10 million rand per day ($500 million dollars per year) to pump water out of the mines and render it undrinkable is not in tune with the needs of a society suffering from a dramatic water shortage. What does make sense is shifting from the culture of cost-cutting to the mindset of generating income by responding to market demand and community needs. This equates to building social capital, and this is what the population that was oppressed by Apartheid deserves from business and policy makers alike. Not only could the water needs of the local population be met, mining companies could operate a subsidiary enterprise providing bottled drinking water.

Because the presence of uranium would be hazardous, chelation technology would be necessary to achieve the safe removal of such elements from the bottled product. In addition, mine management could easily identify those fissures having no taint of uranium and thus tap the water sources offering maximum potential revenue. The creation of a bottled water industry that at the outset sells 100,000 bottles a day is financially attractive. With just a touch of imagination, we can expand that to many other levels of profit, creating a business that provides naturally occurring high-quality drinking water for the local population, and high-end deep-earth bottled water that radiates the positive energy acquired from exposure to gold deposits. It could even include a minute health-benefiting gold flake. There are unquestionably markets for such water.

The implementation plan based on comparable experience from around the world would hardly need feasibility studies. In less that a decade, the Fiji Water Company developed from nothing to occupy a $200 million dollar high-margin niche in the US. In Hawaii, Japanese investors pump water from 600 meters deep, bottle it, and transport 200,000 bottles per day, selling for the Yen equivalent of $10 dollars per bottle in the Land of the Rising Sun. Using select distribution channels, Las Gaviotas in Colombia freely dispenses drinking water to the local population, while profiting from selling bottled water in the capital city of Bogotá.

Water management at a mine site demonstrates how a cost can become an income. Accessing fissure water as a separate, stand-alone business would incur unrecoverable investment costs to reach the water deep in the Earth's crust. On the other hand, the mines must cover these costs to operate their core business of mining gold. By offering inexpensive and safe drinking water to the local population, mining not only turns an expense into a revenue, it also turns attention from the stigma of pollution and sink holes to a demonstration of social responsibility, thereby creating a better international reputation. Even a proverbial "gold mine" can use stronger brand equity.

ELECTRIFYING SAVINGS

Mines need massive amounts of electricity to pump water and air, cool the shafts, produce ice, and transport ore. Huge electrical generation stations are located at the base of each mine. It is only common sense to explore opportunities that would save electrical costs. Perhaps this is the ideal environment for implementing Jay Harman's mathematical model, inspired by the nautilus, to increase energy efficiency by 20-30% in ventilators and mixers, or other applications in either water or air transportation. Perhaps it is also an opportunity for Curt Hallberg's vortex technology. The ice making machines necessary to moderate the high temperatures are placed in deep shafts and must cope with water containing vast amounts of dissolved air particles. Using Hallberg's gravity-based vortex technology to extract these air particles from the water would reliably reduce the energy costs by 10-15%. However, the latest research results indicate as much as 41% energy savings. Furthermore, when water and air must move up and down 4,000 meters, there is room to exploit the forces of gravity. If we consider other innovations based on nature's adaptive technologies, we could save even more energy and reduce the risk of explosions by introducing cold light such as that of fungi and squid, instead of traditional light bulbs. This would save energy and reduce the risk of explosion. In the darkest shafts of the mines, light should not be based on electricity generated with coal through the grid, or heavy fuel for the backup generators, when it could be based on simple chemistry.

POWER FROM AIRFLOWS

Just like water, airflows are by-products of the core business of mining that could easily generate additional revenue. Airflows created by a vacuum exit the mine shafts at high pressure. When a staggering 2,800 cubic meters of air are released into the atmosphere each second, we can easily comprehend how a few highly efficient windmills equipped with an anti-drag device such as that observed in whales would capture some of the power. Pumping the fresh air needed into these deep shafts generates an exhaust air stream, and the vacuum it creates could easily keep a dozen turbines constantly turning. Compared to the price South Africa's national electric company (ESKOM) must charge for electricity from the grid, the return on investment for wind-driven turbines at both the shaft inlet and the outlet exceeds 50% of initial cost. Given this comparison, it would be hard to justify the investment expenditure for back-up diesel generators.

ENERGY GENERATION FROM TEMPERATURE AND PRESSURE

The temperature differences generated by mine operations are another vast source of energy generation. These temperature extremes come from ice making, exhausting hot air, and transporting the ore from deep within the Earth. These become useful sources of energy simply by installing appropriately placed heat exchangers. Heat exchangers are nothing new. However, this technology has not found much application in mines except for the Mine Water Initiative undertaken in old coal mines in the Netherlands and Germany which now operate as district water heating. Gone are the days when electricity in South Africa was either inexpensive or even subsidized. Now the urge to embark on energy efficiencies is paramount. When we consider that nanotechnology enables us to power a cell phone with a half-degree of temperature differential, imagine what could be done with the 36° F differential found in the mines. Such an energy-generating project is already technically and commercially underway in Europe with only a three to five degree differential. More food for thought: at the depth of 4,000 meters what method might be found to convert the piezoelectric potential into a power source?

ENVIRONMENTAL REMEDIATION

The persuasive logic of carbon credits, profitability, and remediation applies to all energy sources: wind generators, heat exchangers, and methane-fueled generators. It is hard to defend leaving any stones unturned when contemplating revenue generation and cost reduction. Indeed, there are more options.

Gold Fields, the corporate proprietor of one of Jo'burg's largest gold mines, owns an astounding 175,000 acres of surrounding land. These holdings were acquired over the years from farmers who could no longer achieve reasonable productivity due to the declining availability of water. (Recall that mining operations require tremendous amounts of water, which lowers the surrounding area's water table.) Although to their credit Gold Fields utilizes some of this acreage to grow roses for commercial sale, much of the acreage could be quickly converted to biodiesel production.

South Africa has a supportive policy for biodiesel that grants producers tax exemptions. Although this is to be applauded, it also raises eyebrows since it is hard to justify planting vegetation for ethanol production when this displaces crops for human and animal consumption. A country that is struggling to feed its children needs to focus its priorities where they belong. If land that should produce food were used for biodiesel, it would increase the cost of food. This particularly affects those who live on the margins of society. Since it carries a recognized risk of uranium contamination, not all the land around the mines could be used to produce food. However it could serve perfectly well for roses and could likewise grow crops for biodiesel production.

If 50,000 acres were put into production, within two to four years it would generate 100,000 to 120,000 tons of biofuel, depending on the species selected for biofuel production. Similarly, water-guzzling invasive tree species like eucalyptus and black wattle *(Acacia auriculiformis)* could be uprooted and replaced by plants and trees that have extractable oils and that would reestablish the water table over time. To further cascade nutrients, mushrooms could be grown on the rich biomass remaining once the oils were extracted, provided there were no measurable contamination or radiation. Alternatively, or even additionally, capturing the methane biogas escaping from the spent crops could be engineered. Unemployment rates in excess of 50% of the adult population in communities around the mines could be dramatically lowered. Carbon credits alone would suffice to initially finance such an operation. Until recently no one thought Africa could generate carbon credits. If the mines were to exploit this biodiesel potential, they could set the stage for a major contribution to the reduction of greenhouse gases.

Turning a mine into a competitive operation that recovers farmland, renews biodiversity, produces biofuels, provides jobs for the community, creates energy efficiencies using available resources and innovative technologies, and supplies water for sale as well as for the needs of local communities is a business that would qualify for "brand equity." This is not a costly public relations initiative aimed at extracting community goodwill and trust. Rather, it is an approach that is part and parcel of the day-to-day management responsibility to increase cash flow by slashing expenses and improving revenues. From a manager's viewpoint, the social capital created in the process of cutting costs and generating income is just icing on the cake. Why not? If such a systems approach became part of management culture, the issues that have typically wasted management's time are no longer a stress factor but a component of efficient resource use and income generation.

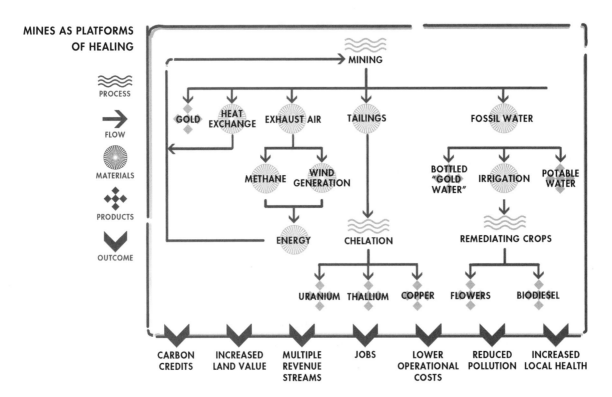

MINES AS PLATFORMS OF HEALING

PROCESS

FLOW

MATERIALS

PRODUCTS

OUTCOME

CHELATING COMPLEX ORES

Now we address the sensitive issue of uranium. Like it or not, uranium is often found in combination with gold. Thallium and copper are also standard by-products of ore processing. These are known as "complex ores." When uranium prices sank to such a low level that extraction was no longer competitive, gold mines stopped producing uranium. Revenue turned to waste and after a few decades of release into streams, uranium accumulated in the wetlands and river beds. According to some activists, this pollution crisis is reaching dramatic proportions and the related clean-up costs could quickly run into the hundreds of millions. While the science is unclear and the costs unaccounted for, companies can discard neither the growing doubt, nor the responsibility for future and potentially significant expenditures. A publicly traded company will be forced to make loss provisions the day the Board is informed of the risks. These risks must be reported to the stock exchange authorities and this immediately pressures the share price. Recall that PCB and asbestos contamination were not considered problematic in the 1960s when their usage was widespread. GE (USA) and ABB (Switzerland) recently settled 1960s-era contamination-related claims for a staggering $500 million dollars and one billion dollars respectively.

The opportunities in energy and water just described are realistic. If managers want to avoid the negative impact on their company's capitalization brought on by declining share prices on the stock exchange, they need to respond proactively to a potential crisis from uranium pollution of the local water and soil. With such a sensitive matter, analysts typically account for the risk of a future clean-up and the subsequent media hysteria by discounting the present valuation of the shares. The shares then suffer from a strong downward trend. The time to invest in innovations that can convert problems into opportunities is well before a risk filing with the stock exchange is required.

Chelating technology has been around for a few decades. This approach to isolating precious metals and toxic compounds like uranium, thallium, and lead is well proven. Chelating ligands bond with metal ions to render the metal inert. The leading provider of this process is the pioneering company Prime Separations, which brought together an expert team of engineers to apply the chelating techniques observed in bacteria. The technology developed alongside other innovative means to recover metals, even those dispersed in minute amounts, like the capacity of the wood ear mushroom (*Auricularia polytricha*) to recover copper and the ability of geraniums (*Geranium spp*) to recover lead. Their efficiency is a million-fold greater than the complex ore smelters that now process these blended ores.

Managers would do well to remember that mines exhaust the available raw materials and thus cannot operate forever. Gold deposits come to an end, as is predicted to occur within half a century. Prime Separations technology benefits the mining operations through a continuous approach to extracting gold, uranium, thallium, and whatever other elements of the periodic table can be sold in pure form. In particular the processing of uranium from both the tailings and the surrounding wetlands could be funded from cash reserves over the next decade or two. This would renew the land and the region for the next generation of economic activity, and avoid the fate of companies like GE and ABB, who had to pay their pollution bill 40 years after the fact.

The chelating technology learned from bacteria is not limited to recovering heavy metals and chromium IV. In geographical conditions where water is very scarce, such as gold mines in Venezuela and Burkina Faso, the Prime Separations know-how could become a key factor in processing ore in a closed-loop water cycle. This technology renders obsolete the need to permit and build pipelines, or to truck water from nearby rivers, or to spend massive sums of money on reverse osmosis facilities and the electricity to keep them running. For new mines that are found to have available thallium, the same technology could purify the metal for sale. Purified Thallium-203 is sold for $1,800 dollars per kilogram by the Los Alamos National Laboratory in the USA. This is real income, stemming from the continuous filtering of the tailings and sedimentation. This is real cost elimination. There will be no cleanup bill due in 40 years. What will be there is bio-regenerated land with considerable value located proximally to a large urban market. Land value was the real payoff of the Las Gaviotas project. In the case of South Africa's gold mines, we can see that augmenting land value is an appreciable way to maintain shareholder value and accrue social capital.

MINES AS BIOREFINERIES

It is an advantage that the tasks of mine management require long-term vision. There is simply no quick buck to be made when you operate a mine. The time between obtaining an exploration license, getting permission to process the ore, then selling the product is often a decade or more. The company must be prepared to invest the trust funds legally required to rehabilitate the land or to provide cash for creating a future beyond the mines. In this sense mine management is acutely aware that the future must be imagined today. Yet the availability of 400,000 acres just 45 minutes from downtown Johannesburg has more potential to benefit the shareholders than has yet been realized.

Agriculture is not the only sector that can imagine multiple cash flows through the concept of biorefineries. Mining can achieve the same benefits, merely by using what is locally available. If we imagine the reprocessing of tailings under a creative financial structure that returns the landscape to its original dramatic beauty, with uranium on its way to the market instead of accumulating in the topsoil and water, then the historic and cultural wealth of the region will be an asset. That asset may well represent the investors' assessments of the ultimate value of gold mines. No one has taken the time to value these surrounding land assets. They are not even valued in the company books of account. Land holdings are considered a cost ready to be dumped to any buyer at any price. What would you pay for land that carries the risk of uranium contamination? What is the value of that land if it is pristine and beautiful?

Sometimes it takes an outsider to show what is extraordinary on your doorstep. If a gold and uranium mine is converted over years into a sophisticated water extraction and energy generation system, combined with the public display of engineering marvels that facilitated mining at 4,200 meters deep, it becomes a potential public attraction that is likely to pay for itself. Jo-burg is one of the most vibrant cities in Africa. Considering the cultural, natural, and industrial sites classified as World Heritage Sites according to the United Nations Education and Cultural Organization (UNESCO), the gold mines, the natural environment, and its historical context certainly qualify for this international recognition.

The necessity for the mines to achieve a sustainable economic basis, combined with the national need to implement sound social and ecological policies and maintain adequate foreign exchange, have seldom been so potentially interconnected as are the possibilities at mining sites around Johannesburg. The probability of immediate and long term benefit is great. Some of the concepts presented are based on existing technologies, others are envisioned and need additional research. What is certain is that the same mines that have been criticized in the past, and that are still rightfully on the radar of governmental and non-governmental organizations today, have seldom been seen in as positive and proactive a light as we have looked at them in this chapter. They are interconnected systems, capable of contributing to society.

A mine that is a World Heritage site, that provides drinking water to the poor, that serves the top of the market with energized, gold-flaked bottled water, that generates additional revenues from carbon credits, that slashes costs by providing a major part of its own energy needs from readily available resources, that diversifies into energy and food production providing much needed jobs, that offers a future to communities that today lack the vision or even ability to dream, is a company that will garner respect, admiration, appreciation, stock value, and public praise from the very first moment it begins to deal with pollution from the past.

FINANCIAL ENGINEERING

It does not take a financial strategist to translate these opportunities into cash flow, nor a business analyst to understand the value of lower business risk compounded with improved social capital. Understanding the array of opportunities is not what is required. What is required is a shift in management culture. Attention now focused on only one major issue must be focused instead upon the interconnections that extend beyond the core business. It is this shift that is likely to be the biggest challenge. The gold mine will remain a gold mine but the multiple inputs and outputs that are so easily outsourced and framed into supply chain management must now be viewed in terms of additional cost reductions, substantial revenue improvements, long-term capital gains, improved market capitalization, reduced business risk from strong cash flow, and a flexible company ready to risk and innovate. These qualities have always characterized the market leaders who are more often than not rewarded for their foresight and vision.

Thus the way forward is based on technological benchmarks elsewhere achieved and on progressive financial engineering applied to the real and future value of all assets. A persuasive rationale based in solid science and economic feasibility awaits the decision of the management and the endorsement of the stockholders. Mining companies in Russia, China, Africa, the U.S., and Latin America can then demonstrate that while there is a regrettable history, there is also a future of hope and a presence of intention.

CHAPTER TWELVE

BUILDINGS DESIGNED
BY FLOWS

It is clear from da Vinci's notes that he saw the city
as a kind of living organism in which people,
material goods, food, water, and waste needed to move and flow
with ease for the city to remain healthy.

— FRITJOF CAPRA, *THE SCIENCE OF LEONARDO*

CREATING AN ECOSYSTEM OF THE DOMICILE

Living species seek to establish shelter, from the egg nest, to the nutshell, to the algal membrane. Everything alive creates subtle borders that delineate exterior and interior. Each creature finds its unique way to achieve inner stability, to control temperature and humidity, to store reserves, and to ensure health and survival.

In recent times the design of human shelter has undergone much transformation, though perhaps not always improvement. The physical constructs of the way we live now far exceed mere shelter. They provide the conveniences that fit our ideas of comfort and contentment. We live in an age of modernity, drifting towards *domótica*, where progress and comfort require ever greater acquisition of electronics and robotics. For most of us, the largest share of our time is passed indoors – at home, at work, at school. We spend about eight hours a day asleep. Perhaps another eight are spent at work or at school, and the remainder commuting or absorbed in household chores and activities. The design of the buildings we inhabit for two-thirds of our lives should reasonably assure health and safety. Surprisingly, the key to a healthy environment is, again, potential hydrogen, pH.

The ocean, with a pH of 8.2, is the cradle of life on Earth. Ecosystems and their life-creating powers thrive in an alkaline environment. Yet much of our environment – indoors as well as outdoors – has reached a high level of acidity. Our excessive use of fossil fuels and the massive volume of carbon dioxide pumped into the atmosphere every day render the air very acidic indeed. There is no escape anywhere in the industrialized world or in any city on the globe. Those who live in rural areas or near a coastline may be less affected. If you live in a megalopolis like New York, Los Angeles, London, Paris, Sao Paolo, New Delhi, or Johannesburg, the atmospheric pH is just above four. Remember, pH is measured on a logarithmic scale; that means that a pH measure of five is ten times higher than four and a pH measure of six is 100 times greater than four.

Consider the remarkable functioning of our digestive system. The food we ingest is taken into the stomach where the highly acidic environment quickly and safely reduces the grains, vegetables, meats, and other comestibles to their basic components. The small intestine, where the nutritive matter is absorbed and made available to the blood for transport to the organs and tissues, is also a significant component of our immune system. It requires an alkaline pH factor to optimally function. Similarly, because a bedroom is where sleep allows the body to repair and regenerate, the air should also have an alkaline pH. Starting at home, we should use our understanding of the flows of air and matter to create an environment supportive of life and health.

If you take the time to check the pH of the air in your house, you will quickly realize that the air in urban areas is acid, and usually does not get better circulating from outside to inside. Unfortunately, it typically gets worse. Interior air quality is degraded by the off-gassing of almost everything in your home or office, even if you have the privilege of living on the beach or atop a breathtaking mountain range. The overall result is simply not good. What is the use of making sure that what you drink and eat offers a healthy balance of acid and alkaline when you breathe acids all day? What is worse is that you inhale acids all night as you sleep. As we power up our Blue Economy, the outside air we breathe will become less polluted and less acidic. In the meantime, the design and construction of our buildings can be such that their interiors naturally evolve to be more alkaline.

THE SEVEN FLOWS OF BUILDING DESIGN AND LIVING SPACE

Architects, along with medical doctors, are potentially the most "connected" thinkers. Yet they too are subject to a rigid compartmentalization of knowledge. As a consequence they conclude that acidity and alkalinity are topics for chemists. Even the most environmentally progressive architect, who has successfully built a LEED Platinum Certified building, is likely unaware of the importance of maintaining the pH factor in buildings. While physics and mathematics figure prominently in the training of architects, life sciences are left to the margin. That is regrettable, since physical structures based on solid math and biology are at the foundation of health and livelihood on Earth.

When the architect receives the specifications for a new building, the volume and the surface area determine its size and functionality; for example, the number of bedrooms, the integration of a kitchen and dining room, the combination of a gymnasium and classrooms, a school solarium, or the pairing of open office space with a kitchenette. Some architects will consider the position of the sun, and propose a south-facing building in the northern hemisphere (and a north-facing building in the tropics). This is straightforward and requires neither much creative insight nor detailed scientific knowledge, or even much inspiration from ecosystems.

Physical buildings cannot be viewed as merely static esthetic structures that meet functional goals and comply with local regulations. Moreover, buildings that are constructed with renewable resources and targeted energy savings are only the first step in redesign. There are seven important flows that must be brought into the design concept: air, light, water, energy, sound, matter, and occupants. Each of these flows influences the dynamic balance that provides the life-promoting conditions that allow us to survive and to thrive. Life enhancement is the driving force behind all these flows. Survival and health must always be the priority, particularly because we spend so much of our time inside. The composition and functionality of our domicile determines our health, our comfort, and our repose.

Air includes matter such as dust. Matter includes the food we eat and what is discarded, while water includes what we drink and what we use to wash away waste. Materials cover the flow of goods that contribute to the functionality and efficiency of our personal environment. These are all important components of our lifestyle and contributors to our comfort levels. Yet, it seems that we design our homes without considering such flows. Accumulated dust can make us ill. Biomass left to rot is a health hazard, and truly a waste. The water in our sewers transports effluent to holding tanks where it is chemically treated to attack accumulated bacteria. The trash generated by our packaging-obsessed consumer society bursts from innumerable landfills outside the scope of our vision or consciousness. These are all literally dead ends. Consider that a flow implies an unimpeded continuity of movement. If we were to enhance rather than obstruct our household flows we could take advantage of a wide portfolio of innovations that would contribute to comfortable and healthful living conditions, reduce costs, and save energy.

Natural systems always design for and with flow. Nothing evolves statically but rather by interaction with everything around it. Insight into this fundamental design principle will reveal connections among disparate phenomena and objectives. This in turn leads to a bundle of solutions that natural systems have adapted and modeled for millions of years. Hence our challenge becomes how to interweave a set of parameters so that we can design with these flows. In short, our challenge is to emulate ecosystems that make use of physics and locally available materials to meet basic needs and to promote greater efficiency and diversity. As we set these goals, and as architects and home designers prioritize health and comfort, then it will then be possible – actually quite easy – to achieve a better balance and more open flows.

To begin, we need to know how to design esthetically pleasing physical spaces that maintain a proper interior pH balance and allow for interplay of the seven flows. If we successfully create a design model that encompasses all these flows, then we will experience a completely new comfort level. The structure would be in tune with its environment, and would thus achieve ideal sustainability with neither extraordinary effort nor higher expense. Such buildings would be more than green; they would reflect more than energy savings from a grass roof or from certified sustainable forestry lumber. As a first priority, these structures would contribute to health and self-sufficiency by drawing from locally available resources and energy sources. They would conform to a healthy and dynamic balance between humanity and the ecosystems on which we depend for the free supply of common benefits like water and air. Such spaces would enhance life.

The first architect to realize the importance of flow as the determining principle in the design of buildings and cities was Leonardo da Vinci. His designs demonstrate a remarkable insight into multiple flows and the need to connect with the surroundings. Moreover, da Vinci imagined the design of cities based on the flows of water, waste, and people. In *The Science of Leonardo*, Fritjof Capra writes:

> *Leonardo's special attention to how movements would flow through his buildings was not restricted to the interiors, but included the surrounding grounds as well, by means of doorways, loggias, and balconies. In fact, in most of his designs of villas and palaces, he considered the garden to be an integral part of the house. These designs reflect his continual efforts to integrate architecture and nature.*

A further extension of Leonardo's organic view of building design and his special focus on their functional integrity is apparent in his pioneering contributions to urban design. When he witnessed the plague in Milan shortly after his arrival in the city in 1482, he realized that its devastating effects were largely due to Milan's appalling sanitary conditions. In typical fashion, he responded with a proposal for rebuilding the city in a way that would provide decent housing for people and shelters for animals, and would allow the streets to be cleaned regularly by drenching them.

THE THOROUGHLY MODERN NURSERY

We start our observations of flows in and around buildings by focusing our attention on the spaces most occupied by infants and young children. While the young are the most sensitive and vulnerable, they are also the potential of our future. Children, like adults with weakened immune systems, are affected more subtly and more easily by the dynamics of multiple flows. This means that where flows are inadequate, or lacking, their potential to complicate health and introduce disease is greater.

Imagine a young child asleep for the greater part of the day in a room filled with formaldehyde from the glue in the particle board; with chemically laden bactericides and fungicides in the flooring and wall paint; with heavy metals from the brightly colored clothes and toys, with bromine fire retardants in the mattress, bedding, curtains, and carpets. The windows are triple glazed and UV protected, with heavy curtains to keep out light and a thick carpet to dampen sound while the child sleeps. Double insulation and an energy-efficient recirculation of heated or cooled air make for an airtight environment to further block noise. The disposable diapers and infant hygiene products are laden with artificial fragrances and parabenes, and colored with chemical dyes and optical whiteners. The water is heavily chlorinated and the air conditioner filter contains chemicals to kill bacteria. The electric wires that pass over or around the bed emit electromagnetic charges that launch dust particles into the air to be inhaled. Artificial squeaks from plastic toys and the crackling of the radio waves from the baby monitor can be heard.

Mind you, everything in this room is individually tested and approved. None has a proven track record of causing harm, even though there are a few exceptions where one toy or another contains toxins that should not have been there. The reality is that the child in this stressful environment is forced to divert too much energy to immune defense. The diversion of energy to process the stress created and accumulated, or to limit damage from the toxic surroundings, diminishes what is available to keep the immune system strong and the child exuberant and healthy. The statistical incidence of respiratory ailments and skin rashes afflicting young children is nowhere close to a comfort zone. To the contrary, we are clearly moving towards an era where more and more problems arise. While there is no one to blame, the system has flaws. The combination of all these broken flows has led to a demonstrable increase in health problems. The National Center for Health Statistics overwhelms you with statistics that underscore this reality.

Thus while all the material conveniences in a thoroughly modern nursery are designed to facilitate the comfort and care of the child, we can see that they actually run counter to an environment that would optimize health and comfort. What is needed is to rethink the whole concept, choosing solutions that create a living environment that strengthens rather than stresses the immune system. What is needed are innovations such as the glue power of the gecko and the mussel, coloration achieved with the photo-optical means used by butterflies and beetles, pH control available from seashells and seaweeds, food-grade chemical fire retardants, fire sensors modeled after the jewel beetle, UV protection from the edelweiss flower, sound control made possible by the ormia fly, and hygiene products made with natural silk polymers, algae polyesters, and lycopenes from tomato seed waste. There is more: the bacterial control in water achieved by vortex technology, biofilm disruption from furanones, electrical power generated from body heat, or outside sound, or pressure on crystals – all without the need for wires or cables.

Today allergies and respiratory ailments affect upwards of 25% of children in urban areas. An immune system that develops normally and naturally, without excessive factors of artificial sound, chemical overload, and stagnant and dust-laden air, will function to protect and maintain the health and growth of the child. We must consider how to best promote life with the solutions nature has devised. We cannot risk the health of our children.

THE FLOW OF AIR AND LIGHT

In earlier times our dwellings were constructed with thatched roofs and tiny windows having no glass. Air flow through such habitation was the norm. More recently, ostensibly to save energy, many buildings are constructed with super insulation so that hardly any air gets in or out. The aim of saving energy is to be lauded, but eliminating airflow is not at all beneficial. The walls do not breathe, the roofs do not seep. The chemical foams used to insulate building walls and roofs are, with a few exceptions, constantly off-gassing acids into the air we breathe. Fire retardants applied to buildings and their material components are another known problem. The risk of fire is considered sufficiently dangerous to mandate the use of flame retardant chemicals even on mattresses and pillows. Of course, each of these chemicals has been approved, one at a time. Each has been tested and although some are deemed possible carcinogens, the health risk is considered worth reducing the risk of death by fire. The unfortunate combination of all these chemicals creates an overdose we should avoid. Every night, all night, we inhale a chemical cocktail we did not need in the first place.

When we block the natural flow of air, we are not connecting the facts and are overlooking the reality of a building. Were we to solve building ventilation with the same methodical approach as the humble termite, a world of connections would unfold. The flow of air, the composition of household materials, and the pH of the air and walls could all contribute, rather than complicate or obstruct. Utilizing insights as to how natural systems succeed at resolving these challenges would allow us to make genuine progress in achieving real sustainability without increasing investment costs.

It is possible to have continuous air flow and save energy at the same time. Ecosystems have been evolving along those lines for millennia. At present, the best way to reduce the chemical load caused by off-gassing, bacterial contamination, and electrically charged dust particles would be to have more air flow through the building. If we design the building so that all the air is refreshed at least once an hour, then exposure to suspected carcinogens in minute amounts will not pose a problem for most people. While opening a modern building to allow the continuous flow of cold, hot, or humid air from the outside would exacerbate energy use, natural systems have reconciled both objectives. What they can teach us will provide multiple benefits.

One of the newer approaches to heating in buildings is radiant floor heating. Hot water circulates through pipes laid in the subfloor, providing heat with greater efficiency than can be achieved by heating the air. A new improvement, less cumbersome as well as less costly, was developed by Korean scientists Young-Suk Shu and Tae-Sung Oh who were inspired by observations of decomposing plant matter in the soil root zone. Ants and termites transport an estimated 15% of all plant material to the second layer of topsoil. Aeration by earthworms, as well as fungi harvesting by ants and termites, assists the further decomposition of plant matter. The heat from decomposition warms the soil around the root zone, increasing the osmosis between the roots and the leaves of the plants, thereby enhancing growth and improving the flavor of the harvested crop.

The Korean scientists developed a thin film of nano-sized carbon fibers that could be placed under a wooden floor or a carpet to produce surrounding temperatures of up to 98° F using only a twelve-volt solar power application. This application was initially tested in Japanese and Korean greenhouses as a method for keeping plant roots warm. Having saved over 70% of the previous heating energy expenditure for greenhouse production, it is now making its entry into home heating applications.

While this innovation is just one advancement, it could be used to enhance ecological carpets such as those made by Interface Global. The most advanced versions are composed of meshed carbon fibers woven throughout a base made from either rubber or PVC. The carpet tiles electrically connect through the micron-size carbon fibers and could even obtain their energy from thin-film dye-sensitized solar cells attached to the windows, generating an ideal comfort level temperature for bare feet. Heating provided by direct current generated through dye solar cells that let light through will tackle mite infestation from two angles. First, the UV radiation will directly kill the mites. Second, the temperature in the carpet will be high enough to dry any scraps, crumbs, or morsels dropped on the floor, eliminating enough nutrient sources to keep mite proliferation under control.

Insect Insights Relative to Humidity

Termites are farmers. They have perfected a system that involves bringing biomass into the deeper soil to farm fungi. Delicate control of temperature and humidity is imperative for success. Over millennia termites have learned that unless the temperature and the humidity are exact, fungi do not proliferate, even when offered an ideal growth medium. Termite nests are always 81°F and the humidity is constant at 61%. Everywhere they live, in every climate, termites have learned to control air circulation by building tunnels and chimneys. Whether in Dallas or Dacca, Oslo or Osaka, and regardless of variation in the outside temperature, termites successfully build their air-regulating infrastructure, maintaining its flow and quality merely by changing the color, width, length, or height of their infrastructure of tunnels and chimneys.

Chimneys warm the air, which rises as exhaust from the nest and creates a vacuum inside. Whether hot or cold, the incoming exterior air is channeled through tiny tunnels built into the underground nest. If the exterior air is hot and humid, it cools and sheds moisture. If it is cold and dry, it warms and absorbs moisture. This is based on the basic laws of physics we learned in high school. Termites know exactly how tall the chimney must be, how long and deep the underground tubes must be, to always maintain the nest temperature and humidity regardless of outside conditions. They acquired this ability over millions of years without a thermostat or the need for energy and pumps.

Humans have been regulating the interior temperature of our dwellings for far less time. Given our much shorter record of experience, we are only beginning to access the mathematical models necessary to construct buildings with a predictable and comfortable air flow. Lacking the tools innate to the termite, we unfortunately chose electricity and fossil fuels as the driving force, neglecting the laws of physics with their wonderful fail-safe characteristics. Nearly all our inventions include moving parts which in a physical world will sooner or later reach a fail state. The termites designed their lasting solution without any moving parts. It is a solution we too can use.

A Living Filter

Flowing air in and out of a building is a great first step. We can also orchestrate flows inside the building to thoroughly cleanse and oxygenate the air. Remember, oxygen brings alkalinity. To do this we must move beyond physics and acquire an understanding of biology in general, plants and microalgae in particular. It is not difficult to recreate an interior environment that precipitates dust and charged particles into the soil. Over two decades ago, a small company named "Living Filters" (Levande Filter AB) pioneered this concept for air filters inspired by the NASA-funded research aimed at cleansing air in space ships.

Professor Lars Thofeldt developed the plant system and since 1998 his Living Filter systems have been installed worldwide. In coordination with the architect, these systems are designed so that air turbulence within the building channels the inside air through a collection of 150 different plants strategically located near the ceiling. The logic of this comes from rainforest ecology, where we observe that rainforests are not only a home for biodiversity and a source of oxygen, they are also massive air filters. In the Amazon, floating dust particles from as far away as Africa can be captured by the rainforest plant matter to precipitate into the soil with the rains and replenish topsoil. The collection of plants in a Living Filter is permanently lit with highly efficient LED lamps. Every 15 minutes, a mist of water is sprayed on the leaves. This unforced mist percolates through the illuminated and moistened plants, cleansing the air while settling dust, even airborne toxins. The result is noticeable: air is oxygen-enriched and nicely alkaline.

Fungi in the Basement

When a building is closed and insulated, humidity is trapped inside. Long, humid summers cause the moisture to condense on basement insulation and mold to grow. Dampness in closed areas without air circulation produces the ideal conditions for fungi to invade a home, especially in the basement. Fungi release spores into the air that can cause respiratory diseases. If your house is made of wood, then both building and occupants are at risk. If you have a steel frame building, then "only" your health is at risk. Expert remediation companies will treat the walls with metal oxides, freeing the building of fungus but emitting chemical gas particulates for a couple of years. These are particles that you should never inhale. This is the superficiality of our "one cause–one effect" way of thinking. It is reminiscent of core business strategy where we abstract all unintended consequences.

If, on the other hand, we design the building to let air flow through the basement and allow full spectrum light (including ultraviolet radiation) to reach the interior, then we eliminate the conditions for fungus growth and actually cleanse the building. Anders Nyquist uses a prisma light to bring natural full-spectrum light into basements. This not only offers free illumination during the day, it also offers a first response to the onslaught of unwanted fungi. With proper ventilation, the spores that cause respiratory problems are exhausted from the building. This is a good start, with a potential that goes beyond merely resolving a problem. A connected world can achieve multiple benefits for multiple partners. There are opportunities for entrepreneurs to seize.

Now we again make the link to pH. Most materials commonly used for walls and flooring exacerbate the stifling effect of insulation and other flow barriers, creating conditions that allow mold and fungi to proliferate. The fungi growing in dark static conditions such as basements thrive in an acidic environment. Thus another way to control fungal growth is to change the pH of the basement to make it more alkaline. If the fungi do not find conditions conducive to their proliferation, they simply remain dormant. Wall and floor coverings could be made from sources of calcium carbonate, such as crushed seashells. If sheetrock were used, the insulation in the wall could be seaweed-based. Both seaweed and seashells are abundant, inexpensive, and highly alkaline. Used as raw material for floor covering and wall insulation, their performance matches the functionality of the materials currently available.

A new understanding of environmental conditions such as air flow, light, and alkalinity can help us eliminate the conditions in which fungus grows as well as lessen exposure to toxins that stress our immune systems. This is how we start weaving information together, connecting insulation to fungi, to air quality, to health, and to the design of a healthy building.

Åke Mård, founder of the innovative MRD Construction Company in Sweden, has another approach to controlling mold in basements. Pittsburgh Corning supplies him with unusable recycled glass. He processes it to create glass foam blocks that are used as structural building materials in Belgium and the Czech Republic. The inputs are air (mainly CO_2) and the recycled glass, and the output is a multi-functional load-bearing structure. Recycled glass enriched with carbonic gas is lightweight and has the advantage of being resistant to acids and molds while simultaneously insulating. Vermin cannot eat their way through. This is exactly how we imagine the economy of the future: use what is available and obtain multiple benefits. These glass foam blocks replace four products in one prefabricated material. They relieve the pressure on bottle makers to produce bottles from recycled glass. Again we see how nature cascades nutrients to other partners in a system.

This innovation goes very much along the lines of the goals of Earthstone, a New Mexico (USA) business which emerged separately from the construction initiatives in Sweden. Earthstone was founded in 1993 by Andrew Ungerleider and Gay Dillingham in response to the destructive strip mining they saw taking place in their region. Earthstone's patented technology takes glass beverage bottles out of the waste stream and puts them to work by creating abrasion products (e.g., substitutes for sandpaper), consumer cleaning products (paint remover), and horticultural products (substituting glass fiber in hydroponics). Their production design emulates natural models, cascading nutrients and energy, and has achieved market share over a decade of success. The new factory is located adjacent to the Albuquerque landfill, their source for waste glass, and part of their energy use comes from the methane gas released from decomposing biomass in the landfill. This project is a clear example of an industrial solution that reduces the adverse impact of our excessive waste generation, putting products on the market that perform competitively, while using available resources.

THE CHALLENGE OF TRIPLE GLAZING

There is more to be said about glass. Homeowners invest in double and even triple glazing to save energy. Often, it is even subsidized through government tax incentives. Though expensive, triple-glazed window panes are considered a sure way to save money and the environment. It is part of a sustainability strategy that requires more investment to save the money needed to pay back the investment. These energy-saving measures are often combined with a window covering coated with a UV-protection film intended to prevent fading of colorful carpets, wall hangings, and pictures. As we have noted, eliminating the UV light is an open invitation to mites. There is no longer any natural physical inhibitor to their growth.

THE FLOW OF WATER

The next flow to consider is water. How do we use water in any building? Without exception, the largest use of water in houses, and definitely in schools and office buildings, is for washing and waste removal. We block the flow of air and light in modern buildings but exaggerate the flow of water through multiple tubes and pipes, some for cold, some for hot, others for gray water and yet again more for black water. Oddly, the first thing we do with digestive waste is to mix it with potable water. Our body's method of acquiring nutrients involves a complex system of stomach, kidneys, liver, bladder, and intestines. We have basically one input pipe with a valve to direct water and solids to the stomach and air to the lungs. There are two output channels, one for liquids and another for solids and gases. It works quite efficiently.

Drinking water is a necessity to life yet not a commodity amply available to all. When we use it to wash away waste matter we are not seeing the connections. Water is the most precious substance on Earth. In many places, drinking water is expensive, more expensive than petroleum even at $100 dollars a barrel. When we have the luxury of easy access to clean drinking water, why do we render it unusable by blending it with human digestive waste? If that were not enough, we add harsh chemicals and chlorinated paper.

You may not think that urine is a remarkable liquid. Yet it is rich in potassium, one of the core nutrients that give our heart the ability to regulate blood flow. Our body cannot accumulate potassium because it is a toxin in our blood stream. Thus it is discharged as rapidly as it accumulates from consuming a healthy diet. Urine should not be wasted but should be returned to the nutrient cycle. In the era of the Roman Empire, it was the emperor himself who had the unique privilege of collecting urine from the citizens' dwellings to be used as a cleansing agent.

Feces are a different matter. Few animal species deliberately drop feces in water, except perhaps birds, such as the flamingo, whose droppings stimulate the growth of algae on which shrimps thrive, and on which the birds in turn depend for nutrients. There are good reasons why our digestive system separates feces from urine. The combined odor of feces and urine is unpleasant. In current custom, urine and feces, along with voluminous quantities of formerly drinkable water, are flushed away and pumped to water treatment systems where the organic matter is expensively devoured by bacteria stimulated by massive amounts of air pumped into the water. If feces and urine were separately collected, as accomplished by our digestive system, there would be little or no odor, provided there was a flow of air to quickly dry the feces.

That is the function of the dry separation toilet designed, operated, and fine-tuned by Dr. Matts Wolgast, a Swedish scientist from Uppsala University. Alternatively, a simple vortex set up to take advantage of the power of gravity could quickly separate solids from liquids. Water cleansing systems such as those evolved by clams would also contribute, as would purifying water using the methods devised by pistol shrimp. Yet even these end-of-pipe solutions go unused in modern buildings. Were we to eliminate the need to use water to transport digestive waste to central water treatment plants where *E. coli* and *Vibrio cholerae* thrive, then we would eliminate not only the risks linked to these potential sources of disease, but the voluminous, industrial-scale quantities of harsh chemicals required to control these harmful bacteria. Although bactericides reduce the risk of disease, they render the waste water totally useless for any form of consumption unless it is subjected to a lengthy and costly recovery process.

At the Laggarberg School in Sweden the on-site operation that processes all toilet waste operates with the logic of an ecosystem. Although flushing toilets are the legal requirement, once liquids and solids are flushed they are immediately separated using a simple vortex. Waste heat is used to dry the solid matter. This destroys all pathogens, parasites, and any excreted antibiotics and hormones before they can have a detrimental impact on humans and their environment. Children at Laggarberg who spend their school years in this learning environment innately comprehend, from day-to-day exposure, the common logic of sustainably managed waste systems.

We think of water as the liquid that flows through pipes from somewhere where it is in abundance to wherever we need it. Cities have established efficient water distribution networks. Imagine the thousands of miles of pipes that bring water from the Colorado River to Los Angeles. Imagine the huge investment New York is making to install septic tanks upstate to preserve its watershed. Now consider what happens to rainwater. It is collected in the sewer pipes buried beneath city roads and simply drained away! Although water is increasingly costly, the State of Colorado even prohibits its urban residents from capturing rainwater from their buildings. How is this possible? How can flushing rainwater into a sewage system be permitted? It is time to think of water as our most precious resource. Prior to birth, we are more than 99% water. Our adult bodies are more than 80% water. Its daily consumption fuels our survival. We treat water the way we do because we do not see the flows. Let us get out of the box (again) and ask the question, "Where is the largest quantity of untapped drinking water on Earth?" It is in the air.

The first and foremost solution to meet our needs for water is to capture rainfall. In every building and on every street there are water catchment areas that could channel water towards its most immediate use, without the need for pumps or chemical treatments, since gravity could do the job. Whether a skyscraper in New York or farm in Colombia, rainfall capture would supply the building occupants' water needs.

Capturing moisture from the air is not seriously considered as a mainstream solution. Yet we would gain fresh insight into rich opportunities to tap water from the air by visiting the driest ecosystems and learn how the local plants and animals survive. The Namibian desert beetle *(Onymacris unguicularis)* catches water from the air through the interplay of hydrophobic and hydrophilic surfaces. The Main's frog *(Cyclorana maini)* from Australia can absorb 30% of its body weight in water and encapsulate it in a cocoon. The Thorny Devil *(Moloch horridus)* accumulates moisture through osmosis into an interior reservoir. The *Welwitschia mirabilis*, a desert plant, shares similar abilities with the desert beetle in condensing water from the air. The cactus thorn sucks water out of the air as do pine trees and the *Guadua angustifolia*, an Andean highland bamboo species. The Garoé *(Ocotea foetens)* laurel tree that grows on the ridge of the summit of the El Hierro Island in the Canary Islands Peninsula produces such streams of water from the clouds that it sometimes looks like a waterfall.

If you have ever observed an air conditioner, you know that it drips water all the time. In a similar fashion, a cooling tower on top of a large office building condenses water vapor that accumulates as sweat along the surface of the tower. To get an idea of how much water is suspended in the atmosphere, consider that if the air expelled every day from the top of a large building were to first flow along a combination of hydrophobic and hydrophilic surfaces, it could funnel as much as 100 cubic meters of water per minute from the roof to the floors below. Interestingly, when we study the flow of air from cooling towers we are discovering the opportunity to let water flow from the top of the building downward. That reduces energy costs. Avoiding pumping by using the force of gravity simultaneously reduces water use. Since water "on top" requires no pumps, we save capital costs. There is a proposal with considerable appeal in an economic crisis: invest less, get more.

Leonardo da Vinci studied water extensively. He was fascinated with water, the flows of rivers, eddies, spiraling vortices, and other patterns of turbulence. He identified two principal forces operating in flowing water – gravity and internal friction or viscosity. At the center of Leonardo's investigations of turbulence was the water vortex, or whirlpool. The vortex was creatively approached in the 20th century by Viktor Schauberger, an Austrian scientist and forester. As we have noted, a vortex has the capacity to cleanse water. The relationship to building design is an easy step. Capture water from the cooling towers, flush a toilet, shine the windows and mop the floors, pump it through a vortex-generating pipe, oxygenate and cleanse through the internal pressure, and each floor down it can be used again, then delivered clean to the basement. This is an efficient use of water that makes a difference.

When we then flow water through a vortex, separating solids from liquids, water from the tenth to the first floor could be reused for toilet flushing ten times. Since flushing toilets are one of the largest water guzzlers in office buildings, a vortex system would save both water and energy. If the surface of the building is covered with material inspired by the physics of the lotus flower or the ability of the abalone to maintain a clean and shining interior shell, then neither water nor chemicals are needed to cleanse it, saving more water. Costly window-cleaning machines could be eliminated from the operational expenses of the building. Are these solutions a reality or a dream? It is up to us. Plants and insects prove they work; many are benchmarked. The water repellent on the legs of water striders is so effective that no moisture ever sticks. It permits these insects to walk on water. These ingenious solutions have been fine-tuned through millions of years of survival in the desert and the pragmatic application of physical laws that work all the time, without exception. Compared to their abilities, our complex systems of pumping water from the mountains through dams, or converting salt water to potable water with the massive energy expenditure required by reverse osmosis, begin to look like archaic technologies.

The combined flow of air and water offers a vast range of opportunities that can be appreciated by understanding the laws of physics and chemistry. Though easy to comprehend, these laws are seldom adapted as solutions. Take the example of a checkered surface with hydrophobic and hydrophilic textures. The massive clouds of air that dissipate from cooling towers could instead flow over a sheet of squares. Some squares are hydrophobic; they "hate water." Some squares are hydrophilic; they "love water." Tiny bubbles of water are rejected from the hydrophobic surfaces before they have time to evaporate. These bubbles collect on the hydrophilic surfaces, forming droplets and flowing downward by gravity alone to fill tanks on the top of a building. This supply may not be enough to satisfy every need. Nonetheless, the idea helps us contemplate vast water resources we have never before considered. If the cooling towers were to expel their saturated air in a swirl, thereby generating a vortex, it could even "press" the water out of the air without any checkered surfaces. The first such systems have been installed by Watreco on the island of El Hierro.

Once we perfect the design of these innovations, we can combine them with the latest insights into the cleansing capacity of a vortex in water pipes. By redesigning the production and consumption models, and taking the time and effort to rethink the entire system, we have a chance to achieve a solution that could save us from massive worldwide water shortages. These innovations, once applied, can cut costs immediately and relieve the stress on scarce water resources that characterize every megalopolis in the world.

The entire coastal zone of California has suffered from water shortages for decades. If there were access to water from the moist air that is always present because of the temperature inversion between the cold ocean currents and the hot inland deserts, the largest economic benefit would be increased land value. Remember Las Gaviotas, a desolate area once considered worthless and now a regenerated rainforest valued at 3,000 times its original cost. An increase in property value based on the inclusion of a commons like abundant water resources would be a welcome reversal to the current trend of property devaluation and speculation. Good land that meets basic needs, starting with drinking water, holds good value.

THE HEAT ISLAND EFFECT

In the sweltering summer heat of New York or Boston, Galveston or Chattanooga, building air conditioners are on full blast. Hot outside air is pushed through these cooling systems and water-saturated heated clouds surround the buildings. The air conditioners produce cool air inside. The warm and humid air exhausts to the outside, rendering the exterior air in the immediate vicinity – including that available for the air conditioning uptake system – likewise warm and humid. Thus the energy required to cool hot, moist air increases. With little wind, the area becomes a heat island. In the summer, when such a heat island effect is at its peak, the warm conditions needed for the spread of *Legionella spp.* (the bacteria responsible for Legionnaire's disease) will be at prime. Rising temperatures cause bacterially proliferated biofilms to get thicker, and consequently the health risks increase. When you enter a building through revolving doors meant to avoid heating or cooling loss, there is no decompression, thus no movement of air. The more people who gather in these airtight buildings, the more heat is captured inside.

Each adult produces about 60 watts of energy every hour. Energy used for heating or cooling adds heat. A meeting room hosting a thousand people can produce 60 kW hours of electricity, and such heat requires proportionally more cooling. Anders Nyquist's design of a sporting hall at the Laggarberg School in Sweden uses an ingenious approach. When heat is emitted by excited spectators during a lively school sports event, the naturally occurring air flows actually bring in the cooler outside air. His design demonstrates that as more people enter the hall, greater airflow occurs, keeping the inside air refreshed and comfortable. That is a systemic design that works!

Building designs create sets of unanticipated problems. The solutions are to serve multiple purposes while producing cost and energy savings and reducing the risks to human health. Healthier buildings that save energy with lower capital and operating costs are the bottom line of this bundling of innovations.

THE FLOW OF SOUND

Prior to birth we are composed primarily of water. The sounds that resonate through the amniotic fluid definitely affect us. In fact, some pediatricians have suggested that pregnant women listen to classical music, or to the chanting of Gregorian or Tibetan monks, because they consider that these sounds enhance an infant's mental development. Alexander Lauterwasser's work in the field of cymatics demonstrated that a flow of sound suffusing a body of water achieves a constant and therefore predictable determination of shape. Sound is a wave; waves produce pressure, and sound waves have different levels or frequencies. Lauterwasser placed a drop of water on a metal plate and applied a sound source. He observed that as sound waves vibrated the water, the water moved. Different waves at different pressures generated different complex patterns of movement. A specific frequency always produced a particular movement and shape of the water at a fixed surface tension. A minimal change in frequency caused alterations in the complex but rhythmic movements.

Each of us knows from experience that pleasant sounds are soothing, and unpleasant sounds can range from mildly annoying to positively unbearable. We can imagine the ambiance of living near a babbling brook or within hearing of ocean waves at the seashore. Living or working next to a freeway or a railroad line requires an accommodation that renders noise awareness subliminal, though wearing.

Since even inanimate objects such as buildings produce noise, exploring innovative ideas that channel the flow of undesirable sounds in our daily environments might help us find ways to reduce the effect such sounds have on us. Scientists study how the streamlined shape of bottlenose dolphins and whales allows these mammals to convert the pressure from water and wind vortices into efficient power. Perhaps we might similarly capture the energy potential of sound and convert it using minute piezoelectric transformers, gaining sufficient electrical energy to power small battery-driven devices such as cell phones. Instead of just blocking noise from the freeway traffic buzzing around the building, we could devise ways to capture and convert it to energy. Thus physical solutions to noise amelioration could also achieve energy savings.

THE FLOW OF ENERGY

The cost of energy delivered to a building depends on two factors: demand and supply. The cases described in this chapter, and throughout the book, demonstrate that a dramatic reduction of energy use can be accomplished by using solutions that require less and provide more. In fact, utilizing only the innovations presently described could potentially reduce the need for electricity in any building, from a gymnasium to a child's room, by 75–80%. To this we may add the wonders of the cold light made by squid and fungi, the self-cleaning demonstrated by the lotus flower, and heat conservation accomplished by the tuna. Technologies provided by the sandfish lizard could give us friction reduction, which is an energy saver, because our incapacity to reduce or overcome friction requires additional energy. As noted earlier, all these ways and means to reduce energy consumption are possible and do not compromise our health, as do any number of current materials. That is good, but there are even better possibilities.

If we turn our focus to supply, as we have already noted, a building has tremendous potential to generate its own electricity. While the pressure from sound and noise will not be enough to power everything in a modern building with electronics, security systems, computer networks, elevators, and air conditioning, we might once again emulate natural systems, welcoming the contributions of all, even the smallest numbers and the tiniest volumes.

We are often inclined to immediately opt for solar; particularly the new dye-sensitive solar cells inspired by the way leaves respond to light. Unfortunately, the sun only shines half the day. Though the purpose of batteries is to store electricity, their materials and production require mined ores and high temperatures, and thus increase our overall fuel consumption. The largest source of energy must be the most readily available power generator, perhaps the source that subjects the whole building to structural compression and requires the tensile strength that dominates the design. Throughout this book we have referred to the great power of gravity. Why not use it in building design?

A redesign of the building structure could set the foundations at each floor on crystals like quartz, silk, or even sugar cane. Based on nanoscale crystals and a ten-story building, it has been guesstimated that the total power from gravity-induced piezoelectricity could reach 6,000 kW/hr. That is not bad. If the quartz energy source were precisely located on each floor, typically under each one of the columns, it would be possible to have electricity available throughout the building with a limited need for cabling. That further reduces the need for copper and mining. It would take only one generation to have these building techniques approved and implemented in new structures. If the science can be demonstrated, then the conservative and risk-adverse construction industry will shift for the better, and buildings will require less investment and achieve lower operational costs. If bamboo were incorporated with reinforced concrete to erect the structure, the building would not only be energy efficient, it would actually sequester carbon dioxide, since the carbon absorbed by the bamboo would offset the emissions from the cement. Now we are talking serious stuff!

A second large potential but unexploited source is to use local gusts of wind, the way a zebra does. Each larger building impacts the local climate, generating turbulence. These turbulences could even be enhanced through planned exterior color choices, not just reflecting the sun but insuring that the light and dark variations provide surface cooling and generate local airflows. It does not make much sense to place windmills in the center of town, since these would make too much noise and not catch sufficient wind. However, it would be possible to place a series of mini- and micron-sized windmills that would constantly generate energy, each equipped with the smart surface that nature provided to whale flippers for the purpose of reducing drag and increasing lift.

Such innovation has been pioneered by Frank Fish through his Canadian company, Whalepower. Because there are temperature differences between the shaded and sunny side, a building has wind on each side. This makes it possible to provide direct current (DC) all the time. Simple wind-powered engines reduce the need for batteries and provide power by capturing the wind currents created by the mere presence of the building. There are many creative wind turbine designs on the market that are not only efficient but also ergonomic, such as the turbine, developed by Walter Presz of FloDesign, which weaves vortices in the air.

This is a powerful potential energy source. A typical ten-story building could have a thousand little ventilators. Provided the blades were efficiently designed to resemble turbulence catchers instead of rather straighter airplane blades, the power could reach 50 kW/hr, another welcome addition to the supply side. If the FloDesign turbine were adopted, the building would squeeze water out of the air at the same time.

Each person in the building emits the energy equivalent of 60 watts of electricity per hour and thus should be considered a source of energy. The technology from the Fraunhofer Institute is capable of capturing energy from even just half a degree of temperature difference between the body and the sensor. Once it is commercially available, this innovation will permit us to move building design another step closer to sustainability. The more people inside, the less additional energy needed. A building with a thousand people inside for eight to ten hours per day would generate an estimated 60 kW/hr during working hours. If this is efficiently transformed, it could power every computer in the building. It works today at laboratory scale. It can work tomorrow in large-scale office buildings, and generate significant quantities of additional local energy for local consumption. The very low distribution costs will convince forward-thinking architects to include sound, pressure, temperature, and micro flows of wind into their designs for optimal energy generation and application. All the scientific confirmation is in place. What is needed next is an entrepreneurial effort to bring a portfolio of these innovations into an integrated design.

THE FLOWS OF PEOPLE AND MATTER

Movement flows of people and product have been studied in considerable detail by systems engineers and city planners and designers. We strive for efficiency and optimal flow in airport or shopping queues, in delivery and removal of goods consumed, in transport of product and people, in consumption of goods and services, entertainment and education. When we link these flows to the other flows we have discussed, we might realize that we could indeed design a building capable of generating nutrients. A bathroom, generally moist and warm, could provide an ideal breeding ground for mushrooms. The starch in our food waste could be converted into bioplastics using only a fungus. Rooftops could become gardens, not only producing locally appropriate fruits and vegetables but reducing the building's surface temperature and energy consumption. Buildings designed to recycle nutrients and augment food security could yield unintended benefits, by providing an energizing and relaxing environment where food crops could flourish and healthful exercise could take place. This would be a building worthy of the genius of Friedensreich Hundertwasser, the brilliant Viennese architect.

The Center for Ecoliteracy in Berkeley, California, and Slow Food in Torino, Italy, have both been active in creating school gardens in urban environments. Now we have the opportunity to surpass this accomplishment and create a self-sustaining environment. Brasilia, the capital of Brazil with two million inhabitants, meets 90% of its fruit and vegetable needs within the city boundaries thanks to the visionary design of Oscar Niemeyer. If access and allocation were designed into the flow of the buildings and the surrounding space, with comfort and sustenance as priorities, then water and nutrients can be abundantly available for our needs. Waste generated from consumption is kept locally available and is contributed to the nutrient stream that simply yet remarkably returns to us as sustenance. It is an elegant cascade that cycles and recycles, benefiting and utilizing all materials. It is a whole systems model perfected by nature and available to meet the needs of all.

SCHOOLS AS SUSTAINABILITY CLASSROOMS

Schools are an ideal testing ground for learning how to work with flows. Between first grade and graduation from high school, children spend an estimated 20,000 hours in classrooms. This is a staggering amount of time, which many feel is inadequately spent. Considering the tremendous investment of time and patience that we require of children, how is it possible that saving money determines how schools and classrooms are designed? Shouldn't the overarching principles be establishing a healthful environment for optimal learning and participation? How much is that worth? We have only touched the surface of these issues. Nonetheless, there are many ready and available options for designing school buildings that are optimally healthy, less costly to maintain, and which avail themselves of the dozens of scientific insights described herein. These are nothing less than shifts in the way we live.

Conditions for good health should not be subject to calculations of financial profit or cost cutting. School buildings are an ideal place to implement principles of health and sustainability and to showcase them in the public domain where they may contribute to the public good. Imagine a school building where over a hundred core concepts in physics, biology, and chemistry are visibly and functionally integrated into the building and the operation of the school. Imagine the connections students would make by seeing these sciences in manifest display. The children and their teachers would have the opportunity to become familiar with the innovations and to learn the science behind their functioning through daily appreciation and exposure. The school itself becomes a living science laboratory. Living what you learn makes acquiring knowledge effortless. Such a school structure would steer society towards sustainability. The obvious differences between the new and old technologies would inspire many youngsters to become tomorrow's innovators and entrepreneurs. This is the springboard from which imagination becomes reality.

In such a building simple and pragmatic combinations of meteorology with the basic principles of airflow maintain constant interior temperature and humidity even as the exterior pressure and temperature change. Highly efficient LED lights shine day and night on a hundred varieties of plants automatically sprinkled every 15 minutes with rainwater collected from the roof. The levels of dust particles and air pollutants entering the building or generated inside are kept low by this misting, decreasing the risk of respiratory diseases. The lights are coated not with mercury but with keratin, inspired by the beetle that creates white without chemicals. Chelating bacteria assist in recycling cast-off metals. The inner walls are composed of crushed seashells and filled with dried seaweed, providing a practical and efficient, highly alkaline, anti-fungal, moisture-wicking sound barrier. Natural airflows in the building pass over these materials, keeping the humidity stable and the pH alkaline. The windows allow passage of UV rays to control mites in the chemical-free carpeting. The carpet tiles electrically connect through the micron-size carbon fibers that obtain their energy from thin-film dye-sensitized solar cells attached to the windows, keeping the floors at an ideal temperature for warmth and dry enough for mite control.

Rather than the mastering of any one technology, implementing a detailed and definitive design plan based on the innovations and technologies introduced here would naturally require insight into a whole system integrated with the local environment. It is the difference between the regenerative and adaptive capacity of an ecosystem and the genius of a single species. Ecosystems simply cannot be reduced to a set of rules. The whole is more than the sum of the individual components.

HOUSING FOR ALL

It is impossible to close this chapter without reflecting on the pioneering design work of Linda Garland, who is based in Bali, Indonesia, and Simon Velez from Bogotá, Colombia. They have done remarkable work with bamboo in designing and constructing affordable, renewable, and attractive housing that could be the most sustainable of all.

From the perspective of its composition, the relative strength of bamboo defies logic. Its marvelous adaptation is to use tensile and compression strength to perfect advantage. Even though bamboo is a grass and not a tree, its fibers outperform any other cellulose source when put to the task of building or paper making. Since we should not speak in absolute terms, we also recognize hemp and flax; however, bamboo is the master for technical functionality. It can demonstrably replace both concrete and steel. With over 2,000 species in the Americas alone, it has qualities that make it capable of effortlessly, ecologically, and inexpensively meeting our growing needs for construction materials. At the end of the 20th century bamboo was still the preferred building material for more than a billion people around the world, especially in the tropics.

After the Kyoto Protocol was signed in 1997, Masatsugu Taniguchi, director of Taiheiyo, Japan's largest cement manufacturer, searched for how to achieve a low carbon footprint using cement. The materials for reinforced concrete are mined and manufactured at high pressure and temperature and leave the Earth's face scarred for centuries. Taiheiyo succeeded by utilizing bamboo fibers. Simply pressing bamboo with cement weight for weight (50/50, or 75/25 by volume), without any additive or chemical, they created a cement board having a neutral carbon footprint. The bamboo itself is farmed and sustainably harvested on 5,000 acres of land next to a factory on the outskirts of Jakarta.

Innovative architects Renzo Piano and Shigeru Ban were inspired by bamboo to create architectural wonders based on the beauty and performance of bamboo. Maestro Simon Velez, the grand bamboo architect of our time, demonstrated that bamboo can comply with the most stringent construction engineering rules of modern society – German building codes. Velez designed the ZERI Pavilion, erected in Manizales, Colombia, which is perhaps the largest bamboo structure in the world (later the most popular pavilion at the 2000 World Expo in Germany). Two severe earthquakes since its construction have merely shifted a few tiles on the roof.

The king of all bamboos is perhaps the *Guadua angustifolia*. When the Spaniards conquered the highlands of Colombia, Peru, and Ecuador, they had to wade through dense bamboo jungles. The life force of bamboo was widely and wildly described by the Spanish colonizers whose letters home told how the native Andean cultures used bamboo defensively in combat, as it would pierce quickly through the body, seemingly without force. These colonizers also quickly learned that their European wood and stone construction techniques did not long survive in the earthquake zones of the southern Americas. They found out the hard way, that *"buildings must dance to the rhythms of the Earth,"* as Simon Velez characterizes the behavior of bamboo. That is exactly what bamboo does: dance.

As this 20-meter tall "grass" was cleared to make space for coffee and cattle farming in the southern Americas, it became the preferred local building material. Two hundred years later, these buildings from colonial times still stand, having survived everything the shaking Earth delivered. This Latin American experience is confirmed in Asia. At 3,000 years and counting, the world's oldest bamboo building stands as an open pavilion in Manchuria.

226

Bamboo does not resist an earthquake but rather moves with it. Neither does a bamboo structure require bracing through cross-links to withstand the chaotic upward and sideward pressures. Curiously, bamboo is hollow. It is flexible enough to stand as long as the building has an inward inclination. The mere reduction of the vertical angle to 85° provides such stability that the tiles on the roof don't even move. It is a pity that the domination of CAD/CAM in the architectural design and construction fields since the late 20th century has demanded 90° angles for all construction, resulting in death and destruction every time the earth trembles.

Lucio Ventania, a well-known Brazilian bamboo artisan, explains, *"As long as structural bamboo is protected from direct sun and never stands in its own water, it will stand, forever."* Hence, the logical design features a large overhang that protects the load-bearing poles from water and sun, the two most destructive atmospheric forces.

Bamboo remains undiscovered by those who live outside its tropical growing range. Not a single species of bamboo grows naturally in the northwestern US or Sweden, where the largest forestry research institutes are located. Thus the focus of the worldwide forestry industry, even in tropical locales, is on species such as eucalyptus and pine, which grow in temperate climates and have nowhere near the renewable potential of bamboo. As awareness of bamboo's sustainable growth habit and building material qualities becomes more widespread, it will serve as an inspiration for innovative architectural projects around the world.

Achieving affordable housing for all is a goal that can be met with the use of bamboo. A 1,000 square foot plot of land in the Andean highlands would be sufficient to grow a house. Planted with the giant *Guadua angustifolia* bamboo, some 60 bamboo poles would be harvestable after three years. This is enough building material to construct a two-story, 650 square foot house with a magnificent balcony and a staircase in the back that permits airflow. Each subsequent year's bamboo harvest would provide enough poles to construct an additional modest home.

Simon Velez's housing design includes a large staircase in the rear, which acts like a termite mound; a heavy roof structure to stabilize the building; and a wide balcony for comfortable ambiance. There are no 90° angles. This prevents a sudden collapse in case of earthquakes, making it an extremely safe design. Instead of trying to build an earthquake-resistant building, the bamboo, and the method of joinery used, move with the erratic powers of the earth. The house is remarkably fresh, with light entering freely. The massive overhanging roof protects the structural bamboo from any deterioration due to ultraviolet light or rain. The rainwater flows around the house, hardly touching the bamboo's surface, collecting in cisterns for drinking water. Although there is wind play, not even a hurricane could lift the house.

The bamboo unused in house construction, considered by many a waste, can be used to produce charcoal. Charcoal production causes noxious gases. Antonio Giraldo from Armenia, Colombia, has developed a method of curing bamboo in its own charcoal gases, much like the traditional curing systems used in Japan. The flow of the gases is channeled to a huge chamber. Under slight pressure bamboo poles 24 feet long are cured with the fumes from their own charcoal. Instead of using toxic chemistry to preserve the bamboo against termites and fungi, it is cured by its own chemistry. The negative flow of contaminates is converted into a positive flow that not only preserves the bamboo but replaces the pollutants that pose health risks. The way the building materials are made and prepared for use is inspired by natural systems, a cascading of nutrients and energy. This same method is what was used at the Picuris Pueblo in New Mexico with small-diameter wood that was slated to be burned.

ALL FLOWS CONSIDERED

An appreciation of how the flow of air, light, water, energy, sound, people, and matter affect our physical space brings a new understanding of how to design structures that interweave and utilize these flows. It gives us some very practical insights into how to build and furnish homes, offices, and schools to achieve true functionality, cost, and aesthetics.

Pioneering entrepreneurs have shown us that sustainable buildings need not be more expensive. Practical applications from the world of science, well researched and well documented, are opening new possibilities that can finally steer us towards sustainability. Architects dedicated to green building design have the ability to turn possibilities into actualities. Public demand and common sense will help authorities revise building codes and approve industry standards that allow integration of innovations based on solid science. When we embrace these innovations as a society, we will be supporting the health of our families, our domiciles, our workplaces, and our environment. We will be creating the industries of the future inspired by the ingenuity of nature. We too can function as an ecosystem, generating what we need from what is available, finding resource in waste, welcoming the contributions of all, and taking part in a cascade of abundance.

50 Technologies Inspired by Nature Integrated into Building Design	
ECOSYSTEM TECHNOLOGIES	**CONTRIBUTIONS BY SPECIES**
Bamboo value chain generating water, topsoil	Bactericides from red seaweed
Pulp-to-Protein cascading nutrients and energy	No-glue adhesion from gecko, mussel, cocklebur
Vortex for water purification	Underwater data transmission as dolphins
Water harvesting from air	Self-cleaning like the lotus flower
Food grade quality fire retardants	Gathering water like *Welwitschia mirabilis*
Silk replacing steel	Electricity inspired by the whale
Building materials from CO_2	Black & white zebra stripes for temperature control
Cleansing water like river banks	Protection against UV by tomatoes and edelweiss
Fibonacci fluid dynamics	Sucking water from air like the cactus thorn
Bioelectricity systems	Reducing friction like the sandfish lizard
Air purification by plants	Waterproofing like the bees
Carbon fiber heating roots	Reducing drag like whale fins
Food waste to plastics	Concentrated solar power like the dragonfly
Split box using one pipe for water or air	Infrared sensors like the jewel beetle
Reduce traffic congestion with swarm intelligence	Water filtration as clams do
White without chlorine	Electric insulation like the electric fish
Polymer plastics from CO and CO_2	Reduce surface heat, obtain water like the thorny devil
Color without pigments	Sound absorption by seaweed
Dye sensitive solar cells	Seashells changing pH
Heating and cooling like termites	Cold light by squid and mushrooms
Mining metals like bacteria	Misting like the bombardier beetle
Soil regeneration from silkworm droppings	Biobattery based on electric fish
	Drag reduction as the bottlenose dolphin
	Heat conservation in tuna
	Sound control by ormia fly

CHAPTER THIRTEEN

CASCADING
A BLUE ECONOMY

The Earth provides enough to satisfy
every man's need, though not every man's greed.

— MAHATMA GANDHI

OPTING OUT OF A DEAD END

Predictability, though considered a prerequisite of economic success, creates an artifice that blinds us to the ramifications of our actions. Adherence to a core competence and reliance on linear calculations and scientific abstractions achieves a monopolistic economic model that leads to more and more transportation and energy consumption to reach the consumer waiting at the end of the supply chain. Tighter supply chain management and just-in-time assembly create a global and interdependent economy that delivers more and cheaper products to consumers. Global free trade is considered the engine of growth, the tool that makes greater efficiency available to everyone in the world. Shipping cookies immersed in preservation gases, air-freighting deep-frozen pralines, or filling tankers with orange juice may be nothing more than excesses of that logic. Yet such methods will never enable the next generation to provide food and livelihood for all players. Unemployment and poverty will be the only enduring outcome.

Traditionally, seasonal foods provided the micro-nutrients needed for a particular time of year. Each fall harvest, Native Americans ate *huitlacoche*, a truffle-like fungus growing on corn, as a boost for their immune system, preparing them for winter's onset. Now *huitlacoche* is a delicacy that can be consumed all year, even when its beneficial effect is primarily seasonal. In reality our appetites are enticed and trained by the marketers and media outlets of our culture. If this is the basis of marketing as defined by the axiom taught by Philip Kotler, *"Supply what the consumer wants,"* perhaps we might more carefully consider our wishes. Excessive stimulation of demand for products that fulfill desires and ignore basic needs creates a linear goal that focuses on garnering greater share of disposable income. We cannot see that it is an unsupportable system advancing along a destructive path. It is a path that leads to a world of carbon emissions, lost biodiversity, profligate use of non-renewable raw materials, and excessive reliance on toxic chemicals. It is a path without a future.

A CURIOUSLY WINDING PATH

Throughout this book we have reviewed the best inspirations that can be found in natural systems for resolving our present economic and ecologic impasse. We have explored successful benchmarked and implemented models, and have examined the potential of others. We have considered how some might fit linked or bundled applications. Everywhere we have discovered tremendous potential to generate more jobs, while increasing material efficiency and productivity beyond the dreams of many. This is remarkable because we have been led to believe that an increase in productivity is only possible by shedding jobs. Nature knows better, transforming apparent scarcity to sufficiency and ultimately to abundance. The cascading of energy and nutrients among the five kingdoms of nature permits multitudes of human-scale production units to provide for all that is needed. While our current focus on maximizing one output leads to scarcity on one hand and poverty on the other, ecosystems always have enough for all.

All players within an ecosystem make their modest contributions dependent on the availability of nutrients, energy, and the impetus to respond to basic needs. Everything evolves and when crises occur, everyone adapts. In natural systems no one has a license to remain out-of-step for too long. Natural environments have no big players dominating the field. There is much more room for small contributors. A tree that grows to 100 feet does not decide on the basis of this achievement to now continue to 1,000 feet. Were it to succeed in the attempt, physical forces would destroy it.

Business pursues a strategy of ever-lower marginal costs, assuming that the cost of making one more unit will always be less, thus justifying the blind race for size and market control. "Growth" based on the consolidation of power triggers unnoticed collateral damage and renders the whole system inflexible, resistant to change.

Ecosystems benefit from a renewing cascade of nutrients and energy. These unending flows permit life to adapt and thrive. Conditions of apparent scarcity progress to visible sufficiency and even abundance. In natural systems, as soon as there is too much food, some species proliferate or new species emerge. Waste removal is handled by passing it down the nutrient stream to be utilized by other players. For a tree, its fallen leaves are nutrients for soil bacteria, ants, and worms whose output in turn becomes nutrients for the tree.

Natural systems have a different approach to chemistry as well. First, the main solvent is water, which is much more benign to the overall system than any of the catalysts that humans have invented. Second, the bonds between two molecules are mainly non-covalent, which means that it is easy to take them apart. They degrade, and can be reused in other molecules. Nature's chemical engineers apply the "zip-unzip" concept to their methods. It is this ability to degrade, separate, and reintegrate that allows the overall system to have such high material and energy efficiency. To produce a stronger web for its offspring, the spider simply reprocesses the polymers of its old web into the constituent amino acids, and spins it anew.

Non-linear models, often equated with chaos, underpin natural systems. In fact, just about everything in natural systems follows non-linear pathways. In his book, *La Nouvelle Alliance*, Belgian author Ilya Prigogine, the 1977 Nobel Laureate in chemistry, describes these natural relationships as "dissipative structures." It is our desire to squeeze everything into straight lines and 90° angles that makes much of what is manufactured energy-inefficient. Nature demonstrates that while the shortest distance between two points may be a straight line, the fastest and most energy-efficient pathway follows the swirls of a vortex.

As we adjust our production and consumption system to emulate natural systems, we must indulge the apparent surprises provided by non-linear models. This does not mean that all is unpredictable. Physics still applies in our universe. It does mean we must seek out the interactive forces and hidden connections that will permit us to gain multiple results with one set of initiatives. This is demonstrated by termites' capacity to control temperature and humidity with great precision by constructing underground micro-tunnels through their mounds. These termites express a deep understanding of how everything interacts. The ultimate result of these complex relationships and seemingly chaotic interactions is that termites have food because an edible fungus thrives in the underground environment they create. Using what is locally available results in a marvelous system that secures basic needs for the termites while warming the roots of the plants that will grow the leaves, well masticated by the termites, on which the fungus thrives.

We will need to understand and appreciate symbiosis – how species work together to achieve the common goals of a whole system. The renewal made possible at Las Gaviotas came from recognition of the symbiosis between pine trees and mycorrhizal fungi. An appreciation of how natural forces always evolve towards the best use of resources within an ecosystem allows us to recognize the regenerative capacity of natural systems to overcome calamities that are often the result of our own ignorance. Nature does not calculate cash flow. While we are obsessed with monetarization (to our own benefit) natural systems generate multiple revenue flows best measured in protein, drinking water, energy sources, and defense systems. Nature produces betterment through the calculation of an integrated benefit flow. Such synergies lead to common benefits, such as free, abundant, and unpolluted water and air. If entrepreneurs in these new competitive businesses were to include such outcomes in their goals, then it would continuously build common benefit and realize enormous social capital. Perhaps, like the nation of Bhutan, we could monitor our National Happiness Index, rather than our Gross National Product.

The linear economic model prescribes placing a market value on everything, calculating the costs of each input, allocating overhead for every output, and converting cost centers to profit centers that are made to compete for internal resources through outsourcing. The resulting calculation is derived from the logic of consolidation – basically adding it all up while eliminating double counts. This does not unveil synergies amongst different divisions of the same company, nor identify the commons that are considered free, and thus without economic value. Neither does it put a price on the externalized costs that are imposed on society, which is located outside the logical framework of the core business. Nor does this disclose the lost opportunities that simply cannot be considered because they are not part of the core business. Most commonly, we simply impose the costs on future generations who are not made aware nor informed in detail that we are exploiting the Earth beyond easy repair and leaving the problems for them to resolve. Thus climate change occurs without any real understanding of the urgency to undertake corrective action.

In business, companies opt to maximize profits and target market share regardless of social cost to a local community by producing wherever the costs for a single product are lowest. Industrial and policy decisions never consider prioritizing full employment a viable option. In contrast, natural systems employ everyone; no one is considered too old or too young. Where ecosystems clearly promote innovation, collaboration, patience, and perseverance, the current economic model is rather insensitive to any change not initiated by or not serving the interests of the dominant players themselves. Market leaders with their streamlined production and distribution systems fiercely resist any change that risks the existing processes and revenue streams, including of course bonuses.

We often forget that species and ecosystems have coped with numerous disasters in the past and have rapidly evolved to adjust to new and even dramatically changed circumstances. This is the approach we must take to carbon dioxide emissions and other so-called greenhouse gases. If we isolate CO_2 and do not see the whole system, then we are likely to overlook the real solutions. The harvesting of CO_2 for the production of biofuels by microalgae is a simple yet brilliant solution that generates multiple benefits, including the continuous harvesting and reuse of carbonic gases in photo-biorefineries and the making of polyesters without sulfuric acid. If, on the other hand, we only think about the gas and the problems it causes, and decide that we must find engineered solutions for its elimination, then constructs like nuclear energy and the disposal of vast quantities of CO_2 into the deep oceans may sound logical and obvious, at whatever cost, and paid for by the taxpayer. These expensive choices are only obvious when the capacity of ecosystems to provide for solutions is abridged to a single concept presented in over-simplified targets such as lowered emission rates. This eliminates the opportunity to balance risks or create new long-term options. It leaves people to scramble for quick-fix solutions that cannot predict long-term collateral effects.

In an evolutionary model where changes are recognized as what is normal, flexibility is also the rule. Risks inherent to inevitable changes are mitigated because a natural system will evolve with a simple yet complex algorithm: always search to reduce material and energy needs so that more life, and more diverse life, can populate the system and render it resilient.

The opportunities for entrepreneurship inspired by the power of ecosystems mark the goals of a Blue Economy. What we see unfolding before us goes beyond the genius of each species. The total is more than the sum of its parts. A world that is home to these marvelous ecosystems that cascade nutrients and energy endlessly is a world that can accept the challenge to resolve poverty and misery, inequality and waste. Focusing merely on a hundred innovations that draw from of nature's remarkable examples, we envision that it is possible to generate as many as 100 million jobs over the next 10 years.

Let us inspire the creativity and the determination of entrepreneurs around the world who will find in these innovations multiple opportunities to build a renewed economy. If we shift our gaze and our focus to find inspiration in the marvelous workings of nature, we can move from capacity to competency, from scale to scope, creating a Blue Economy for a blue planet.

A QUALITATIVE COMPARISON	
NATURE'S MBA – ABUNDANCE	**CORE BUSINESS MBA – SCARCITY**
1. Everyone has a job to do and contributes their best.	Unemployment is part of the system.
2. Thousands of small contributors; many opportunities for entrepreneurship.	Power concentrated among a few. Giant multinationals are the rule.
3. Everything is used: cascading of nutrients and energy.	Minute parts used, the rest is wasted, abandoned in landfills, indiscriminately incinerated.
4. Predictable physics provides the first source of power.	First source is non-renewable fossil fuels. Climate change guaranteed.
5. Water is the primary solvent. Chemistry has limited, secondary use.	Heavily reliant on chemistry. Aggressive solvents used to create covalent links.
6. Biodiversity is time and place specific. Biology always has exceptions.	Biology is cloned.
7. Diversity flourishes.	Standardized and predictable output.
8. The constant of change is the basis of evolution.	Resistance to fundamental change. Innovative technologies are considered disruptive.
9. What is locally available is put to use.	Centralized manufacture requires global sourcing.
10. Even unnoticed, the basic needs of all are met.	Vast numbers of the population are left out even when a majority lives in wealth.
11. With few exceptions nearly all models are non-linear.	All calculations are linear.
12. All materials degrade over time.	Covalent molecular bonding gives us components that do not degrade, even those with one-time use.
13. Everything is connected, evolving in symbiosis.	All is a stand-alone. Synergies are discouraged, except in finance.
14. Clean air and water are free and abundant.	Everything can be sold for profit, even basic necessities like water.
15. One initiative generates multiple benefits for several partners.	One project equals one cash flow, only for the progenitor and controlling partners.
16. Risks are shared.	Risk hampers innovation.
17. Material and energy utilization is maximized; taxation does not exist.	Taxation to redistribute wealth.
18. Optimize the system.	Maximize one critical success factor.
19. Negatives are converted into positives.	Negatives are mitigated at high cost, or ignored, or passed on, unresolved, to future generations.
20. Economies are based on scope.	Economies are based on scale.

EPILOGUE

REALIZING A DREAM

I see skies of blue, and clouds of white,
The bright blessed day, the dark sacred night.
And I think to myself... what a wonderful world.

— *COMPOSED BY* ROBERT THIELE & GEORGE DAVID WEISS
— *PERFORMED BY* LOUIS ARMSTRONG

239

ERIN CURRIER

n 1994 the Zero Emissions Research Initiative pioneered the conversion of coffee pulp waste from the farm into protein by using the waste to grow mushrooms for human consumption and feeding animals the spent substrate. It took nearly a decade of research before each step in the process from farm to consumer was certified. Twenty scientific publications provide the backbone of the "Pulp-to-Protein" program. There are over 10,000 people working with mushrooms in Colombia along with dozens of villagers in Zimbabwe who base their livelihood on these simple and sustainable practices. In addition, Indian villages used this technique to become self-sufficient in food production following many years of malnutrition and hunger. In 2008 alone, training programs introduced the systems approach to farmers in Tanzania, Congo, South Africa, Cameroon, Mozambique, and the USA.

"Coffee waste is an amazing substrate for mushrooms, rich in fibers and caffeine," explains Emilio Echeverri, the former Vice-President of the Colombian Coffee Federation. Echeverri supported the Pulp-to-Protein program from its inception and was later elected governor of the coffee growing state of Caldas. In a caffeine growth medium, mushrooms reach maturity three times faster than if they were farmed on oak, thus offering the potential to save oak forests throughout China and elsewhere.

Carmenza Jaramillo undertook research on farming white button mushrooms *(Agaricus bisporus)* in 1978. After six years of research and peer-reviewed articles published in both English and Spanish international journals, she was completely committed to the goals of the initiative. She started her own mushroom farm in Manizales, Colombia, and trained many, many others. By now Carmenza's students, like Francenid Perdomo, have become the experts, generously training others, cascading the knowledge to help many others achieve food security.

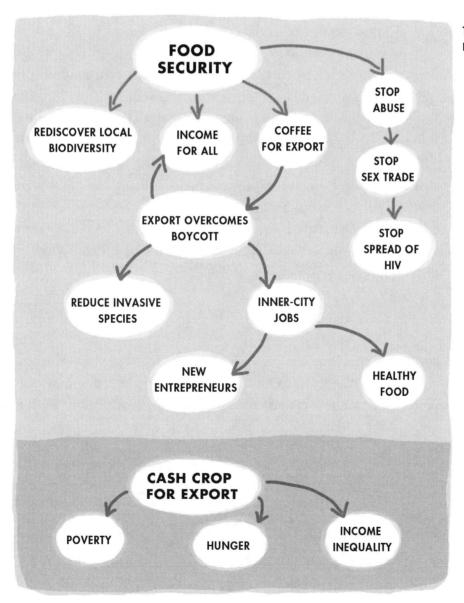

THE FUTURE OF HOPE IN ZIMBABWE

In parallel, Chido Govero, a Zimbabwe-born orphan who survived for years on a bowl of peanuts a day, learned this method of farming mushrooms at the age of twelve. She went from poverty to self-sufficiency in just a few months' time. Chido had the unique opportunity to spend a two years at the Africa University in Mutare, Zimbabwe. Under the guidance of Margaret Tagwira at the University's horticultural laboratory, Chido perfected her knowledge of mushroom tissue culture. It is evident that Chido has the proverbial "green thumb." What she touches produces food.

Paul Katzeff is a social entrepreneur who created Thanksgiving Coffee in Mendocino, California, and was the first in the US to sell certified Fair Trade coffee. His company was the first in California to become carbon neutral by offsetting emissions through planting 75,000 trees in Ethiopia. As well, they were the first to operate their corporate car fleet fueled by biodiesel. Katzeff introduced all his colleagues in the Specialty Coffee Association of America (SCAA) to the "Pulp-to-Protein" concept developed by ZERI. According to Katzeff, *"We have always been stuck between the cash crop and local development. But now, the waste of the cash crop is providing food security. This is the economic model to follow."*

SUCCESS IN CALIFORNIA

Following the economic crisis of 2008, the ZERI Foundation proposed the conversion of coffee grounds into mushrooms as a rapid and pragmatic response. The idea was enthusiastically greeted by Mrs. Makini Hassan, director of the Marin City Community Development Corporation. Her statement was emphatic. *"We are going to do this!"* she exclaimed, after learning the details. *"With unemployment reaching 11% in California, we need to create jobs, now!"*

Chido Govero and Carmenza Jaramillo were present to speak before the Specialty Coffee Association's conference held in Atlanta, Georgia in April 2009, where ZERI received the Association's 2009 Sustainability Award.

Subsequently they traveled to San Francisco to demonstrate how to convert the coffee grounds waste from local coffee shops into an ideal mushroom-growing medium. They took their expertise to Marin City, an urban area between Sausalito and Mill Valley. The response from Mrs. Makini Hassan was effusive. *"Seldom is there an opportunity such as this to pursue a social enterprise that provides a creative and meaningful way for youth and young adults to generate revenue, meet a viable market need, and learn from this hands-on entrepreneur, Chido Govera, a brilliant method of providing sustainable produce."*

Chido and Carmenza also helped Nikhil Arora and Alex Velez – both top students in their class at the UC Berkeley's Haas School of Business – to inoculate the first 500 pounds of coffee grounds with mushroom spore and launch Back To The Roots Ventures (BTTR Ventures), their entrepreneurial effort to achieve sustainable income from sustainable practice. *"If it works in Zimbabwe and Colombia where the conditions are tough, then it can definitely work here,"* concluded Arora, who dropped a well-paid consulting job to join Velez and pioneer this business model in the Bay Area. *"The beauty is that coffee grounds have only been touched by steam and boiling water. This means the substrate is sterilized and as such, 80% of the energy cost for preparing the growth substrate for mushrooms is eliminated,"* explained Velez.

The raw material is free, the energy demand is tiny, and product demand is huge. All these factors mean that these young entrepreneurs can offer expensive mushrooms below market price, garnering them a greater market share. In addition, the caffeine causes the mushrooms to fruit faster. That generates better cash flow and achieves more product than competitive mushroom-growing operations. The mushroom substrate that remains after harvest is rich in protein and serves as great fertilizer or as feed for chickens, goats, and even bison, as a pilot project with the Picuris Pueblo in New Mexico has demonstrated. However, in the San Francisco Bay area, where livestock is rare, it likely has a better future as compost for community gardens.

COFFEE, INVASIVE SPECIES, AND LOCAL BIODIVERSITY

A third opportunity subsequently emerged. I met with Charles Higgins, the Executive Director of Slide Ranch, an organic farm located within the Golden Gate Recreational Park along the Marin County coast. Almost immediately we began collaboration on an extension of the Pulp-to-Protein project right along the beach. One of the Park Services' goals is to remove non-native invasive species. Such an undertaking requires significant time and money. However, if these invasive species are blended with coffee grounds, which have been generously supplied by Equator Estate Coffees & Teas in nearby San Rafael, they become edible mushrooms. Chido, who was able to successfully farm mushrooms on grass clippings, broken branches, and corncobs, looked at the invasive species and concluded, *"It is like being in Heaven. We have never had such a wealth of biomass in Zimbabwe."*

Having three trial units operational in a mere two weeks is indicative of the potential of the Pulp-to-Protein model. According to Arora, *"Only eight to ten coffee shops suffice to create a production unit, each of which can generate about ten jobs."* Realizing that the Bay Area has an estimated eight million inhabitants, the potential is such that mushrooms could become a protein source comparable to and as readily available as chicken. At the same time, it generates good income, creates thousands of jobs, and offers inexpensive, high quality food. The goal for BTTR is to create 250 jobs. The sky is the limit but some estimates suggest that coffee grounds alone could generate 50,000 jobs in America. Why wait to try it out?

More recently Arora and Velez were selected by Newsweek as one of the Top 25 Entrepreneurs younger than 25. They were selected as runners-up in the BBC World Challenge, a global competition aimed at finding projects or small businesses from around the world that have shown enterprise and innovation at a grass roots level. The business model inspires.

Wild mushrooms that may cost $25 per pound in season, and are impossible to get out of season, may soon be available year-round, thanks to coffee grounds and invasive species blended with the entrepreneurial approach of Velez and Arora. Such an approach reduces landfill, reduces methane gas production, and increases consumer awareness of the solutions to sustainability to be found in their own backyard.

While briefly residing in Mill Valley, I often visited Muir Woods. I was continually amazed by its rich biodiversity evident just in the assortment of fungi I observed. The search for endemic mushrooms in local forestry areas is not something new for ZERI. It has already done this in New Mexico where it led to the creation of the first ever "State Mushroom Spore Bank" in the United States. The Spore Bank was initiated by Lynda Taylor, one of my first students in America. At a time when Americans are increasingly aware of the need to eat healthy food, mushrooms that are rich in protein and all essential amino acids, and are very low in cholesterol and saturated fatty acids, offer an excellent option. The production scheme proven elsewhere, and now tested by BTTR Ventures the Bay Area, will provide the basis for nationwide production.

OVERCOMING AN UNJUST BOYCOTT

Both Chido and Carmenza returned to their native countries following their contribution to job-generating schemes in America. When Chido attended the local church service during her stay in Marin City, she was asked by one of the parishioners, "Do you like America?" Although she responded in the affirmative, Chido added that she had a mission in Zimbabwe and wished to return. She has made a promise, to reach out to the orphan girls, and train them to achieve food security and self-sufficiency with nature as their helpmate. The last day of her visit in the US, Chido met with Helen Russell and Brooke McDonnell, the co-founders of Equator Estate Coffees & Teas, the women-led coffee wholesaler in San Rafael, California. The idea emerged to create "Chido's Blend" and for the first time in perhaps a decade to bring premium coffee from Zimbabwe to the United States. After years of boycott, farmers from Zimbabwe would have the opportunity to sell their exceptional coffees to US consumers!

The plan that is being developed empowers everyone in the process. The coffee farms in Zimbabwe can receive the opportunity to export for sale under the brand name "Chido's Blend" only when they commit to training the orphaned and at-risk girls living in the communities around their farms. The cash crop is now an export commodity, providing more work opportunities. The conversion of coffee waste into mushrooms and the waste of mushroom farming to animal feed provides food security. Food security for girls, especially orphans, reduces the risk of abuse.

The first buyers of Chido's Blend coffee in the USA were given a complimentary copy of Chido's book, *The Future of Hope, a Message from an African Orphan to a World in Turmoil*. After living like a nomad, sheltering wherever she could for 15 years, the sale of just a thousand copies of her book will permit Chido to build her own house. Actually, she is building her second house; the first one she built is for the mushrooms! The coffee sales are progressing, and Chido will not only be able to build a house for herself at Kufunda Village, she may one day be able to finance traditional houses in villages where orphans can live and learn from each other. Chido's dream is that from there they will travel by bus to other African coffee farms. At each stop Chido will make the same proposal: *"We will help you access the US market, if you will help make it possible to train the young orphan girls in your community."* As Chido points out, *"We know how to train them. I was just like them, and had nothing but hunger and the desire to feed my little brother and blind grandmother."*

Chido hopes that over the next decade she can reach thousands of girls throughout Africa. She has pledged not to rest as long as orphans are abused. They are desperate for access to a well with water, an earthen hut, and a small plot of land to tend as a vegetable garden to feed themselves. The usual price they must pay is submitting to abuse, most often by their own relatives. As orphans have neither a living mother, nor a father who will pay a dowry, few can ever get married. However, if these orphans have a skill that makes them able feed their family, this supersedes the need for a dowry.

From these experiences we can realize that the world is replete with connections. In natural systems everything is connected to everything else. We see that in in our modern society we can connect surmounting a trade boycott with the export of a cash crop, the waste of which becomes food security, and which generates jobs, both in Africa and in American inner-cities. Food security makes independence and self-sustenance possible. Eliminating dependency can eliminate the preconditions for abuse, and promote conditions for health and prosperity. All this can be made possible by coffee drinkers in the US who purchase Chido's Blend coffee from Equator Estate Coffees & Teas. It is a profound example of how individual consumer choices can carry us far toward affecting economic outcomes in far away places. In the same way, Chido's work as mentor to Zimbabwean orphans and to ecologically dedicated entrepreneurs is a profound example of how one individual can affect the lives of many.

We may hope that these small successes can inspire others to greater achievements, and that individuals everywhere will realize the meaning and importance of contribution to a Blue Economy in their own lives. A Blue Economy embraces the contributions of all. A Blue Economy cascades in endless innovation and evolution, utilizing all contributions and benefiting all participants.

FROM ZERI TO 100

I established the Zero Emissions Research Initiative (ZERI) Foundation in 1996 to explore, imagine, and discover strategic levers to development that would promote true sustainability. My ongoing work is to mentor individuals, businesses, and even nation-states to become aware of the perfection that nature achieves and to understand that a Blue Economy will lead to an energetic and sustainable success for the people and places of the planet. My current work in Bhutan and El Hierro, Canary Islands, allows me to mentor *in situ* economic development from the scope of a Blue Economy. Using innovations from the growing portfolio of environmental innovations means that developing nations can leapfrog over the developed world's mistakes, eliminating the propagation of poverty, pollution, and disease. A country like Bhutan, or an island like El Hierro, Canary Islands, can embark on a pervasive strategy to steer society towards sustainability.

The population of El Hierro has turned down proposals for the installation of a satellite launching platform or a radar monitoring station. They have sought alternatives that could meet their most important criteria: to provide a sustainable future rich with opportunities for future generations. They have opted for 19 of the 100 innovations described in this book. The public and the private sector have raised the cash needed to make the entire island of El Hierro self-sufficient in water and energy by the end of 2011. The farmers have agreed that all agriculture will be produced to organic and sustainable standards within seven years. All agro-waste will be dedicated to mushroom cultivation. Spent substrate will become compost, or will be cascaded to animal feed. Ivanka Milenkovic has committed her support to this goal. In addition, they intend that within a decade every single car on the island will be electrically powered, and all energy requirements will be met by harvesting the power of the ocean waves using a device that moves like the giant kelp. The investments required are calculated and the core funds needed are guaranteed.

The approach in Bhutan is similar. On a recent extended visit, it was clear that the challenge facing this small Himalayan nation is that their primary revenue source – glacier-generated hydropower – will disappear over the next 20 years of climate change. This pristinely beautiful land has begun to feel the stress of waste and consumerism. In consultation with their leaders I have identified 15 innovations that could provide them a solid economic foundation for decades to come. A portfolio of these innovations will convert all agro-wastes into bioplastics. The cultivation and harvesting of raw silk will build a new industry in health care while keeping their agricultural soils robust. Wind, locally a rich source of energy, will be captured with tiny turbines. The government has given its complete support to a strategy for building design and construction that is rooted in providing energy savings hand-in-hand with sustainability. Anders Nyquist, the brilliant Swedish architect, has committed his support. Notably, as soon as the opportunities were articulated, entrepreneurs and investors emerged.

I am also pleased to be commencing a weekly webcast (beginning in February 2010) that will feature a new business model inspired by one of the innovations described in this book. One business model will be presented each week for 100 weeks. These discussions will be disseminated worldwide to local populations in local languages. It is hoped that these electronic lectures will offer further information and resources to those who are serious about moving toward a Blue Economy.

While these successes and ventures seem modest, a decade of worldwide effort could achieve major changes. There is no doubt that growing numbers of regions and nation-states are becoming aware of and beginning to embrace sensible solutions and innovations that empower people and sustain communities. As initiatives emerge and collaborators share their successes, many will have the confidence to take the next step. Just as Javier Morales in Spain and Thinley Choden in Bhutan have the vision to enact new ideas and bring them to fruition, thousands of others will step forward with similar vision and strength. We may hope that these ongoing efforts can inspire others to greater achievements, and that individuals everywhere will realize the meaning and importance of contribution to a Blue Economy in their own lives. Cascading in endless innovation and evolution, a Blue Economy embraces the contributions of all.

The principles of economy are the principles of community. The principles of community are the principles of ecosystems. The success of our economies, of our communities, and of our planetary habitat depends on a collaborative effort to envision and achieve the abundance of a Blue Economy.

APPENDIX 1

A Table of 100 Innovations Inspired by Nature

CASCADING LIKE ECOSYSTEMS				
RANKED INNOVATION	POTENTIAL OPPORTUNITIES	RESEARCH/ BUSINESS LOCALE	DEVELOPER	SPECIES
1. Rainforest regeneration	Water, food and fuel, carbon credits, export goods, local livelihood security	Gaviotas, Colombia	Paolo Lugari	*Pinus caribbae* and *Pisolithus tinctorius*
2. Cascading farming and food processing	Locally farmed & processed food, clean water, biofuels, urban garden	Songhai, Benin	Father Godfrey Nzamujo	Maggots
3. Pulp-to-Protein	Mushrooms, biofuel, animal feed, export crops, local food	Hong Kong, Colombia, Serbia, Zimbabwe	Shuting Chan, Carmenza Jaramillo, Ivanka Milenkovic, Chido Govero	Plants, mushrooms, animals
4. CO_2 to nutrients and biofuels	Carbon harvesting, food, biofuel, bioplastics	Universidade Rio Grande do Sul, Brasil	Jorge Alberto Vieira Costa, Lucio Brusch da Fraga	Spirulina *Arthrospira platensis*
5. Cascading brewing systems	Beer, mushrooms, bread, sausages, biofuels, water	Namibia; Germany, USA, Japan, Sweden	George Chan, Jim Lueders	Plants, animals, mushrooms, algae, bacteria
6. Silk for topsoil	Steel and titanium substitute, medical devices, various consumer products from razors to cosmetics	Oxford Biomaterials, UK, Germany	Fritz Vollrath	Silkworm, golden orb spider
7. Bamboo housing	Water, carbon harvesting, building materials, biochemicals	Manizales, Colombia; Bali, University of Bremen, Germany	Simon Velez, Carolina Salazar Ocampo, Sabine Bode, Linda Garland, Ing Klaus Steffens	Bamboo *Guadua angustifolia*
8. Building material for quick, inexpensive housing	Recycling paper into renewable building material, fabricating emergency shelter	Japan	Shigeru Ban	Wood fibers of any species
9. Ecological waste-water treatment	Water, mushrooms, biogas, fertilizer	John Todd Ecological Design, USA	John Todd	Plants, algae, mushrooms, fish, bacteria
10. Food-grade fire retardants	Agro-waste reuse, health enhancing products, mining	Trulstech AB, Sweden; Deflamo AB, Sweden	Mats Nilsson	Citrus peel, grape pomace

RANKED INNOVATION	POTENTIAL OPPORTUNITIES	RESEARCH/ BUSINESS LOCALE	DEVELOPER	SPECIES
11. Unrecyclable glass to building material	Multipurpose building material, consumer and agricultural products	Earthstone, USA; MRD AB, Sweden; Pittsburgh Corning Europe	Andrew Ungerleider, Gay Dillingham, Åke Mård	Silicon dioxide (silica)
12. Air flow as in a rainforest	Tree nursery, air filtration, energy savings, interior design	Levande Filter AB, Sweden	Lars Thofeldt, Christer Swedin	Rainforest ecosystem
13. UV-radiation protection	Multifunctional materials for coloration, cosmetics, health	Facultés Universitaires Notre Dame de la Paix da Namur; Belgium. Oxford Univ., UK	Jean Pol Vigneron, Andrew Parker	Edelweiss and tomatoes
14. Plastics from food-waste starch	Bioplastics, landfill reduction, animal feed, biofuel	Kyushu Institute of Technology, Japan	Yoshihito Shirai	Fungus *Rhizopus oryzae*
15. Wood to food	Charcoal, mushrooms, animal feed, preserved wood for construction, mulch	Picuris Pueblo, New Mexico, USA; Colombia	Lynda Taylor, Robert Haspel, Antonio Giraldo Maya	Trees, fungi, animals
16. Prairie biofuels	Tourism, biofuels, biodiversity	Land Institute, USA	Wes Jackson	Oil-bearing plants and fruits

SUBSTITUTING SOMETHING WITH NOTHING

RANKED INNOVATION	POTENTIAL OPPORTUNITIES	RESEARCH/ BUSINESS LOCALE	DEVELOPER	SPECIES
17. No batteries	Electronics, medical devices, games and toys, clothing, shoes	Fraunhofer Institute, Germany; Colombia	Peter Spies, Jorge Reynolds	Warm-blooded animals
18. No smelting	Pure metals, energy efficiency, e-waste processing, mining	Prime Separations, USA	Henry Kolesinksi, Robert Cooley	Bacteria
19. Physics as a substitute for harsh chemistry	Drinking water, bactericide substitute, ice-making, irrigation, blending systems	Watreco, Sweden	Curt Hallberg, Ove Mortenson	Vortex caused by gravity
20. No refrigeration	Vaccines, medicine, food preservation	Cambridge Biostability, UK (Newco)	Bruce Roser	Water bear, resurrection fern
21. No glue	Consumer and industrial applications	Velcro, USA	George de Mestral	Cocklebur
22. No bactericides	Agriculture, oil & gas, food processing, consumer products, health care, medicine	Commonwealth Biotechnologies, USA; Venturepharm (VPL), China	Peter Steinberg, Staffan Kjellberg	Red seaweed *Delicea pulchra*

RANKED INNOVATION	POTENTIAL OPPORTUNITIES	RESEARCH/ BUSINESS LOCALE	DEVELOPER	SPECIES
23. Water reclamation without osmosis	Drinking water, heat island effect mitigation, energy efficiency	QinetiQ, UK	Andrew Parker	Namibian desert beetle
24. Cleansing without soap	Construction, paints, car design, flat sheet glass	University of Bonn, Germany	Willhelm Barthlott	Lotus flower
25. No lubricants or ball bearings	Mechanical friction in machinery, cars, house appliances, microelectronic mechanical devices	Technical University of Berlin, Germany	Ingo Rechenberg, Abdullah Regabi	Sandfish lizard
26. Pigment-free coloration	Cosmetics, paints, crystals, textiles	Oxford University, UK	Andrew Parker	Birds and beetles
27. Propulsion without CFCs	Medical, cosmetics, safety equipment, mining	University of Leeds, UK	Andy McIntosh	Bombardier beetle
28. Air conditioning without machinery	Real estate development, housing, schools, office & public buildings, retirement homes, industrial parks	EcoCycle Architects, Sweden	Anders Nyquist	Zebra, termite
29. Heating from the roots (greenhouses and homes)	Floor heating, horticulture, tree nurseries	Republic of Korea	Young-Suk Shu, Tae-Sung Oh	Root zone heating from vegetal decomposition
30. Calcium Carbonate from CO_2 Exhaust	Cement industry, coal-fired power stations, smelting, ceramics,	CO_2 Solutions, Canada	Norman Voyer, Sylvie Gauthier	Natural carbonic gas fixing
31. No aluminum packaging	Food, drinks, medicine, cosmetics	University of Queensland, Australia	Rebecca Cramp	Desert burrowing frog
32. Heat-free ceramics	Microelectronics, engines, defense industry, energy efficiency services	University of California, USA	Robert Ritchie	Abalone
33. Chemical-free paper	Paper, consumer goods (e.g., disposal diapers & paper products), insulation materials	Lawrence Berkeley National Laboratory, USA	Steven Chu	Termite
34. Mercury-free light	Illumination (especially in mines)	Marine Biological Laboratory, Woods Hole, USA	Roger Hanlon	Jellyfish and fungi
35. Solvent-free solutions	Chemistry applications of all kinds	University of Belgrade, Serbia	Ivan Vilotijevic	Red algae (*Dinoflagelattes*)

RANKED INNOVATION	POTENTIAL OPPORTUNITIES	RESEARCH/ BUSINESS LOCALE	DEVELOPER	SPECIES
36. Painless needle injections	Diabetic care, vaccination, veterinary applications	Okano Kogyo, Japan; Terumo Medical	Masayuki Okana	Mosquito
PLATFORM TECHNOLOGIES				
37. Maggot therapy	Abattoirs, feed, health care	Advanced Gel Technologies, UK	Stephen Britland	Maggots
38. Water purification	Microelectronics, food processing, emergency water supplies	Aquaporin, Denmark	Peter Agre	Aquaporin or protein cells
39. Water filtration by collidal graphite	Urban and industrial water treatment systems	Marathwada University, Aurangabad, India	U.H. Mane	Clams
40. Water purification	River restoration	University of Florida, USA	Rudolph Scheffrahn	Bald Cypress
41. Water purification	Microelectronics, pharmaceuticals, misted chemicals, cosmetics, food and drinks	University of Twente, Netherlands	Michel Versluis	Pistol Shrimp
42. Impact control by diatom frustules	Construction industries, mine engineering	Alfred Wegener Institute, Germany	Christian Hamm	Diatoms
43. Plastics from CO and CO_2	Microelectronics, designer plastics, food packaging	Novomer, USA	Geoffrey Coates	Citrus fruits
44. Polyesters from algae	Cosmetics, food packaging, nano-scale polymers	Universidade Rio Grande do Sul, Brazil	Michele Greque de Morais	Spirulina (*Arthrospira platensis*)
45. Biobattery from electric fish	Miniaturized and mobile electronics	Medical College of Virginia, USA	Michael N. Sheridan	Torpedo marmorata, *T. ocellata*
46. Algorithm for energy conservation	Home climate control, agriculture (greenhouses)	University of Adelaide, University of Iwate	Roger Seymour, Anna-Maria Angioy Kikukatsu Ito	Flowering plants
47. Lead capture	Waste management, water purification, micro-electronics, car battery recycling	Plant Cell Technology Laboratory, University of Guelph, Canada	Praveen Saxena	Yellow geranium

254

RANKED INNOVATION	POTENTIAL OPPORTUNITIES	RESEARCH/ BUSINESS LOCALE	DEVELOPER	SPECIES
48. Copper capture	Electric wiring, color pigments, electronic waste, car recycling, soil decontamination	Fungi Perfecti, USA	Paul Stamets	Wood ear mushroom
49. Applying Fibonacci code turbulence	Ventilation, mixing liquids, water treatment, computer cooling	Pax Scientific, USA	Jay Harman	Nautilus shell
50. Adhesion without glue, nuts or bolts	Aerospace industry, automotive industry	British Aerospace, UK	Stanislav Gorb	Gecko
51. Formaldehyde free glue	Wood processing, multilayer packaging	Oregon State University; Columbia Forest Products, USA	Kaichang Li	Mussel
52. Natural antibiotics	Food processing, cleaning products, personal care (mouth wash)	Northeastern University, Boston, USA	Kim Lewis	Barberry
53. Avian flu control	Building management (public places), air filtration, heating and cooling	Virginia Polytechnic, USA	John Coleman	Vultures
54. Repellent for yellow fever	Health management of public places, e.g., schools, hotels, restaurants	University of Liverpool, UK	Andrew Evans	Asian gaur
55. Anti-fungal chemistry	Building management, food processing, wood processing, agricultural chemicals	Chinese University of Hong Kong	T. B. Ng	Red kidney bean
56. Drinking water from condensation	Agriculture and irrigation systems, ornamental plants, office building management	Instituto Venezolano de Investigaciones Cientificos	Ernesto Medina	Cactus thorn
57. Desalination	Urban water supply, emergency water production, maritime transport, oil and gas	British Antarctic Survey, UK	Andrew Rankin, Eric Wolff	Penguins
58. Salt membrane	Water supply in coastal zones, maritime transportation	University of British Columbia, Canada	Daniel Mosquin	Polynesian box fruit
59. Potable water from the air	Building management, agriculture	Oxford University; University of Namibia	Keto Mshigeni	*Welwitschia mirabilis*

RANKED INNOVATION	POTENTIAL OPPORTUNITIES	RESEARCH/ BUSINESS LOCALE	DEVELOPER	SPECIES
60. Self-cleansing surface	Sanitary ceramics	INAX, Japan	Emile Ishida	Abalone
61. Ceramic composites	Engines, micro-electronics	University of California-Santa Barbara, USA	Herbert Waite	Glycera worm
62. Lubricants	Microelectronic mechanical systems (MEMS) like airbags	Vienna University of Technology, Austria	Ilse Gebeshuber	Diatoms
63. Creating white	Food, cosmetics, chemistry, plastics, paper	University of Exeter, UK	Peter Vukusic	*Cyphochilus beetle*
64. Stress-resistant packaging	Packaging, electronics	Case Western University, USA	Christoph Weder	Sea cucumber
65. Expandable packaging	Drinks, fuel containers, liquid pharmaceuticals	Station Biologique de la Tour du Valat, France	A. J. Crivelli	Pelican
66. Waterproofing	Bioplastics, water containers, building materials (roofing)	Agricultural College, Devon, UK	Glynne Jones	Bees
67. Wood degradation for paper	Paper, disposable consumer paper products, insulation materials	Russian Academy of Sciences	Vladimir Zverlov	White rot fungus and bacteria
68. Blue light for HIV test kit	Medical devices	Beacon Biotechnology, USA	Fred Mitchell	Deep sea crustaceans
69. Pipes and tubes for buildings	Construction industries, urban planning	Splitvision AB, Sweden	Björn Bellander	Human respiratory and digestive system
70. Thin-film solar cells	Textiles, greenhouses, buildings, chemical industry (substitute to anti-corrosion)	Politechnique de Lausanne; Konarka UK	Michael Graetzel, Alan Heeger	Plant leaves
71. Concentrated solar power	Water heating, electricity generation	University of California-Santa Barbara, USA	Luke Lee	Dragonfly
72. Heat conservation	Textiles, underwater engineering	University of Florida, USA	Brian McNab	Tuna
73. Drag reduction	Wind power, aerospace, automobile design	Whalepower, Canada	Frank Fish	Dolphin and whale

RANKED INNOVATION	POTENTIAL OPPORTUNITIES	RESEARCH/ BUSINESS LOCALE	DEVELOPER	SPECIES
74. Aerodynamic efficiency	Automotive design	Mercedes Benz, Germany	Klaus Matthek	Box fish
75. Solid-state energy	Security systems	Imperial College, UK	J. W. Millbank	Lichen
76. Biocatalysis	Chemistry, food processing	University of Exeter, UK	Sir Christopher Evans, OBE	Marine algae
77. Energy from waves	Energy for mobility management, coastal zone development	Biopower, Australia	Tim Finnigan	Giant kelp
78. Traffic congestion reduction	Telecommunications, mobility and queue management, automotive (GPS)	Science University, Munich, Germany	Darya Popiv	Swarm intelligence of insects
79. Self-heating	Agriculture (horticulture and greenhouses)	University of Cagliari, Italy	Ana Maria Angioy	Dead horse arum
80. Anti-freeze	Automotive, food preservation, pharmaceuticals	Queens University, Canada	Virginia Walker	Mealworm beetle
81. Silicon deposits	Electronics, cosmetics	NT-MDT, Russia	Viktor Bykov	Sea sponge
82. Distortion-free lenses	Optics, electronics, security devices	Harvard University, Cambridge, USA	Joanna Aizenberg	Brittle star
83. Self-assembly of chips	Microelectronics	University of Regensburg, Germany	Nils Kröger	Diatoms
84. Conductivity	Medical devices, mobile microelectronics, bio-sensors	Whale Tracking Research, Colombia	Jorge Reynolds	Whales
85. Conductive gel	Medical devices, mobile microelectronics	Marine Biological Lab Woods Hole, USA	R. Douglas Field	Sharks
86. Thin film lenses	Security systems, telemonitoring, traffic control	Case Western University, USA	Anna Hiltner	Octopus
87. Infrared sensors	Fire safety, defense industry, domotica, kitchen equipment	University of Bonn, Germany	Helmut Schmitz	Jewel beetle

RANKED INNOVATION	POTENTIAL OPPORTUNITIES	RESEARCH/ BUSINESS LOCALE	DEVELOPER	SPECIES
88. Radar airport security	Security systems, traffic control	Smith & Co (Farran), UK	Tony McEnroe	Bats
89. Sonar location device	Hearing aids, security systems	Cornell University, New York USA	Ron Hoy, Ron Miles	*Ormia ochracea* *(fly)*
90. Acoustical lenses	Hearing aids, security systems, hydrophonics	University of California-Santa Cruz, USA	James Aroyan	Pink dolphin
91. Sound transmission	Medical devices, hearing aids	Stanford University, USA	Caitlin O'Connell	Elephant
92. Fiber optics	Light management, telecommunications	Harvard University, USA	Joanna Aizenberg	Sea sponge
93. Underwater data transmisson	Telecommunications, entertainment	Berlin Technical University, Germany	Rudolph Bannasch	Dolphins
94. Water repellent	Skin care, fine chemicals, textiles, shoes	University of Bonn, Germany	Zdenek Cerman	Water strider
95. Dehumidification	Building management, medical treatment, food preservation	University of Bath, UK	Julian Vincent	Desert cockroach
FOOD FOR THOUGHT				
96. Malaria control	Substitute for pharmaceuticals	University of Canterbury, New Zealand	Ximena Nelson	Jumping spider *(Evarcha culicivora)*
97. Radiation resistance, DNA repair	Cosmetics, alternative to plastic surgery, pharmaceutics, radiation remediation	Université de Paris Sud France	Nicolas Leulliot	*Deinococcus radiodurans* bacteria
98. Shock buffer	Automotive, elevators, building design in earthquake zones	University of Kanazawa and Toyota Japan	Juhachi Oda, Kenichi Sakano	Woodpecker
99. Body fat reduction	Health care, food processing	University of Texas, USA	Chen Chi Lee	Hibernating animals
100. Reduction of gastric acidity	Pharmaceuticals, functional foods	University of Adelaide, Australia	Michael Tyler	Gastric brooding frog

APPENDIX 2

100 Innovations Inspiring Competitive Business Models

> Go confidently in the direction of your dreams.
> Live the life you have imagined.
>
> — HENRY DAVID THOREAU

The original concept for this project was to find and promote the best and most elegant solutions from nature that could be applied to solving to our current economic and environmental challenges. Our research for this book reviewed the emerging business model and the shifts in the economic system it would engender. The microeconomic changes and the new macroeconomic reality derived from hundreds of small opportunities. This list offers the reader a numbered overview (1–100) of some of the relevant cases that demonstrate what is really possible. Although the choices were complex, by assessing each for its capacity to respond to multiple needs with lower investments we narrowed our selection to the few dozen listed here. Omissions or errors indubitably occur and may hopefully be forgiven in future editions.

Most of the developers named are researchers, scientists, and innovators with whom I have had personal contact and exchange. Many other individuals as well have been involved in the observation, discovery, and implementation of the innovations we feature below. Some applications described are mere possibilities. Others have been successfully trialed and have reached marketability and sustainability. I invite you to join me for my ongoing webcast series beginning in February 2010 and continuing through February 2012. Each online segment features additional descriptions and background of one innovation and an exploration of possible or developing applications.

Each of these groupings is assessed for the capacity to generate employment. To date these one hundred innovations have generated approximately 20,000 jobs. Worldwide, when translated into solid projects by dedicated entrepreneurs and professionals, the potential during the coming decade is an additional 100 million new direct and indirect jobs. Some, such as coffee and silk, can achieve major

impact, while others may contribute fewer jobs but greater sustainability. A Blue Economy allows for gradual (and non-linear) evolution while encompassing the potential to achieve levels of cooperation and contribution that will benefit all.

CASCADING MATERIALS, NUTRIENTS, AND ENERGY LIKE ECOSYSTEMS

This first group of innovations cascades nutrients, matter, and energy to effectively generate more income, employment, and social capital than a core business approach. These are concrete examples that emulate ecosystem principles where waste of one is a food or nutrient for another, effectively integrating multiple activities so everything contributes to the fullest extent. In economic terms, this clustering and cascading means that scarce and expensive yet desirable materials and products become abundant and affordable. This will easily out-compete the present reality, where too often the lowest quality is all that is affordable or available. Perhaps one of the greatest contributions that Blue Economy models can offer is making affordable and plentiful what is most needed and most desired. Such outcomes require collaboration, vision, commitment, and flexibility. Yet the results – full employment, freely available commons, and substantial levels of socioeconomic benefit – make entire communities robust and successful.

In addition, the cases described in this first section have the greatest potential for job generation, quickly responding to multiple needs, generating multiple benefits over and above competitive advantage, producing cash flow, and even accumulating of social capital. These cases have been implemented around the world and clearly signify a new trend. They are inspired by ecosystems that cascade materials, nutrients, and energy in endless cycles, assisted by an abundant supply of gravitational and solar energy. These are certainly not the only cases in the world. Though there are dozens of others we have limited ourselves to a mere hundred in this first edition, focusing on those more immediately in our personal experience, and for which we have been able to evaluate long term potential.

The job generation outlook for these cases is impressive. Even if we overshoot the estimate by a factor of ten, the impact remains tremendous. Each project or business enterprise demonstrates a way forward that is within the carrying capacity of our planet's resources. While there is no single solution, each case illustrates the diversity of approaches that emulate ecosystems by valuing all inputs and wasting nothing. It is fair to say that each of the projects and businesses mentioned actually deserves a book of its own.

INNOVATION:	**Las Gaviotas (1)**
BENEFIT:	Rainforest Regeneration
DEVELOPER:	Paolo Lugari (Colombia)
DATE:	1984
JOBS POTENTIAL:	15,000,000

Starting with 20,000 acres of barren savannah that had suffered 450 years of slash and burn agriculture, Paolo Lugari transformed Las Gaviotas, in Vichada, Colombia, into a rich and verdant rainforest. Begun in 1984, this long-term initiative succeeded by making use of the symbiosis of the Caribbean pine tree and mycorrhizal fungi. Las Gaviotas is an oasis of peace, filled with the luxurious biodiversity of over 250 tropical flora, 90% of Amazonian origin. Water, tree resins, and biofuels are all harvested for cash flow. The population garners health benefits from regular exercise (all transport is on bicycles) and everyone receives free drinking water. Housing, health care, energy provision, livelihood, and food security are all positively impacted by the development at Las Gaviotas. It also increases social capital. By the latest count Gaviotas supports approximately 2,000 people through direct or indirect jobs. Were a comparable approach applied to 15 million acres of similar land in Colombia the potential would be in excess of one million jobs. If this model were applied to the 200 million acres under consideration in Venezuela, Brazil, and Peru, it could generate 15 million jobs while capturing the annual equivalent of Japan's carbon emissions.

INNOVATION:	**Songhai Center (2)**
BENEFIT:	Food and health security
DEVELOPER:	Father Godfrey Nzamujo (Porto Novo, Benin)
DATE:	1986
JOBS POTENTIAL:	500,000 (Africa), 5,000,000 (Worldwide)

Songhai Center, initiated by Father Godfrey Nzamujo, demonstrates the capacity to create an integrated farming and food processing center in an African peri-urban zone. The food security project follows the successful model of cascading nutrients and energy. The core products generating cash flow are food for local consumption and export, while biogas complements electricity from the grid. The population benefits from improved hygiene, thanks to digesters and water treatment facilities that utilize indigenous and invasive plants and bio-waste. All animal wastes from the abattoir cascade to the maggot farm where they become nutrient matter. Maggots are harvested as feed for quails and fish. Further income

potential can be realized from supplying maggot enzymes at a fraction of the cost to innovative health care companies like Advanced Gel Technologies (3).

Once again we see a cascading model that positively impacts the availability of clean water, food, health care, and energy. It creates local employment and gains significant social capital. In 2009, 250 people were directly or indirectly employed at Songhai. A comparable facility located at every slaughterhouse in Africa would provide in excess of 500,000 jobs. Worldwide, this approach could provide five million jobs. The result would be much greater availability of highly desirable goods and services of benefit to everyone, even those well-to-do.

INNOVATION:	**Pulp-to-Protein (4)**
BENEFIT:	Food security
DEVELOPER(S):	Carmenza Jaramillo (Columbia), Shuting Chang (Hong Kong), Ivanka Milenkovic (Serbia), Chido Govero (Zimbabwe)
DATE:	1992
JOBS POTENTIAL:	50,000,000 (coffee waste only)
	100,000,000 (coffee plus tea, corn, straw, orchard pruning, water hyacinth)

The coffee waste Pulp-to-Protein initiative was undertaken and scientifically substantiated by Carmenza Jaramillo at the behest of CENICAFE. This initiative converted wasted biomass on coffee farms into food and achieved food security. The coffee research started in 1994 and built on the pioneering work of Prof. Shuting Chang of the Chinese University of Hong Kong, who grew as many shiitake mushrooms on coffee waste substrate as could be grown on logged and shredded oak trees. Research conducted by Ivanka Milenkovic at the University of Belgrade established that the spent substrate could be used as a high-quality livestock feed.

Both the mushroom fruiting body sold for consumption and the spent substrate used as animal feed build local food security and increase disposable income through export sales. Today an estimated 10,000 people have direct and indirect employment through this initiative. The program in Zimbabwe, headed by Chido Govero, lifts orphans out of poverty and abuse. The potential exceeds 50 million jobs if all the coffee farms around the world were to cascade nutrients like ecosystems do. If this program were extended to tea farms and apple orchards, the potential could double to 100 million. The capacity to generate food exceeds the present tonnage from fish farming.

INNOVATION:	**CO₂ to Micronutrients and Biofuel (5)**
BENEFIT:	Food and Fuel Security
DEVELOPER:	Jorge Alberto Vieria Costa (Brazil),
	Lucio Brusch da Fraga (Brazil),
	Michele Greque de Morais (Brazil)
DATE:	1995, 2007
JOBS POTENTIAL:	2,500,000

CO_2 to Micronutrients and Biofuels, a program initiated in 1995 by Jorge Alberto Vieira Costa from the Federal University of Brazil in Rio Grande, was implemented in partnership with a team headed by Prof. Lucio Brusch da Fraga and funded by the Fundaçao Banco do Brasil. This program has taught local farmers to grow spirulina using the water from local lakes. The sales generated from production and harvest provide the farmers with much-needed income. The spirulina is provided to low-income families as a nutritional supplement, helping eradicate malnutrition. After the success of this program its scope was expanded to include harvesting CO_2 using the available infrastructure of a local coal-fired power station to grow algal biodiesel. The pilot plant was inaugurated in 2007.

Again we see a system that positively impacts food, health care, energy, even the production of esters, and generates local employment. By the latest count approximately 100 jobs have been generated by this undertaking, including a dozen academic posts. The production of biodiesel at coal-powered electricity-generating facilities is a sensible adaptation of ecosystem logic to an industrial production model. If all the coal-fired power stations around the world were to capture their CO_2 exhaust to grow algal biodiesel, an additional 2.5 million jobs could be created.

INNOVATION:	**Integrated Biosystems Breweries (6)**
BENEFIT:	Food, energy
DEVELOPER:	George Chan (Namibia), Jim Leuders (USA)
DATE:	1995, 2002
JOBS POTENTIAL:	1,000,000

Integrated Brewing Systems in Tsumeb, Namibia, was initiated by Professor George Chan in 1995, in cooperation with Namibian Breweries and in partnership with Werner List and the University of Namibia. Starting with brewery waste, this ingenious cascading of nutrients integrates the five kingdoms of nature, increasing

brewery revenues through animal husbandry, mushroom production, fish farming, and biogas generation. When the brewery closed in 2003 because of a lack of demand for sorghum beer, the principles of the system had been solidly benchmarked in very harsh circumstances: without water, in a desert location, with cold winters, and without qualified staff. The pioneering experience has been applied to the principles of beer brewing around the world by companies including Storm Brewery (St Johns, Newfoundland, Canada), Great Lakes Brewery (Cleveland, Ohio, USA), Shinano Brewery (Nagano, Japan), Visby Brewery (Gotland, Sweden), and Meierhof (Ottbergen, Nordrhein Westfalen, Germany).

The full application of the system commenced in the summer of 2009 in Stevensville, Montana, initiated by master brewer Jim Lueders at the Wildwood Brewery. This cascading model provides food, recycles water, generates jobs, and creates additional income, particularly from the sale of bread, mushrooms, and sausages at the local market. The number of jobs created at existing micro-breweries is estimated at 250. If all breweries around the world were to cascade waste to nutrients, it would generate at least an additional one million jobs.

INNOVATION:	**Silk for Topsoil, Oxford Biomaterials (7)**
BENEFIT:	Soil fertility, silk substitution for metals
DEVELOPER:	Fritz Vollrath (UK)
DATE:	1992
JOBS POTENTIAL:	12,500,000

Professor Fritz Vollrath, from Oxford University Department of Zoology, has demonstrated the potential to replace high-performance metals like titanium with silk. His initial *Scientific American* publication in 1992 set the stage for a renewed demand for silk spun by the mulberry worm. Vollrath and his team reprocess worm-spun silk in a similar manner to the method used by the golden orb spider, using water and pressure only. They have created a portfolio of medical devices introduced to the market through Oxford Biomaterials (OBM) and its affiliated companies.

If silk were to replace just the stainless steel and titanium used in household consumer goods, it would increase demand for silk beyond the present production capacity, while lowering landfill accumulation of these mined metals. Since the silkworm derives its food from the leaves of the mulberry tree, extensive plantings of mulberry trees on arid land could provide food, energy, jobs, and soil regeneration. Although the technology is still in its early stages, the applications have proven viable in the medical field and will soon expand into consumer goods. Within a

decade, the number of jobs created through reforestation, topsoil regeneration, and silk processing could expand to 1.25 million for each 250,000 acres of mulberry plantations, making silk production a major economic driver. If one million tons of silk were produced (matching historic production levels), these agricultural and industrial sectors would provide a livelihood for 12.5 million families.

INNOVATION:	**Bamboo Housing (8)**
BENEFIT:	Housing, topsoil, water, paper recycling, refugees
DEVELOPER:	Shigeru Ban (Japan), Sabine Bode (Germany), Simon Velez (Colombia), Carolina Salazar Ocampo (Colombia)
DATE:	1995
JOBS POTENTIAL:	10,000,000

Shigeru Ban imitated the form and the structural strength of bamboo using recycled paper, creating a building system inspired by bamboo and using the cellulose from one waste stream to provide raw materials for construction. He designed a paper-made building structure for the Japanese pavilion at the 2000 World Expo in Hanover, Germany. This design could quickly be adapted to the creation of solid and inexpensive shelter for disaster victims.

Bamboo is an abundant and rapidly proliferating species native to tropical climates. It has significant potential to favorably impact housing needs when used in developing nations as a structural building material. For durability and performance it is comparable to steel and reinforced cement. However, it is much less costly, far more available, and rapidly self-renewing. Its ecological impact is carbon-neutral. Increased demand for bamboo would also lead to reforestation in compromised tropical areas. This would reduce and eventually reverse soil erosion while replenishing surface water through bamboo's capacity to retain moisture.

Simon Velez **(9)** is considered the Maestro of bamboo construction. Using the insights of Prof. Dr. Ing Klaus Steffens from the University of Bremen (Germany), Simon Velez and his team coordinated with Sabine Bode and Carolina Salazar Ocampo to design, permit, and construct the ZERI pavillion at the 2000 World Expo in Hanover, Germany. The structure utilized bamboo, recycled cement, copper, and a mixture of terracotta, cement, and bamboo fiber panels.

INNOVATION:	**Integrated Wastewater Treatment (10)**
BENEFIT:	Waste recovery
DEVELOPER:	John Todd (USA)
DATE:	1986
JOBS POTENTIAL:	250,000

John Todd (John Todd Ecological Design) designs ecological wastewater treatment systems with plants, algae, and bacteria to cleanse municipal and industrial sewage. This technique evolved into what is known today as "Eco-Machines." These convert polluting organic matter into nutrients. In 2001, John Todd and his colleagues included mushroom cultivation in their South Burlington, Vermont sewage treatment facility, completing a low cost, low energy operating system that integrates beneficial input from four kingdoms of nature.

Innovative components to the water treatment process could potentially include bacterial sublimation with vortexes, water filtration with colloidal graphite and clams (**11**), the cleansing technology of the pistol shrimp (**12**), and the water purification technique of the bald cypress tree (**13**).

At present John Todd Ecological Design employs a dozen staff. However, there is vast worldwide potential for systems that convert polluted water to a resource through biological processes and the bundling of naturally derived technologies. Such an industry could generate an estimated 250,000 jobs within a decade.

INNOVATION:	**Trulstech AB (14)**
BENEFIT:	Food grade fire retardant
DEVELOPER:	Mats Nilsson (Sweden)
DATE:	2004
JOBS POTENTIAL:	2,000

Trulstech is the first company to offer fire and flame retardants made from food-grade ingredients. Mats Nilsson designed these substitutes for toxic ingredients based on his understanding of the Krebs Cycle. The capacity to produce fire retardants using ingredients derived from waste streams like citrus peels and grape pomace places green chemistry into a systemic context. This technology cascades waste to generate cash flow and service multiple markets, from flame retardants for textiles, interior design components, and automotive materials, to the control of forest fires and even the reduction of explosion risk in mines. These

food-based chemicals are competitive in price and available through the start-up company Deflamo AB. This group employs a dozen staff today. The substitution of toxic constituents with these food-grade alternatives could represent a net job generation of a few thousand.

INNOVATION:	**Earthstone (15)**
BENEFIT:	Agriculture, housing
DEVELOPER:	Andrew Ungerleider, Gay Dillingham (USA)
DATE:	1993
JOBS POTENTIAL:	50,000

Andrew Ungerleider and Gay Dillingham founded Earthstone to make products that replace strip-mined pumice, used as a household and commercial abrasive, with reconditioned unrecyclable glass. Ungerleider heated a blend of green, brown, and white glass, injecting it with CO_2 to convert it to a structural material. The Earthstone facility is located on the Albuquerque, New Mexico municipal landfill. A portion of the facility's energy requirement is supplied by the biogas generated from decomposing biomass at the landfill. Recycled glass can be substituted for fiberglass in agriculture, and for numerous industrial and consumer products.

MRD AB (Sweden) goes beyond these developed markets and converts unrecyclable glass into structural building materials based on the innovative construction techniques of Åke Mård. This lightweight material with a micron-sized air bubble structure imitates diatom frustules **(16)**, the hard and porous cell walls of minute algae. It is marketed as pre-fabricated units that permit rapid construction, a big advantage in cold climates.

These companies, along with Pittsburgh Corning Europe (manufacturer of cellular glass thermal insulation products) have already generated over 400 jobs by recycling glass into building and consumer products. If all recycled glass were reclaimed by this technique, it would generate an estimated 50,000 jobs while reducing the load on landfills, replacing energy-intensive building materials, and reducing strip mining. This system increases the amount of glass recycled, relieving bottling companies of the extra costs for transport and sterilization of recycled glass, and promises a potential worldwide job increase in excess of 100,000.

INNOVATION:	**Living Filters (17)**
BENEFIT:	Air purification and biodiversity
DEVELOPER:	Christer Swedin (Sweden, USA)
DATE:	1998
JOBS POTENTIAL:	10,000

Levande Filter AB (Living Filters), designed by Lars Thofeldt and commercialized by Christer Swedin, achieves the control of air-suspended particles, from dust to charged carbon and even carbon monoxide, using a rainforest ecosystem model. To clean the air in a building a Living Filter system utilizes a wide variety and number of tropical plants and a misting system that imitates the rainfall in a rainforest. Whether for an office, school, or even an airport, this technique is facilitated by the optimal use of air flows as well as the misting of humidity into the plant zones. The low energy and maintenance cost is competitive with the cost of ornamental plants commonly used as decoration in office buildings.

The Living Filter system is particularly efficient in eliminating charged particles, which are known causes of respiratory diseases. Widespread use of Living Filter systems would generate a large number of jobs in both installation and maintenance. As an added benefit, it would increase not only building ambiance but appreciation of plant biodiversity. The greatest job generation, estimated at 10,000, would likely be in the expanded need for plant nurseries around the world.

INNOVATION:	**Tomato Waste Reprocessing (18)**
BENEFIT:	Food waste to UV protection
DEVELOPER:	Jean Pol Vigneron (Belgium), Andrew Parker, UK
DATE:	1994
JOBS POTENTIAL:	2,000

Ultraviolet radiation protection from tomato skins is based on ground-breaking research by Professor Jean Pol Vigneron at the University of Namur (Facultés Notre Dame de la Paix de Namur) that offers researchers a new direction for products that protect from excessive sun exposure. Professor Vigneron's original findings came from studying the edelweiss plant. They shed light on how we might use naturally derived substances to protect from excessive sun. Separately, Professor Andrew Parker's research concluded that the least costly and most secure supply of UV-protective agents can be derived from tomato skins. Not only are these materials that can be easily reclaimed from the massive waste stream generated by producing

tomato sauce and ketchup, they can be obtained and manufactured at costs below the present price of titanium oxide, today's standard sun protection agent. This generates potentially thousands of jobs.

INNOVATION:	**Plastics from Food Waste Starch (19)**
BENEFIT:	Waste to plastics
DEVELOPER:	Prof. Yoshihito Shirai (Japan),
	Geoffrey Coates (USA), Michele Greque (Brazil)
DATE:	2000, 2004
JOBS POTENTIAL:	10,000

Yoshihito Shirai from the Kyushu Institute of Technology studied the potential for making plastics from food-waste starch. He did not use cornstarch because of its importance in maintaining food security in many developing countries. He reasoned that if growing corn for biofuel or plastics production pushed the price of corn higher, it would be less available as a food and thus more people would go hungry. Shirai designed a system that took food waste from restaurants in his local area, Kita-Kyushu, and used a fungus to convert the waste, at nearly room temperature, into polylactic acid. Because landfill costs in Japan are high, such bioplastics are financially viable. Shirai's laboratory research led to the construction of a pilot plant that has been operational since 2004. As production expands it will further reduce the load on the landfill. As a further cascading benefit, the residue from bio-plastics production is used as animal feed.

Meanwhile, in the US, Novomer (20) is developing plastic products derived from CO and CO_2, capitalized by investment funds from Unilever and DSM.

In Brazil, Michele Greque de Morais is researching the production of polyesters (21) extracted from algae as a by-product of spirulina (human nutrients) and algal oil (biodiesel). Successful results would be an important contribution to making full use of this developing field.

INNOVATION:	**Wood to Food (22)**
BENEFIT:	Waste into Nutrient
DEVELOPER:	Lynda Taylor (USA), Robert Haspel (USA)
DATE:	2001
JOBS POTENTIAL:	40,000

Lynda Taylor and Robert Haspel are not your everyday scientists. They are activist citizens dedicated to making a difference where it counts. Each dry season, New Mexico, like Colorado and California, suffers massive forest fires. At the Picuris Pueblo, north of Santa Fe, Lynda and Robert undertook a project to demonstrate that the removal of small-diameter wood can not only reduce the risk of forest fires, it can be a source of income through the production and sale of quality products. The small-diameter wood that is cleared becomes the raw materials for two products. Part of the wood is converted to charcoal in ovens made from metal shipping containers. Using a technique developed by Antonio Giraldo Maya, the captured combustion smoke from the charcoal can be used to preserve wood used for construction. The wood not suitable for charcoal production or construction is chipped, then inoculated with native mushroom spore and spread over the tracks left by wood-cutting equipment and trucks. The mushrooms are harvested and the spent substrate is fed to the Pueblo's bison herd. Over the course of the year the decomposing mulch eradicates the equipment tracks.

This cascading of nutrients, supported by a capital outlay from the State of New Mexico, generates jobs and products for sale that could potentially replace the gambling casinos currently driving economic development on Native American land. If this strategy were applied to all forests endangered by imminent fire hazard, it would provide forest protection and at the same time generate food and job security.

INNOVATION:	**Biofuels from Prairie Perennials (23)**
BENEFIT:	Energy
DEVELOPER:	Wes Jackson (USA)
DATE:	2007
JOBS POTENTIAL:	10,000

Wes Jackson from the Land Institute calculated that the biofuel potential from naturally occurring Midwestern prairie perennials could generate more energy (and biodiversity!) than monocultures of corn. Although this has only been developed as a concept and has neither been commercially implemented nor produced any intellectual property, the scientific base and the detailed logic underpinning the proposal invites a fundamental rethinking of how our industrial society can proactively respond to basic energy requirements now that fossil oil production has peaked. The biodiversity of the prairie includes oil-bearing plants and fruits. These species offer a harvest of lipids and oils without requiring irrigation or genetic manipulation to increase yields. Because it relies on natural systems already in place, this approach could quickly replace biofuel harvesting from corn, soybeans, or other cultivated crops. The investment monies thus released would be available to fund biofuel production from truly renewable resources.

SUBSTITUTING SOMETHING WITH NOTHING

This second group of innovations includes those that shift the standard business model, since one (or more) of the current industry standard materials (often toxic or non-renewable) is simply no longer needed. There are 20 such examples in this grouping. They contain possibilities for truly significant industrial initiatives. This portfolio of innovations affects an estimated 200 sectors of the economy. At an entrepreneurial level many would perhaps commence more modestly, covering specific niche markets and operating locally. However, their scope is such that all economic sectors would be influenced.

In economic circles there is much debate about the need for rational levels of material consumption. A thoughtful assessment of all the innovations that emerge from mirroring ecosystems reveals that what we often consider indispensable is simply not needed in nature. This is why we present this category of innovations that highlight how something, which today may be the market standard, may actually be unnecessary. This implies that we can reduce the negative factors such as high cost and unacceptable collateral damage inherent to the way we respond to market demand.

Several substitutions are generic, and numerous species demonstrate skills that achieve similar results. However they accomplish this with different techniques. That is why several technologies are described together, though listed separately in the table in Appendix 1. The end result is a fascinating list that allows us to envision considerable improvement in meeting market needs with fewer materials. The infamous axiom known as the rebound effect – that a reduction of materials triggers more demand – is based on an assumption of scarcity and not likely to apply under these circumstances.

The "substitution effect" changes the dynamics and even the logic of economies of scale. As we have seen, the materials that can often be eliminated are major occupational health hazards and environmental risks that increase the need for management and require centralized handling. However, substituting something with nothing opens opportunities for entrepreneurs to develop products that are non-polluting and toxin-free, and to access markets competitively. This goes along with the logic of "investing less, generating more," and is bound to have a positive effect on employment.

INNOVATION:	**No batteries (24)**
BENEFIT:	Energy, health, mining
DEVELOPER:	Peter Spies (Germany), Jorge Reynolds (Colombia)
DATE:	1986
JOBS POTENTIAL:	5,000

Peter Spies and his colleagues, in association with the Fraunhofer Society, are researching how to replace batteries with energy systems that operate without batteries. He is designing electronic devices such as cell phones that are powered by body heat and the pressure wave of our voice.

Jorge Reynolds (**25**) uses his insights on how the whale generates and conducts electricity to eliminate the need for batteries in medical devices ranging from monitoring equipment to a substitute for the pacemaker that eliminates the need for surgery. Without batteries and wires such production and consumption models no longer create massive waste streams. Innovations that employ physics like natural systems can reduce the need for mined material, reducing costs and saving energy. This type of innovation can spur the redesign of other devices and even toys. The electric fish (**26**) provides additional ideas for insulation and bio-batteries as does the lichen (**27**) with its solid-state energy provision.

INNOVATION:	**No smelting (28)**
BENEFIT:	Energy, mining
DEVELOPER:	Henry Kolesinksi (USA), Robert Cooley (USA)
DATE:	2002
JOBS POTENTIAL:	50,000

Henry Kolesinski and Robert Cooley, former researchers with Polaroid and with Waters Corporation, and now principals at Prime Separations, developed a thin-film technology that chelates up to 18 metals the way bacteria do, eliminating the need for mining and smelting. The 400 million tons of accumulating and polluting electronic waste are the raw materials for this application. It is even possible that waste processing facilities could use existing and mainly defunct complex ore crushing plants to convert cast-off CD-players, cell phones, and printed circuit boards into a 70-micron sized powder that could be "chelation mined" for its metals. This would relieve landfills of toxic waste, offer pure metals at a low energy cost, and save massively on energy consumption. Since the processing facilities could be proximally located to landfills, transportation to central sites would not be required as is the procedure today. This would significantly reduce climate change impact.

There are other technologies like the capture of lead by geraniums **(29)** and of copper by the woodear mushroom**(30)**, but nothing competes with the wide field of application for the chelating process on thin film developed by Prime Separations. The decentralized recovery of electronic waste is expected to generate jobs similar to the recycling of glass into building materials and consumer goods.

INNOVATION:	**Physics as a substitute for harsh chemistry (31)**
BENEFIT:	Energy, health
DEVELOPER:	Curt Hallberg (Sweden); Jay Harman (USA)
DATE:	1997
JOBS POTENTIAL:	250,000

Curt Hallberg's mathematical models of the vortex, inspired by the pioneering work of Viktor Schauberger, allowed him to develop a variety of products that use the force of gravity and the conformation of a vortex in a system that either aerates water or expels air from water. In effect, he uses physics to substitute for harsh chemistry. The plethora of possible applications would permit the redesign of numerous consumer and industrial systems as well as change the way we consider water consumption in buildings, waste treatment, irrigation, ice production, disinfection, anti-corrosion, and dozens more fields.

Hallberg's fundamental insights are complemented by the separate work of the Australian inventor Jay Harman (USA) whose work at Pax Scientific **(32)** achieves vortex-like designs based on the Fibonacci code. Entrepreneurial opportunities in nearly 50 sectors of the economy are likely to create a major employment boost once his innovations are more widespread.

INNOVATION:	**No refrigeration (33)**
BENEFIT:	Energy, health, food
DEVELOPER:	Bruce Roser (UK)
DATE:	1998
JOBS POTENTIAL:	1,000

Bruce Roser observed the minute tardigrade and the resurrection fern and formulated a method for preserving vaccines without a cold chain. Previously, delivering life-saving vaccines to children where there is no electrical service has meant reduced availability and doubled costs. The value of this invention, initially commercialized by Cambridge Biostability Ltd., is increased by a vaccine

production process that relies on the same freeze-drying equipment used for food processing. While this innovation provides the means to dramatically reduce energy requirements, reduce CO_2 emissions, and improve health care, it also opens future avenues to apply this knowledge to food preservation.

Cambridge Biostability could not raise funds for clinical trials, even though their first priority was vaccine accessibility for developing nations. The patent portfolio was sold to a new investor, and progress towards achieving improved health care delivery and lower CO_2 emissions awaits the approval of financial managers. Additional job creation as a result of this innovation would be in the manufacturing sector. Ideally the realized cost savings could be allocated to funding other humanitarian services.

INNOVATION:	**No glue (34)**
BENEFIT:	Material efficiency
DEVELOPER:	George de Mestral (Switzerland)
DATE:	1958

George de Mestral has developed an impressive range of products that stick without glue. These gluing effects can even be done and undone like a zipper, offering a longer life to the components. Subsequent variations such as gecko-inspired tape **(35)** have been widely described and even tested, and have recently been brought to the Japanese market by Nitto Denko.

A similar product that has reached the market is a formaldehyde-free glue, inspired by the mussel **(36)** and commercialized by Columbia Forest Products. Since the production of glue or its substitutes is not a labor-intensive activity, the impact on the labor market is minimal. However, the decreased use of toxic components would be a substantial benefit.

INNOVATION:	**No bactericides (37)**
BENEFIT:	Reduced need for harsh chemicals and drugs
DEVELOPER:	Peter Steinberg (Australia)
DATE:	1995

Peter Steinberg from the University of New South Wales in Sydney observed that *Delicea pulchra*, a red seaweed growing in the Tasman Sea, had no bacterial biofilm

on its surface structure. With Staffan Kjelleberg, a Swedish scientist living in Australia, he was able to ascertain that the seaweed remained bacteria-free merely by interrupting the bacteria's intercommunication. Unable to communicate, the bacteria did not invade a host.

An innovation that eliminates the need for antibiotics and bactericides provides a welcome alternative to industrial chemicals and pharmaceuticals that spur the evolution of untreatable mutations which defy the vast majority of current medicines. Here we have a platform technology with applications in agriculture, consumer goods, industrial supplies, medical devices, and pharmaceuticals. This technology will likely be further clinically trialed by Commonwealth Biotechnologies Inc., a NASDAQ listed company, a subsidiary of Venturepharm China (VPL). Because the active ingredient must be approved by the authorities as a novel molecule, the major challenge is to pass the approval procedures. This has been a significant obstacle in the path from concept to patent to market.

There are other technologies inspired by how natural systems achieve results that provide solid alternatives to the harsh chemistry that is now the rule. These include barberry-based antibiotics (**38**), bactericides produced by fungi, and specific applications like a repellent for mosquito-born yellow fever (**39**) and anti-fungal chemistry from red kidney beans (**40**). As is often the case with innovation, contrary to common wisdom and contrary to what we expect, species have capabilities that are extremely important. Whereas one can indeed claim that vultures spread illnesses, vultures themselves are never infected by avian flu (**41**). Perhaps their secret – whether an antibody, a pH factor, or some unknown quality – may one day be discovered and put to good use.

INNOVATION:	**Water Reclamation without Osmosis (42)**
BENEFIT:	Water, energy
DEVELOPER:	Andrew Parker (UK)
DATE:	2001
JOBS POTENTIAL:	100,000

Water availability is a worldwide challenge. With the majority of the world population inhabiting coastal areas, the obvious solution is thought to be the reclamation of fresh water from seawater. However, the process is energy intensive. When Andrew Parker from the Department of Zoology at the University of Oxford studied the Namibian beetle, he did not immediately realize that what he learned would offer a viable alternative to reverse osmosis water reclamation. The Namibian beetle gave him an initial insight on how to capture water from the air, a

feat that the cactus thorn (**43**) had already mastered, the thorny devil had achieved, and many other species including plants like the *Welwitschia mirabilis* (**44**) had successfully developed. Water that can be extracted from the air, then flow with the force of gravity to where it is needed without pumping, potentially eliminates diverting rivers, constructing dams, or installing reverse osmosis equipment. It thus provides major energy savings.

Innovations based on these species adaptations might well contribute to mitigating the heat island effect common to large cities such as Tokyo, London, or Chicago, thus significantly reducing carbon emissions. The potential for job generation is substantial. If fully applied this technology would complement all existing technologies, while permitting a better response to critical global water shortages.

The possibilities go beyond potable water reclamation. These insights could one day be bundled with other desalination methods that we might learn from the mangrove ecosystem or from the Polynesian box fruit (**45**), which is perfectly able to drift for months in the Pacific Ocean without any salt permeation. Penguins can drink seawater (**46**). They have glands under their eyes that remove all the salt.

INNOVATION:	**Cleansing without Soap (47)**
BENEFIT:	Water, material efficiency
DEVELOPER:	Willhelm Barthlott (Germany), Emile Ishida (Japan)
DATE:	1993
JOBS POTENTIAL:	100,000

Willhelm Barthlott of the Nees Institute at the University of Bonn can be credited as a nature tech pioneer and entrepreneur based on his contribution to our fundamental understanding of how the lotus flower never needs soap to clean itself. Actually no species in nature uses cleaning surfactants. In the case of the lotus flower, its physical makeup simply does not permit dirt particles to adhere for long and if they do, a small dewdrop will remove them immediately. This "lotus effect" has been used in an estimated 100 commercial products, with the German company Sto AG taking the lead since 1999.

The self-cleaning capacity of the abalone (**48**) is such that it never accumulates interior dirt. Emile Ishida, a professor at Tohoku University in Japan, adapted this capacity into a product design for INAX, the Japanese household ceramics company. The invention helps reduce the use of chemicals, as well as the subsequent contamination of water bodies. Although the job potential is slight, it scores highly for material productivity.

INNOVATION:	**Frictionless Movement (49)**
BENEFIT:	Energy, mining
DEVELOPER:	Ingo Rechenberg and Abdullah Regabi (Germany)
DATE:	2004
JOBS POTENTIAL:	5,000

Ingo Rechenberg, with the support of Abdullah Regabi El-Khyari from the Technical University of Berlin, has made impressive breakthroughs in achieving friction reduction without lubricants, ball bearings, or diamond dust. The inspiration comes from the sandfish lizard, which literally swims through desert dunes without accumulating heat. The lizard's nearly friction-free movement is facilitated by its keratin-based outer skin. This provides a fascinating new parameter for the design of energy-efficient systems that outperform the lubricants made by diatoms **(50)**. It has been estimated that as much as one percent of the world's GDP is lost in friction. All available options rely on fossil fuels and/or mined materials, processed at high temperatures. This insight sets the stage for a new generation of bionics. Since the production of ball bearings, lubricants, and industrial diamonds is highly automated, few jobs will be lost. Providing frictionless movement capability for the vast numbers of moving parts in our daily lives offers enormous possibilities.

INNOVATION:	**Pigment-Free Coloration (51)**
BENEFIT:	Energy, mining, health
DEVELOPER:	Andrew Parker (UK)
DATE:	1998
JOBS POTENTIAL:	2,000

Andrew Parker from Oxford University developed a platform based in natural physics that offers a broad set of optics applications permitting elimination of color pigments most often derived from heavy metals. Such mastery of optical effects has been successfully implemented in the design of security systems for bank notes. Achieving color effects without color pigments is a major breakthrough that would significantly impact the paint industry. Their entrenched market position and regulatory framework indicates that this innovative use of optically achieved color effects to replace chemistry will likely be initially implemented in the cosmetics industry.

Teijin (under the brand name Morphotex®) and BASF have already streamlined the manufacture of fibers that are colored and yet pigment-free. To date the mass

marketing necessary to create a new standard for the color market is not in place. One optical color, white, could possibly replace more than color pigments. An understanding of how we perceive white has led to the replacement of an optical brightener, based on a benzene ring, which is one of the main chemicals used in the detergent and the paper industries. The bright white Cyphocillus beetle from Indonesia **(52)** provides additional proof of this concept. The job generation potential is moderate since this technology implies the substitution of one coloring system by another.

INNOVATION:	**Propulsion without CFCs (53)**
BENEFIT:	Energy, material efficiency
DEVELOPER:	Andy McIntosh (UK)
DATE:	2004
JOBS POTENTIAL:	2,000

Andy McIntosh at the University of Leeds (UK) has developed a mechanical device, inspired by the bombardier beetle, that resolves the problems of propulsion gases. By replacing chlorofluorocarbons (CFCs), which have created havoc in the ozone layer, we acquire a unique opportunity to redefine industrial solutions. Even harmful gases substituted with less harmful gases are nonetheless a chemical solution. This platform technology could well find its first market in medical applications, especially for patients suffering from asthma and cystic fibrosis for whom relief requires immediate and fine medication misting. Because car engines emit toxic gases from incomplete combustion, the same technology could make fuel injection systems more effective, thereby reducing toxic exhaust.

The technology has not yet arrived on the market. With the proactive investment role of Lars Uno Larsson, it may soon have a portfolio of applications that will end the need for propulsion gases. This is another example of how physics replaces chemistry by using existing physical forces to attain the same objective. The elimination of chemistry is not expected to result in major employment opportunities. On the other hand, the installation of mechanical devices requires more labor, reduces material intensity over time, and eliminates the "throw-away" concept. This technology could be bundled with anti-bacterial products from seaweeds in medical applications, and with the vortex technology for fuel injection systems.

INNOVATION:	**Air Conditioning without Machinery (54)**
BENEFIT:	Energy, health
DEVELOPER:	Anders Nyquist (Sweden)
DATE:	1990
JOBS POTENTIAL:	10,000

While on an extended trip through Africa in the late 1950s, Bengt Warne documented the advanced architecture of termite mounds. He used his detailed understanding to create "envelope houses" that managed the precise entry and exit of air. An innovative Swedish architect, Anders Nyquist, then expanded Warne's experience, which has since been successfully implemented around the world. Although Nyquist lives just under the Arctic Circle, he has learned by observation and deduction that there is no real need for heating and cooling systems, provided we are prepared to learn from the zebra and the termite.

The office buildings of Daiwa House in Japan, the Laggarberg School in Timrå, Sweden (both designed by Nyquist), a hospital at Las Gaviotas in Colombia (designed by a local Gaviotas team without outside assistance), and the Eastgate Office and Shopping Complex in Harare, Zimbabwe (designed by Arup) all borrow from the termite, and to some extent from the zebra, to achieve buildings with healthy and energy efficient airflow. Several of these buildings successfully eliminated expensive heating and cooling systems altogether; others installed back-up systems and air pumps (Arup).

The particular advantage of the zebra effect, which creates micro-gusts of wind on the roof, is that it removes heat from the exterior, thus reducing the need for chemically saturated insulation. Widespread use of these temperature and humidity control systems is likely to decrease sales for major energy system providers. However, the energy savings and the enhancement of occupants' health will release resources for more productive investments and products.

INNOVATION:	**Heating from the Roots (55)**
BENEFIT:	Energy, food, health
DEVELOPER:	Young-Suk Shu, Tae-Sung Oh (Republic of Korea)
DATE:	2001
JOBS POTENTIAL:	50,000

Young-Suk Shu and Tae-Sung Oh observed that the underground composting of plant debris, stored by ants and termites, achieves a rich soil nutrient base for plant

growth. It also warms the soil through radiant heating. They realized that warming the root zone of plants increased osmosis, while protecting plants against freezing. They transformed this insight into a greenhouse heating system that heats the roots instead of the air. This method reduces energy consumption, thereby eliminating the need for air heating in greenhouses.

In 2007 when the technology was first introduced in Japan, it quickly gained favor with tomato and strawberry farmers. Once the heating effect was perfected using thin carbon fibers, its field of application grew beyond agriculture. It is now positioned as an inexpensive alternative to radiant floor heating that uses fluid-filled plastic piping.

For this application, a carbon mesh blended with cellulose is joined to the rubber base of a carpet, which is connected to thin-film dye-solar cells placed on windows. This floor-heating strategy cuts energy consumption by at least two-thirds. Since the energy source could be solar, it would have a low carbon footprint and a high level of comfort. Panasonic has decided to commercialize this product for home applications in Japan. This type of floor heating will make heating accessible to parts of the world where winter weather is relatively mild and conventional heating costs are proportionally high. This innovation is expected to generate a considerable number of jobs, perhaps comparable to photovoltaic solar panel installation.

INNOVATION:	**Calcium Carbonate from CO_2 Exhaust (56)**
BENEFIT:	Energy, material efficiency
DEVELOPER:	Normand Voyer (Canada), Sylvie Gauthier (Canada)
DATE:	1998
JOBS POTENTIAL:	100,000

Research conducted by Normand Voyer and Sylvie Gauthier makes it unnecessary to mine calcium carbonate for the manufacture of cement. They devised a process that captures carbonic gases with enzymes, delivering a pure CO_2 that can be used to manufacture calcium carbonate. The carbonic gases can be captured from coal-fired power stations, and even from the manufacture of cement. CO_2 Solutions, quoted on the Toronto Stock Exchange, markets technologies and engineering solutions that achieve this cyclical production and consumption of greenhouse gases. Another company, Novomer, views the industrial generation of CO and CO_2 from the same positive angle: this is a raw material we can be paid to receive and recycle.

Since the raw materials for manufacture can be obtained from the smokestacks of coal-fired power plants, their innovation represents an exceptional opportunity to

replace the costly mining of calcium carbonate. The technology has been tested at a semi-industrial scale and is ready to be marketed. Some retrofitting of power stations, cement plants, incinerators, and similar facilities is required to adapt the technology to existing infrastructure. Thus, government incentives (in this case especially from Canada), could do much to bring these technologies to market. This technology is certain to generate major employment opportunities both in initial retrofitting and in manufacture and delivery.

INNOVATION:	**No Aluminum Packaging (57)**
BENEFIT:	Energy, material efficiency
DEVELOPER:	Rebecca Cramp (Australia)
DATE:	1977

Today's food and drink industries maintain product freshness and appeal with packaging made of thin aluminum foil. Vast numbers of shelf-ready products from cookies and coffee to potato chips and juice drinks are delivered in packaging made of this non-ferrous metal. Although convenient and effective as packaging, manufacturing these foils uses a great deal of energy. Worse, they most often end in land fills after a single use.

Rebecca Cramp at the School of Biological Sciences, University of Queensland, studied the Australian desert burrowing frog and concluded that it holds the key to a new type of packaging that requires no aluminum. She designed a packaging system for liquids that can be manufactured using thin layers of keratin, one of the most common and abundant proteins. It is simple, and free of metals.

If we add the pelican's expansive capacity **(58)** to the genius of the burrowing frog, and if the packaging could also respond to stress by hardening quickly, the way the sea cucumber does **(59)**, then we could achieve totally new packaging concepts. Perhaps we can even include waterproofing as do bees **(60)** and expand the design concepts from packaging to housing. Jobs in the present aluminum industry would be reduced and replaced by the innovative systems that would emerge. Though predictable numbers of new jobs cannot be anticipated, this type of packaging would dramatically reduce the load on the environment, reduce the need for mining, and cut carbon emissions.

INNOVATION:	**Cold-process ceramics (61)**
BENEFIT:	Energy, material efficiency
DEVELOPER:	Robert Ritchie (USA)
DATE:	1977
JOBS POTENTIAL:	3,000

Robert Ritchie is chair of the Department of Materials Science and Engineering at the University of California, Berkeley, USA. His observation from ceramics research was that ceramics in nature are made at ambient temperature and pressure, whereas the industrial versions require high heat and pressure. Both the abalone and the glycera worm **(62)** produce extremely hard ceramic composites at ambient temperatures.

Such ceramics could be produced even on a small scale, since the energy requirements are limited and the required infrastructure is modest. This would permit hundreds of small businesses to produce specialty ceramics, such as those in high demand by the electronics industry, not least the emerging market for nano-devices. High-performance ceramics produced at ambient temperature would be stronger than Kevlar™, the famous bullet-proof ceramic. Thus it would save energy, lessen adverse climate impact, and offer better quality to the consumer.

INNOVATION:	**Chemical-free paper (63)**
BENEFIT:	Energy, material efficiency
DEVELOPER:	Steven Chu (USA)
DATE:	2004
JOBS POTENTIAL:	250,000

Steven Chu is a Nobel Laureate and Secretary of Energy for the Obama administration. Earlier in his career he worked at the Lawrence Berkeley National Laboratory. He studied the symbiosis of termites and bacteria in processing wood. His research forms the basis for a technique that could make paper without chemicals. It is an approach that could reverse the need for the massive pulping plants that are industry's answer to the complexities and hazards of production.

The process for paper manufacture is to chemically burn all the non-cellulose by immersing chipped wood in an acid bath. The residue, called "black liquor," is typically incinerated because of its toxicity. The hemi-cellulose is discarded alongside the lignin, even though it could be recovered as xylan and xylitol, tree sugars that help prevent

tooth decay since they do not attract bacteria. A process developed by the Wood Chemistry Research Institute of Latvia uses a pressure-based wood separation method **(64)** that cascades hemicellulose, lignin, and lipids, leaving cellulose as a clean residue.

The production of paper from wood, using methods perfected by termites, white rot fungi **(65)**, and bacteria, also creates a re-use cycle for CO2 that decreases its contribution to climate change. Thus this approach could make small-scale paper production much more feasible, generating a considerable number of jobs especially in China and India where demand for paper is rapidly increasing and where automation and bulk capacity have created significant job losses. China closed down 10,000 paper mills between 1995 and 2004 to address uncontrolled factory pollution. We might even see the reintroduction of bamboo and straw as raw material stock for paper instead of monocultured pines and eucalyptus, which would add further job-creation opportunities.

INNOVATION:	**Mercury-free light (66)**
BENEFIT:	Energy, material efficiency, health
DEVELOPER:	Roger Hanlon (USA)
DATE:	2004
JOBS POTENTIAL:	150,000

Manufacturing energy-efficient light bulbs today requires the use of minute amounts of mercury. Even the compact fluorescent lights heralded for energy savings depend on this heavy metal. In a society with the goals of health and sustainability, the release of mercury without a guarantee for recovery, even in minute amounts, is unacceptable. This explains the importance of bright light produced without mercury.

When Roger Hanlon, from the Marine Biological Laboratory at Woods Hole, Massachusetts, studied how jellyfish, squid, and fungi produce light, he found that the brightness was activated by calcium working like a light switch to activate a protein which releases energy in the form of light. The source of light and the power of its brightness is not a heavy metal but rather two renewable materials that are available in abundance. This generates a rather blue light although standard preference is for white light. However, white can be obtained through optical effects rather than additional chemistry. The blue light generated in this way, especially the brightest version found in deep sea crustaceans **(67)**, also has applications like the curing of adhesives.

Along the same line as termite-inspired papermaking, the elimination of a toxic component like mercury from the production process facilitates entrepreneurship and local production. Multiple efficiencies can be achieved and the elimination of mercury would be an important reduction of collateral costs that were previously borne by society.

INNOVATION:	**Solvent-free solutions (68)**
BENEFIT:	Health
DEVELOPER:	Ivan Vilotijevic (Serbia)
DATE:	2005
JOBS POTENTIAL:	150,000

Ivan Vilotijevic studied at the University of Belgrade and at the Massachusetts Institute of Technology. His research into the catalytic action of red algae dinoflagellates provides a remarkable insight for how industry could one day replicate this effect, using only water to achieve what now requires chemical solvents. In industrial production, solvents are considered critical to speeding reactions and securing faster output. Algae can produce esters using water as a solvent where typical polymer manufacturing relies on sulfuric acids. Seaweeds also produce biocatalysts that speed up the process in water **(69)**. In fact, water offers high yields for nearly every chemical reaction on which natural systems depend. This approach would eliminate occupational hazards and reduce environmental damage. It would also reverse the trend towards further concentration of production, and permit more diversity in manufacturing while generating more high quality jobs.

INNOVATION:	**Painless needle injections (70)**
BENEFIT:	Improved health care
DEVELOPER:	Masayuki Okano (Japan)
DATE:	2004

Masayuki Okano, President of Okano Kogyo Corporation, is known as the "metalwork magician." He designed a painless injection needle based on the shape of a mosquito's proboscis. The prototype was a super-thin conical roll of stainless steel welded at the seam to make a leak-proof conical cylinder with a fine tip. Today his Nanopass 33 Syringe, manufactured by Terumo Corporation, is the standard for pain-free hypodermic needles. The Nanopass 33 is especially popular among millions of diabetic patients, making it perhaps the second most widely used product (after Velcro™) inspired by the workings of nature.

PLATFORM TECHNOLOGIES ACCELERATING SUSTAINABILITY

This third group of innovations provides a fresh insight into an assortment of possibilities that are developing individually but are presented as possible combinations, a symbiosis of achievements with the potential for greater impact, particularly on job creation.

The portfolio of innovations described range from innovative businesses that have succeeded in the marketplace to a group of technologies that represent great ideas but will require more time to achieve commercial success. The key is to bundle these and other technologies so that synergies will translate to strategic market advantage.

INNOVATION:	**Water Purification (71)**
BENEFIT:	Water, health, energy
DEVELOPER:	Peter Agre (USA), Andrew Rankin, Eric Wolff (UK)
DATE:	2003
JOBS POTENTIAL:	300,000

Peter Agre from John Hopkins Malaria Research Institute (USA) received the 2003 Nobel Chemistry Prize for his discovery of aquaporins, proteins integrated into cell membranes that regulate water flow at a rate of one trillion molecules per second through the membranes. His research paved the way for a multitude of biochemical, physiological, and genetic studies of water channels. The Danish company Aquaporin A/S aims to provide a proof of concept and start marketing the first applications in 2011. Since using aquaporins to purify water is one highly useful application, long-term investment would likely be a safe bet.

There are hundreds of species ranging from bacteria to plants and animals that have the capacity to purify water. The penguin is one fascinating case study. Andrew Rankin and Eric Wolff traveled to the Antarctic on a special expedition for the British Antarctic Survey and became fascinated by the capacity of the glands under the penguins' eyes that remove salt. The glands function much as do human kidneys but much more efficiently. Researching such remarkable examples from nature can give us potential solutions to suffice our basic needs. Technologies that replace reverse osmosis are certain to generate income and jobs for communities and industries around the world.

INNOVATION:	**Pipes and Tubes for Buildings (72)**
BENEFIT:	Health, energy, material efficiency
DEVELOPER:	Björn Bellander (Sweden)
DATE:	1990
JOBS POTENTIAL:	500

Björn Bellander observed how human respiratory and digestive systems constructively utilize input and output channeling mechanisms to handle air, water, and discarded matter. In effect, they combine piping for solids, liquids, and gases. Based on these observations he designed a series of simple valves to dramatically simplify the pipes, tubes, and lines required to regulate inflow, throughput, and outflow as well as interior distribution through a structure. Today his designs are marketed by Splitvision AB (Sweden) under the brand name Split Box™. The overall technology reduces the energy loss in both household air circulation and water heating, and handles all sewage as well. Material requirements, labor, and energy are all conserved. Production, installation, and maintenance of the control unit will likely generate the same number of jobs as those that are eliminated; however, income will likely be at a higher level.

INNOVATION:	**Thin-film Solar Cells (73)**
BENEFIT:	Energy, material efficiency
DEVELOPER:	Michael Graetzel (Switzerland), Alan Heeger (USA)
DATE:	2003
JOBS POTENTIAL:	500,000

In 1991 Michael Graetzel, from Politecnique de Lausanne (Switzerland) discovered and patented a solar cell that generates energy from a leaf dye. Graetzel's novel approach represents a paradigm shift away from photovoltaics, which require a huge energy input. His cell is simple, cheap, and energy efficient to make. Another giant in research, Alan Heeger, the 2000 Nobel Laureate in Chemistry from University of California at Santa Barbara, assisted the product to market through Konarka, which licensed the technology from Graetzel. Heeger added his own rich portfolio of know-how and patents. Konarka is now operating at full capacity from a facility in Wales, UK.

The improvements for solar energy are multiple, with concentrated solar power inspired by the dragonfly (74) as another avenue that the Spanish firm Abengoa has benchmarked and for which they have made major plans for further expansion.

These are clearly technologies that will dominate the market in the future and may well displace photovoltaics. Since the thin-film solar cell units will be smaller and the concentrated solar power facilities will be much larger, there will be no net change in terms of overall job generation.

INNOVATION:	**Energy Conservation through Heat Recovery (75)**
BENEFIT:	Energy, material efficiency
DEVELOPER:	Brian McNab (USA)
JOBS POTENTIAL:	50,000

Brian McNab, Professor of Biology at the University of Florida, studies physiological ecology, the diversity of animals and the impressive variety of mechanisms that enable them to live everywhere from Antarctica to the Sahara Desert, from tropical rainforests to the depths of the oceans. He studied energy generation to explain an organism's physical, chemical, and cellular responses to survival challenges. Animals scale their metabolism to cope. Some use osmosis, gas exchange, or endothermy. The bluefin tuna withstands temperature differentials of up to 68° F. It has a thermal barrier equipped with a counter-current heat exchanger between its blood and gills. While efficiencies in industrial heat recovery reach 95%, natural systems that operate in cascades of energy reach 99%. This implies that most heat expended today could be recovered, generating heat or cold on site, with the option to convert it to electricity. Novel approaches to heat exchange are a business of the future, and the generation of jobs will quickly follow.

INNOVATION:	**Algorhythm for Energy conservation (76)**
BENEFIT:	Energy, material efficiency
DEVELOPERS:	Roger Seymour (Australia), Ana Maria Angioy (Italy), Kikukatsu Ito (Japan)
JOBS POTENTIAL:	20,000

Roger Seymour, a zoologist at the University of Adelaide, studies heat generation in plants. Plants generate physical heat, so much so that warm flowers can melt snow. All plant tissues so far found to warm themselves have reproductive functions. The dead-horse arum lily (*Helicodiceros muscivorus*) **(77)** outperforms all others, even the much-heralded sacred lotus, famed for its ability to maintain a flower temperature between 86-97° F, even when the environmental temperature drops as low as 50° F. The physics and biochemistry at play in plants and cold-blooded animals may change the way people manage heat. Dozens of options fine-tuned by

such fauna and flora will inspire new patents and offer services for different needs, just as in natural ecosystems. Kikukatsu Ito from Iwate University has obtained patents for the algorithm that allows plant heating systems to adjust to time and light. This could easily replace the outmoded 60-year-old Honeywell air conditioning algorithm.

INNOVATION:	**Drag Reduction to improve Lift (78)**
BENEFIT:	Energy, noise pollution
DEVELOPERS:	Frank Fish (Canada), Tim Finnigan (Australia)
JOBS POTENTIAL:	10,000

Frank Fish, professor at West Chester University in Pennsylvania (USA), observed how whales reduce drag. He reasoned that these insights on drag could be combined with wind power to improve lift. In wind tunnel tests, the bumpy flipper of the humpback whale was shown to have less drag and increased lift when compared to the smooth and straight lines of airplanes and wind electric generators. Marketable applications being developed by Whalepower, Fish's Toronto-based company, could reduce the noise pollution typically associated with wind turbines. There are similar applications under development that could reduce friction and drag while increasing lift. These will help us achieve a more efficient energy production system.

The Mercedes Benz car design inspired by the ocean-dwelling boxfish (*Ostracion cubicus*) **(79)** appears counter-intuitive. Like its reef-dwelling counterpart in nature, the square-looking automobile hardly seems aerodynamic. Yet the boxfish and its automotive replica combine structural integrity and low body mass to achieve maximal strength to energy expenditure, maneuverability, and stability.

A new innovation comes from studying the capacity of giant kelp to capture motion from ocean waves caused by tidal ebb and flow. A Sydney-based Australian start-up, BioPower Systems, has developed modular devices that collect the energy from the undulating movements of wave and tide **(80)** and convert them into utility-scale grid-connected renewable energy. Their bioWAVE™ and bioSTREAM™ devices are positioned beneath the ocean surface. When the currents are too strong, they flatten just as the kelp.

These innovations in energy efficiency and generation go beyond the familiar and yet are just a first look at the broad portfolio of energy sources that will emerge. This can usher in yet another platform for entrepreneurship that will reduce the monopoly of large power generating systems and insure that local systems are competitive and diverse enough to meet the local needs as evolution has always done.

INNOVATION:	**Optics (81)**
BENEFIT:	Energy, noise pollution
DEVELOPER:	Joanna Aizenberg (USA)

Joanna Aizenberg graduated from Moscow University with a degree in physical chemistry and soon achieved a new and broader understanding of how sponges create glass fibers that transmit light better than fiber optics. It is even possible to knot these fibers. The core revelation of her work is the multi-functionality of materials. Apart from transmitting light, these glass fibers demonstrate great tensile strength, while maintaining great flexibility. She discovered that the chemistry was simple because life in the deep ocean must work with what is locally available. Aizenberg's research could revolutionize the carbon footprint of the telecommunications industry. Fiber optics requires high temperature and acid chemistry, whereas the sea sponge uses ambient temperature and alkaline chemistry. Glass fiber would be a replacement for the present standard of fiber optics, and therefore might not generate additional jobs, merely the benefit of energy savings and reduced noise pollution. Perhaps the dolphin's ability to accomplish underwater communication at high precision and speed **(82)** is a skill we might come to understand and apply to the field.

INNOVATION:	**Oceanlife Optics (83)**
BENEFIT:	Energy, noise pollution
DEVELOPER:	Joanna Aizenberg (USA)
JOBS POTENTIAL:	3,000

Joanna Aizenberg expanded her studies to the brittle star, which manufactures, at ambient temperature, perfect bio-lenses that minimize aberration, optimize light intensity, increase focus, and detect light from particular directions. This understanding could permit the control of crystallization in advanced electronics manufacture, since these require ceramics and semiconductors, all manufactured through bio-mineralization.

Optics inspired by nature's designs have an enormous potential for transforming the process of image collection. These new materials show promise for optical systems that have fewer, lighter lenses than traditional lens systems. The latest examples include single lenses inspired by octopus eyes **(84)** and a three lens, wide angle system for surveillance systems.

The logic of these lenses could be extended to acoustical lenses designed by the pink dolphin **(85)**. Because their underwater habitat offers limited visibility, dolphins use sounds – a focused beam of clicks – that are reflected from objects and modulated by their melon organ. Their biosonar works because the melon organ is composed

of lipids of different density than the surrounding water, acting like an acoustic lens. Once we develop and bundle these nature-inspired technologies into pragmatic solutions, each can complement others to achieve a wide range of useful products and services.

INNOVATION:	**Hearing Aids from Elephant Feet (86)**
BENEFIT:	Health
DEVELOPER:	Caitlin O'Connell-Rodwell

Caitlin O'Connell-Rodwell, a research associate at the Stanford University School of Medicine, has studied the elephant's vocal call and has discovered that it is composed of two distinctive sounds – one that is airborne and another that travels through the ground much like a seismic wave. The vibration that moves through earth can carry roughly twice as far. Furthermore, the vibrational waves generated by an elephant stomping its feet can carry up to 20 miles away. Elephants can effectively communicate using such signals.

O'Connell-Rodwell's research work may lead to breakthroughs in hearing-aid design and engineering. Combining that innovation potential with a micro-battery operating from temperature variables would be a boon to the hearing impaired who annually purchase 2.5 million hearing aid devices in the US alone.

INNOVATION:	**Silica Production (87)**
BENEFIT:	Energy, material efficiency, cost reduction
DEVELOPER:	Nils Kröger (Germany)
JOBS POTENTIAL:	70,000

Nils Kröger, a diatom biologist at the University of Regensberg in Germany, was first to identify a silica-forming protein in diatoms. When working with the protein, silica spheres formed in minutes instead of hours. Joanna Aizenberg added to this fundamental breakthrough. Their research may herald the means by which the micro-electronics and telecommunications industry could become sustainable.

Diatom-like self-assembly of chips producing silica in a certain order introduces the possibility of low toxicity, low waste, and low energy alternatives to what is now a material- and energy-intensive industry. The method of depositing silica as perfected by the sea sponge is an innovation that has been commercialized by the Russian start-up company NT-MDT. If this innovation succeeds in redefining the investment capital and the operational expenses for the integrated circuit industry, this will reduce the investment costs as well as the environmental load.

INNOVATION:	**Acoustics (88)**
BENEFIT:	Energy, noise pollution
DEVELOPER:	Ron Hoy (USA), Ron Miles (USA)
JOBS POTENTIAL:	1,000

Ron Hoy and Ron Miles of Cornell University studied the Brazilian ormia fly and realized that the fly can locate sound, something that hearing aids cannot do. The fly couples mechanics and acoustics to know exactly how to escape a hungry cricket. Understanding and adapting this ability, along with eliminating batteries based on the innovations of Jorge Reynolds, would make way for hearing aid designs that would be optimally functional and systemically sound. Beyond hearing aids, combining the generation of electricity from pressure with ormia fly acoustics could bring any number of small electric devices to the market that would perform better and more discretely than present models.

Bats **(89)** demonstrate an ability that could provide useful improvements to technologies used for airport security. Working together with the National Microelectronics Research Centre in Ireland and Fraunhofer Institute in Germany, Farran Technology, an Irish components company, has devised a security imaging system that can image all objects, not just those made of metal. The Tadar camera (actually named after the Brazilian *Tadarida* bat) uses a three-millimeter wavelength learned from bats to help detect and identify suspicious objects hidden under clothing. It can also be used to see through clouds or fog, in the same way that the bat uses high-frequency signals to navigate and locate insect prey in the dark. Tadar's sensors detect energy naturally emitted or reflected energy from objects. These wavelengths are completely harmless. A thermal contrast between the body's natural radiation and any hidden object, whether metallic, non-metallic, plastic, or liquid, is detected and identified by a clear image derived from the object's frequency response.

The abilities of the jewel beetle *(Melanophila acuminata)* **(90)** could help us devise a better early warning system for fire. According to scientific observations made by Canadian entomologist William George Evans, the tiny pits on the beetle's underside can detect infrared radiation from the flames of a fire as much as 50 miles distant. Scientists at the University of Bonn in Germany are conducting research to study this ability and to design prototype sensors that adopt these features. Their goal is to manufacture an inexpensive mechanical device that would warn of forest fires, although commercial, military, and consumer applications would also be possible once the optimal design and functionality were achieved.

INNOVATION:	**Temperature Control (91)**
BENEFIT:	Energy, material efficiency
DEVELOPER:	Virginia Walker (USA), Brandon Brown (USA)
JOBS POTENTIAL:	2,000

Working at Queen's University in Kingston, Ontario, Canada, Virginia Walker and her research colleagues have found a new approach to energy efficiency: producing antifreeze sustainably. The yellow mealworm beetle *(Tenebrio molitor)* produces a protein that is upwards of a hundred times more effective as antifreeze than is glycol, the current market standard. Glycol is a petroleum-based toxin, whereas the mealworm works with amino acids.

Research conducted by Brandon R. Brown at the University of San Francisco found that sharks produce a special gel that senses minute temperature differences **(92)**, which indicate nearby prey. Perhaps the shark has developed electro-sensors to identify feeding zones by converting minor temperature gradients to electricity with sufficient voltage. Brown found that a variation as small as 1.8° F would produce a voltage as large as 300 microvolts. Such gels offer another potential energy source that is worthy of investigation. The use of gels and proteins with these performance levels offers many industries a platform for innovative applications and custom solutions.

INNOVATION:	**Water Control (93)**
BENEFIT:	Water, energy, material efficiency
DEVELOPER:	Julian Vincent (UK, USA)
JOBS POTENTIAL:	2,500

Julian Vincent from the University of Bath has a broad range of expertise that extends from string instruments to desert cockroaches. His studies of the bladder-like structures of the desert burrowing cockroach *(Arenivaga investigata)* suggest they have a dehumidifying ability that achieves condensation when demand exceeds supply, and evaporation when supply exceeds demand. This is the case of the water spider **(94)** and the water strider as well. Both have an extremely hydrophobic wax that covers the hairs on their legs. This lets them walk on water without breaking the surface. The highly precise functioning exhibited by these insects suggests possible solutions of particular interest to the microelectronics industry as well as emerging microelectro-mechanical systems (MEMS) developments, such as devices that trigger airbag release.

INNOVATION:	**Traffic Management (95)**
BENEFIT:	Energy
DEVELOPER:	Darya Popiv (Germany)
JOBS POTENTIAL:	25,000

Traffic congestion not only causes stress and tension for those on the road, it also has negative economic and ecological impact. Darya Popiv from the Science University of Munich has conducted extensive research on insect swarm intelligence. She proposes that the interaction among cars in traffic flow patterns fits the parameters for swarm intelligence modeling. Her models use the SuRJE (Swarms under R&J using Evolution) traffic simulation software developed by Ricardo Hoar and Joanne Penner at the University of Calgary (Canada). This software applies the principles of swarm intelligence. Popiv has introduced pheromones, the tools of chemical communication among members of an insect colony, into the algorithm. She proposes that cars in swarm-based traffic micro-simulation are able, just as are ants, to emit and receive pheromones. The physical interpretation of stronger pheromones equates to visual and perceptual signals such as brake lights, turn signals, and acceleration or deceleration.

Other applications have followed, such as the reduction of queues at ski lifts. A brief look at the commercial software indicates that this business application is not only profitable but is expanding quickly and generating a considerable number of well-paid jobs.

EXTRAORDINARY FOOD FOR THOUGHT

Finally, we offer a few inspirational discoveries that encourage us to dream. The previous cases demonstrate the capacity to inspire our economic system and business models using systems and bundles of natural technologies that will accelerate innovation and respond to the basic needs of all. The tally of potential job generation edges just under 100 million, a number difficult to overlook. Readers may note that the last entry in this section describes a species of frog that is now extinct. This is the reality of our modern society. In our hurried advance we can cause unintended consequences and miss the chance to learn solutions that natural systems have developed through millions of years of evolution.

These last few inspiring projects offer both perspective on what is to come and a warning of what we will miss if the tremendous biodiversity that surrounds us is not preserved and allowed to evolve according the rhythms determined by the forces of the universe, which nature adapts to the advantage of all.

INNOVATION:	**Shock Absorption (96)**
BENEFIT:	Safety
DEVELOPER:	Juhachi Oda, Kenichi Sakano (Japan)

In 2002, Professor Ivan Schwab at the University of California–Davis was the first to ask how the woodpecker avoided headache. When Japanese ornithologists made a complete study of the beak, skull, and body of the woodpecker, they quickly realized the ingenuity of this long-beaked bird. It has a sac of fluid behind its beak that absorbs the shock of its constant hammering as it feeds, constructs its nest, and drums. Juhachi Oda from the University of Kanazawa and Kenichi Sakano from Toyota became acquainted with the woodpecker's remarkable abilities and were inspired to design new automobile shock absorbers. Though contributing to the safety and comfort of the vehicle passengers, this innovation will not create new jobs – perhaps only greater respect for another of Earth's remarkable species.

INNOVATION:	**Repair after Irradiation (97)**
BENEFIT:	Health
DEVELOPER:	Nicolas Leulliot (France)

Nicolas Leulliot, Professor at the Université Paris Sud, along with his Swiss colleagues from the University of Zurich, has discovered that a bacterium named *Deinococcus radiodurans* is not only resistant to radiation, it is capable of repairing radiation damage. Where *E. coli*, the standard bacterium in the human gut, can repair a few of the damaged links in cell DNA, *Deinococcus* is capable of repairing about 500. As we have noted, the capacity to self-repair is one of the unique features of natural systems. Whatever the error or unintended damage, the life force can recover just as a broken bone or an open wound can heal. This bacterium's ability to repair DNA at such a rate and intensity calls for years, if not decades, of further research.

INNOVATION:	**Burning Fat not Sugars (98)**
BENEFIT:	Health
DEVELOPER:	Chen Chi Lee (USA)

Chen Chi Lee, molecular scientist at the University of Texas, confirmed what John P. Craven, the former chief scientist of the US Navy, has suggested: it is possible to switch the human metabolism from burning sugar to burning fat by simply inducing a state of torpor, or temporary hibernation. Some animals can drop their

normal body temperature and activity levels at night to conserve energy. During these periods they draw on layers of fat which act as their energy source. Whereas Craven tested his hypothesis and successfully reduced excess body fat by packing his wrists and ankles in icepacks at night, Lee proposes a complex phosphate to induce temporary hibernation. This chemically induced state of torpor would cause the body to draw on its stores of fat. It offers a natural means of treating high blood pressure, diabetes, and coronary disease.

INNOVATION:	**Eradicating Malaria (99)**
BENEFIT:	Enhanced health care
DEVELOPER:	Ximena Nelson (New Zealand)

Ximena Nelson, working at the University of Canterbury at Christchurch, New Zealand, observed how the sensory system of the East African jumping spider give it the ability to select its preferred meal – mosquitoes infested with the parasites that cause malaria. Having superbly sharp vision, this five-millimeter spider can distinguish mosquitoes better than any human, and attacks them with great precision. In future we may further research the eyesight of the jumping spider. We may further study its ability to climb up or across practically any terrain, including glass; or how its color perception extends to the ultraviolet range.

INNOVATION:	**Stomach acidity (100)**
BENEFIT:	Health
DEVELOPER:	Michael Tyler (Australia)
DATE:	1985

Michael Tyler from the University of Adelaide discovered the unique abilities of the female gastric brooding frog *(Rheobatrachus silus)*. Following the male's external fertilization of her eggs, the female would take the eggs into her mouth and swallow them. The jelly that surrounded each egg contained a special substance that halted the production of hydrochloric acid in the mother's stomach. During the 6-week period that the offspring were present in her stomach the frog did not eat. Had further study been possible, it is almost certain that the *Rheobatrachus* held a practical solution for excessive stomach acidity that affects the health of millions. Diseases attributable to acid-loving bacteria might have been effectively resolved by research and study of the gastric brooding frog's ability, had it not become extinct. May this loss encourage us to honor, support, and renew our planet's biodiversity.

BIBLIOGRAPHY AND REFERENCES
Books and Journals

Alexandersson, Olaf, *Living Water: Viktor Schauberger and the Secrets of Natural Energy*, Warrington, UK: Newleaf Books, 2002.

Anon., *International Journal of Medicinal Mushrooms, Volumes I – XI*, Redding, CT, Begell House, 2000-2009.

Asit K. Biswas, et al., *Environmental Modelling for Developing Countries,* Dublin: Tycooly Intl, 1990.

Ayensu, Edward S, *Ashanti Gold, African Legacy of the World's Most Precious Metal*, London, UK: Marshall Editions, 1998.

Barksdale, Jelks, *Encyclopedia of the Chemical Elements, "Titanium,"* New York: Reinhold Book Corporation, 1968.

Bartholomew, Alick, and David Bellamy, *Hidden Nature: The Startling Insights of Viktor Schauberger*, Kempton, IL: Adventures Unlimited Press, 2005.

Benyus, Janine, *Biomimicry; Innovation Inspired By Nature*, New York: Harper Perennial, 2002.

Brown, Lester R., *Plan B 4.0: Mobilizing to Save Civilization*, New York: W.W. Norton, 2009.

Buswell, John, *"Development of the World Mushroom Industry: Applied Mushroom Biology and International Mushroom organizations,"* *International Journal of Medicinal Mushrooms, Volume X*, Redding, CT, Begell House, 2008.

Capra, Fritjof, *The Science of Leonardo: Inside the Mind of the Great Genius of the Renaissance*, New York: Anchor Books, 2008.

_____, *Steering Business towards Sustainability*, Tokyo, Japan: United Nations University Press, 1995.

_____, *The Web of Life: A New Scientific Understanding of Living Systems*, Boston: Shambhala Books, 1997.

Chang, S. T., and John Buswell. "Development of the World Mushroom Industry: Applied Mushroom Biology and International Mushroom Organizations," *International Journal of Medicinal Mushrooms*, Redding, CT: Begell House, 2000-2009.

Donachie, Matthew J., *Titanium, A Technical Guide, Metals Park*, OH: ASM International, 1988.

Fleischmann, Wimm, et al., *Maggot Therapy: A Handbook of Maggot-Assisted Wound Healing*, New York: Thieme Publications, 2004.

Fredriksson, Marianne, and Bengt Warne, *På akacians villkor. Att Bygga Och Bo I Samklang Med Naturen (On the Conditions of the Acacia, to Build and Live in Harmony with Nature)*, Göteborg: Warne förlag AB, 1993.

Gabriel, Julie, *Green Beauty Guide: Your Essential Resource to Organic and Natural Skin Care, Hair Care, Makeup, and Fragrances*, Deerfield Beach, FL: HCI Press, 2008.

Govero, Chido, *The Future of Hope*, Tokyo, Japan: ZERI Foundation, 2009.

Gravitis, Janis, "Biomaterials and Bioenergy from Photosynthesis, within Zero Emissions Framework, published in Frano Barbir and Sergio Ulgiati, Sustainable Energy Production and Consumption: Benefits, Strategies and Environmental Costing," *NATO Science for Peace and Security Series C: Environmental Security*, New York: Springer Verlag, 2008.

Greatbatch, Wilson, *The Making of the Pacemaker: Celebrating a Lifesaving Invention*, Amherst, NY: Prometheus Books, 2000.

Ishida, Emile, *Nature Technology: Channeling the Forces of Nature* (in Japanese) Tokyo: Kagaku Douijin, 2009.

Kamm, Birgit, et al., *Biorefineries - Industrial Processes and Products: Status Quo and Future Directions (2 Volume Set) (v. 1)*, Weinheim, Germany: Wiley-VCH, 2006.

Lovins, Amory, et al., *Natural Capitalism*, Boston, MA: Back Bay Books, 2008.

Margulis, Lynn, *Five Kingdoms, An Illustrated Guide to the Phyla of Life on Earth*, New York: W.H. Freeman & Company, 1998.

Margulis, Lynn, and Dorion Sagan, *Acquiring Genomes: The Theory of the Origins of the Species*, New York: Basic Books, 2003.

_____, *What Is Life?*, Berkeley: University of California Press, 2000.

Margulis, Lynn, and Karlene Schwarz, *Five Kingdoms: A Multimedia Guide to the Phyla of Life on Earth*, W.H. Freeman Company, 2003.

McDonough, Bill, and Michael Braungart, *Cradle to Cradle*, San Francisco, CA: North Point Press, 2002.

Meadows, Donella, et al., *Limits to Growth*, Report to the Club of Rome, New York: Universe Books, 1972.

Miles, Philip G, and Shu-Ting Chang, *Mushrooms: Cultivation, Nutritional Value, Medicinal Effect, and Environmental Impact*, Boca Raton, FL: CRC Press, 2004.

Molisson, Bill, and Reny Mia Slay, *Permaculture: A Designers' Manual,* Tasmania, Australia: Tagari Publications, 1988.

Panati, Charles. *Extraordinary Origins of Everyday Things*, New York, Harper Collins, 1989.

Parker, Andrew, *In the Blink of an Eye: How Vision Sparked the Big Bang of Evolution*, New York: Basic Books, 2004.

Posamentier, Alfred and Ingmar Lehmann, *The (Fabulous) Fibonacci Numbers*, Amherst, NY: Prometheus Books, 2007.

Priya, Shashank, and Daniel Inman, *Energy Harvesting Technologies*, New York: Springer Verlag, 2008.

Rangers, Jorgen, and Dennis Meadows, *Limits to Growth: The 30-Year Update*, White River Junction, VT: Chelsea Green, 2004.

Rau, Thomas, and Susan Wyler, *Swiss Secret to Optimal Health: Dr. Rau's Diet for Whole Body Healing*, New York: Berkley Books, 2009.

_____, *Biological Medicine: The Future of Natural Healing,* Marion, MA: Biological Medicine Network, 2003.

Rodríguez Lledó, Camilo, *Bioconstrucción* (Spanish Edition), Madrid: Ediciones Literarias Mandala, 2009.

Rozema, Jelte, Yiannis Manetas, and Lars Olof Björn, *Responses of Plant to UV-B Radiation (Advances in Vegetation Science)*, New York: Springer Verlag, 2001.

Rubio Luna, Germán, *Arte y Mañas de la Guadua, Una guía sobre el uso productivo de un bambú gigante, Art and Skill of the Bamboo: Guide to the Productive Use of Giant Bamboo*, Bogotá: Ino Arte, 2007.

Schauberger, Viktor, *Nature As Teacher: How I Discovered New Principles in the Working of Nature* (Eco-Technology Series), Dublin, Ireland: Gateway (Gill & MacMillan), 1999.

Schauberger, Viktor, and Callum Coats, *Water Wizard: The Extraordinary Properties of Natural Water*, Dublin, Ireland: Gateway (Gill & MacMillan), 1998.

Stern, Lord Nicholas, *The Economics of Climate Change: The Stern Review*, Cambridge, UK: Cambridge University Press, 2007.

Todd, Nancy Jack, and John Todd, *From Eco-Cities to Living Machines: Principles of Ecological Design*, Berkeley, CA: North Atlantic Press, 1994.

van Dieren, Wouter, *Taking Nature into Account: A Report to the Club of Rome*, New York: Springer Verlag, 1995.

Velez, Simon, et al., *Grow Your Own House, Simon Velez and Bamboo Architecture* (English and German Edition), Weil am Rhein Germany: VITRA Design Museum, 2000.

Vieira Costa, J. Alberto, et al., "Improving *Spirulina platensis* Biomass Yield Using a Fed-Batch Process," *Bioresource Technology*, St. Louis, MO: Elsevier, 2004.

Vollrath, Fritz, *Spiders Weird and Wonderful*, London, Hodder Children's Books 1992.

von Weiszäcker, Ernst, and Amory Lovins, *Factor Four: Doubling Wealth*, London, England: Earthscan Ltd, 1998.

von Weizsacker, Ernst, et al., *Factor Five: The Promise of Resource Productivity*, London: Earthscan, 2010.

Weisman, Alan, *Gaviotas: A Village to Reinvent the World*, White River Junction, VT: Chelsea Green, 2008.

White, Richard E., and Gloria Eugenia Gonzalez Marion, *Las Gaviotas: Sustainability in the Tropics*, Worldwatch Institute, June 2007.

Wiesel, Elie, *Night*, New York: Bantam Books, 1982.

Wijkman, Anders, *Unmitigated Disasters: the Victims of Man-made Catastrophes*, Bourton on Dunsmore, UK: Practical Action Publishing, 2008.

Wilkes, John, *Flowforms: The Rhythmic Power of Water*, Edinburgh, UK: Floris Books, 2003.

Winans, Stephen C., and Bonnie Bassler, *Chemical Communication among Bacteria*, Herndon, VA: ASM Press, 2008.

Worldwatch Institute, *State of the World 2008: Toward a Sustainable Global Economy*, Washington, DC: The Worldwatch Institute, 2008.

Worldwatch Institute, *State of the World*, Washington, DC: Worldwatch Institute, 2009.

Yang, Jiashi, *Analysis of Piezoelectric Devices*, Hackensack, NJ: World Scientific Publishers, 2006.

OTHER WORKS BY GUNTER PAULI

Pauli, Gunter, *Breakthroughs,* Hanslemere, UK: Epsilon Press, 1995.

_____, *Crusader for the Future: A Portrait of Aurelio Peccei, Founder of the Club of Rome*, Oxfordshire, UK: Pergamon Press, 1987.

_____, *Out of the Box: Zeri Management Stories*, Tokyo, Japan: ZERI Publications, 2007.

_____, *Upsizing: The Road to Zero Emissions, More Jobs, More Income and No Pollution*, Sheffield, UK: Greenleaf Publishing, 2000.

Pauli, Gunter, Gunter's Fables Series, Gland, Switzerland: ZERI, 2006
Animal Medicine Medicina Animal
Can Apples Fly? Manzanas Voladoras?
Cold Feet Pies Frios
Don't Eat Me Alive! No Me Comas Vivo!
Forest Drinking Water Aqua Potable del Bosque
Grow a House Cultiva una Casa
How to Take it Apart Como des Baratarlo
Oranges from Soap Jabon de Naranjas
Red Rice Arroces Rojos
Shiitake Love Caffeine Los Shiitake Aman la Caffeine
The Ant Farmer La Hormiga Agricoltura
The Bear and the Fox El Oso y el Zorro
The Five Kingdoms of Nature Los 5 Reinos De La Naturaleza
The King of Hearts El Ray del Corazones

The Magic Hat Sombrero Majico
The Smart Mushroom El Hondo Sabiondo
The Strongest Tree Arbol Mas Fuerte
The Zebra Aircon Ventilador de las Cebras
Tree Candy Dulce del Arbol
Walking on Water Caminando Sobre El Agua
Where is Home? Donde Esta Mi Casa?
Who is the Most Beautiful? Qien es el mas Bello?
Why Can't I Steal Less? Por Que no Puedo Robar Menos?
Why Don't They Like Me? Porque no me Qiere?

ADDITIONAL INFORMATION

Contact Dr. Gunter Pauli:
Zero Emissions Research Initiative (ZERI):
info@zeri.org

Further information related to THE BLUE ECONOMY:
www.zeri.org
www.blueeconomy.de
www.TheBlueEconomy.com

Order copies of THE BLUE ECONOMY:
www.paradigm-pubs.com/catalog/detail/BluEco

> By Mail:
> Paradigm Publications, 202 Bendix Drive, Taos, NM, USA 87571
>
> By Phone: +1 (575) 758-7758
>
> By Fax: +1 (575) 758-7768

INDEX
The Blue Economy